LAND OF THE DAWN-LIT MOUNTAINS

A JOURNEY ACROSS ARUNACHAL PRADESH – INDIA'S FORGOTTEN FRONTIER

ANTONIA BOLINGBROKE-KENT

SIMON & SCHUSTER

London · New York · Sydney · Toronto · New Delhi

A CBS COMPANY

First published in Great Britain by Simon & Schuster UK Ltd, 2017
A CBS COMPANY

3 5 7 9 10 8 6 4 2

Simon & Schuster UK Ltd
1st Floor
222 Gray's Inn Road
London WC1X 8HB

www.simonandschuster.co.uk
www.simonandschuster.com.au
www.simonandschuster.co.in

Simon & Schuster Australia, Sydney
Simon & Schuster India, New Delhi

The author and publishers have made all reasonable efforts
to contact copyright-holders for permission, and apologise
for any omissions or errors in the form of credits given.
Corrections may be made to future printings.

A CIP catalogue record for this book
is available from the British Library

Paperback ISBN: 978-1-4711-5656-4
eBook ISBN: 978-1-4711-5657-1

Typeset in Bembo by M Rules
Printed and bound by CPI Group (UK) Ltd, Croydon, CR0 4YY

MIX
Paper from
responsible sources
FSC® C020471

For Marley

Contents

Prologue   1

PART ONE: THE WILD EAST
  1. The Forgotten Land   5
  2. All I Need Is a Hero   17
  3. Tea and Unicorns   34
  4. Where's John?   49
  5. Into the Wild   66
  6. Opium Country   86
  7. Monsoon Come Early   103
  8. Tribal Gathering   120
  9. Secrets of the Tsangpo   137
 10. Last of the Igu   159

PART TWO: TOUCHING TIBET
 11. Searching for Shangri-La   175
 12. The King   192
 13. The Heart of the Lotus   211
 14. The Cheerful Mountain   227
 15. Goodbye to Pemako   242

PART THREE: UP AND OVER
 16. Easter in the Hidden Land   259
 17. A Risky Business   275
 18. The Sela Pass   294
 19. Sister Act   315
 20. Yak to the Plains   331

     Acknowledgements   343
     Glossary   347
     List of Tribes in Arunachal Pradesh   354
     Endnotes   355
     Select Bibliography   360
     Index   363

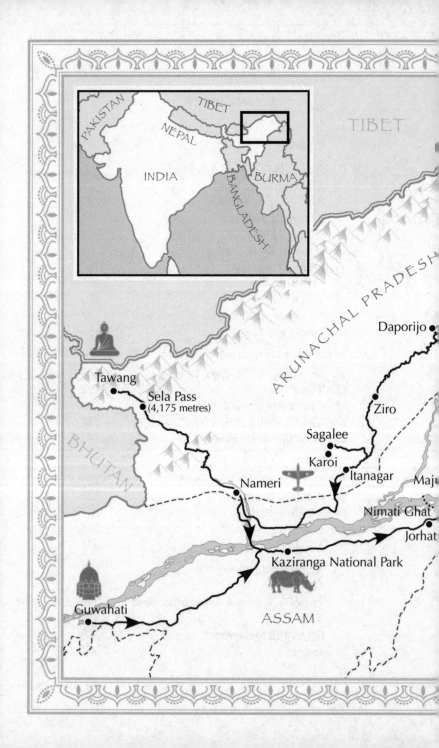

AUTHOR'S NOTE

During the course of my journey I encountered and spent time with people from numerous different tribal groups, among them Idu Mishmi, Khampa, Monpa, Adi and many more. When I am writing about someone from a distinct tribal group I always refer to them as Idu, Adi or Monpa etc., as opposed to simply 'Indian'. When talking about tribal people in general I occasionally use the term 'tribals', which is a term commonly used in India, both by tribal and non-tribal peoples. When I am writing about people from the states of Assam, Bihar or Bengal, I refer to them as Assamese, Bihari or Bengali. In cases where I write about non-tribal Indians in a generic manner I simply refer to them as Indian, or 'mainland Indian' – a common term used by the tribal people of Arunachal Pradesh to describe non-tribal people from outside the state. In a very few instances, names have been changed to protect people's identities.

PROLOGUE

The priest chivvied us into the dark, humid interior, muttering mantras and incantations as he went.

'You are so lucky!' said Manash. 'This is the least crowded I've ever seen it. Normally you have to queue for hours.'

But it was hard to contemplate a bigger crowd. Age-blackened walls sealed us into Kamakhya's crush of devotees, the mass of humanity shuffling and chanting as it moved through the tunnel towards the subterranean inner sanctum, the air thick with incense, sweat and expectation. Priests rocked and chanted next to bronze platters piled with notes, streaking our foreheads with vermilion as we passed. Crimson deities loomed out of the shadows, their stony features lit by the flickering of dozens of little butter lamps. Hemmed in by rock and flesh, I pressed on through the guttering gloom, hands raised in supplication, lips mouthing mantras I didn't understand, senses charged with an unseen energy.

In a small cave at the heart of the temple lay the holy of holies, Sati's *yoni*, or vagina, a slab of black granite carved with a ten-inch fissure kept constantly moist by a spring in the rocks above. Here the crush and heat and fervour reached a

1

crescendo as people pushed towards the holy pudenda. Call it the goddess, imagination or claustrophobia, but the cramped, ancient chamber seemed to pulse with the power of something beyond my understanding, as if we'd stepped into the womb of the divine mother herself.

Breathless, bewildered and trampled on, I knelt before the sacred slit, obeying the attendant priest as he motioned for me to touch the pool of water, smash a coconut on the rock, donate some rupees and throw a handful of marigolds. *Please, goddess, look after me on the journey ahead*, I repeated, as he thumbed my head with more vermilion, gave me a scrap of red cotton and hustled me out of the way. A minute later we were blinking in the daylight and greedily gulping at the air, daubed red and garlanded with marigolds.

As we left the temple compound I grabbed a passing baby goat for a cuddle. It looked at me with cold, capricious eyes and proceeded to munch on my marigolds. Sacred vaginas, holy goats and a lucky absence of crowds – the omens were good. This was fortunate, for I was about to depart on a journey that had fired my dreams and fears for the past two years. Given the remoteness of where I was going, and the events of the past year, I needed all the divine luck I could get.

PART ONE

THE WILD EAST

1

THE FORGOTTEN LAND

Curled beneath the eastern ramparts of the Himalayas broods a wild land of unnamed peaks and unexplored forests: the Indian state of Arunachal Pradesh. The largest and least populous of the Seven Sisters – the septet of states that make up India's turbulent, tribal Northeast – it lies folded between the Tibetan plateau, the steaming jungles of Burma, the mountains of Bhutan and the flood-prone plains of the Brahmaputra Valley. Remote, mountainous and forbidding, here shamans still fly through the night, hidden valleys conceal portals to other worlds, yetis leave footprints in the snow, spirits and demons abound, and the gods are appeased by the blood of sacrificed beasts. More tribes live here, and more languages are spoken, than anywhere else in South Asia. A goldmine of flora and fauna, its unparalleled altitudinal range provides sanctuary to a fabulous array of exotic and alarming creatures. Snow leopards prowl along frozen ridges. Royal Bengal tigers pad through the jungle. Burmese rock pythons slither through the loam.

Yet Arunachal Pradesh remains almost unheard of outside India and little known by those within it. Cordoned off from the outside world from 1873 until the end of the 1990s, today the harshness of its terrain, a sensitive political situation and the need for expensive and restrictive permits still make it a little-visited region.

Much of this isolation is down to simple geography. This violent landscape was formed around fifty million years ago when the Eurasian and Indian landmasses collided in an almighty tectonic smash, the old continents welding into a naturally forbidding architecture of plunging ravines and densely packed peaks, all rent and skewed and tumbling, the very earth itself fighting for space. In the seam between the former continents rose a great river, the Tsangpo, coursing along the suture of the Indian and Eurasian plates. Landlocked, topographically impractical and soon covered by thick forests, this was not a corner of the planet designed for human habitation.

Who came here first, and where they came from, nobody really knows, but what is certain is that by the time the East India Company annexed the region – then known as Assam – from the Burmese at the Treaty of Yandabo in 1826, this isolated Indo-Tibetan border area was home to numerous tribes of singularly fearsome repute. Major John Butler, a British Political Officer who travelled everywhere with two glass windows to fit into the bamboo walls of the huts he stayed in, described it as a 'wild, uncivilized foreign land' occupied by lawless savages with a nasty proclivity for opium. In 1837 J. M'Cosh, a surgeon stationed in Calcutta, wrote of its 'straggling hordes of barbarians'. Another colonial wag noted how these 'rude and barbarous people' were 'very averse to strangers' and notably fond of removing the heads of unwanted interlopers. The warlike Ahom, Tai invaders who'd ruled Assam for 600 years, had wisely left these headhunting hill dwellers alone and, unless provoked, the British did too.

In 1873, after half a century of intermittent raids on their lucrative interests in Assam, the British introduced the Inner Line Permit. Designed to prohibit movement between the Brahmaputra Valley and the surrounding mountains, it was essentially a peace deal with the tribal populations of the hills, a clever way of saying: 'You stop interfering with our tea, oil and elephant trades and we won't meddle in your affairs.' By now Assamese tea was big business and, with so much at stake, the British did not want their profits dented by troublesome tribesmen. From then on – the odd skirmish and light butchery aside – the 'savages' kept to the hills, the British to tending their tea on the plains.

This *laissez-faire* attitude came to an end in 1910 when the Chinese invaded Tibet, deposed the Dalai Lama and looked set to march into eastern Assam too. Russian imperialist ambitions in the East were bad enough but now, with the Chinese jabbing at their unprotected Achilles heel, the British quickly set to mapping and monitoring these neglected frontier zones. Surveying parties led by colonels with bristling moustaches and perfectly pomaded hair marched north from the plains, their trains of bandy-legged porters buckling under the weight of hampers, tents and gramophones. As the British explorer and botanist Frank Kingdon-Ward later wrote, these parties were instructed to not only 'explore and survey as much of the country as possible', but also find the 'Pemako Falls' and settle 'the question of the Tsangpo and Brahmaputra rivers'. Whether the two great rivers of Tibet and Northeast India were one and the same, and if they hid a colossal waterfall in their unexplored inner gorges, was one of the greatest geographical mysteries of the nineteenth century. The British were determined to find the answer before the Russians or Chinese.

Not wanting to dilly-dally, in 1914 Sir Henry McMahon, the foreign secretary of the British-run government of India, boldly inked a new Indo-Tibetan border along the ridge of the eastern Himalayas. Until then, British colonial interests officially extended only to the edges of the Brahmaputra Valley, but now we were laying claim to the ungovernable mountainous tracts beyond. Stretching 550 miles from Bhutan to Burma, the 'McMahon Line' was rejected by the Chinese delegation at that year's Simla Conference, who walked out after maintaining that Tibet and a significant chunk of Assam belonged to them. Sidelined by the confusion of the Great War and its aftermath, the issue reappeared in 1943 when the Chinese produced a map reiterating their claim to these territories. Despite the British responding with a renewed bout of mapping and exploration of the disputed frontier, the matter still wasn't resolved by the time India lurched to Independence in 1947.

At this point, Jawaharlal Nehru, India's first prime minister, had more pressing issues to consider than his fledgling country's remote, tribal Northeast. Rather than complicate matters, he opted to keep Britain's Inner Line Permit system in place – a system that remains to this day. As a man who claimed to have a 'strong attachment to the tribal people' of his country, he was, perhaps, partly driven by a desire to preserve the unique cultures of the North East Frontier Agency, as Arunachal Pradesh was then known. But it could also have been a case of taking the most expedient path – a path that was muddied when India's accommodation of Tibet's fugitive Dalai Lama in 1959 contributed to the Sino-Indian War of 1962. In October of that year, Mao Zedong's People's Liberation Army launched a surprise assault across the McMahon Line, temporarily occupying parts of the region and advancing as far south as Tezpur in Assam. Fortunately, a month later, they announced a ceasefire and withdrew.

Since then the two nations have eyeballed each other over the parapet of the Himalayas, missing few opportunities for border braggadocio, spying and diplomatic spats. China has never accepted the McMahon Line and continues to lay claim to the region, referring to it as South Tibet and including it on official government maps – a slur which India takes very seriously indeed. As I write this in May 2016 the Indian government is drafting a new law that could lead to not only a hefty jail sentence but also a fine up to $15 million (no, that's not a typo) for any careless cartographers who publish an inaccurate map showing disputed territory, such as Arunachal Pradesh, Kashmir and Ladakh's Aksai Chin, as lying outside its borders. The Indian customs declaration form, which all visitors to the country must fill out on entry, puts 'maps and literature where Indian external boundaries have been shown incorrectly' above 'narcotic drugs and psychotropic substances' in their list of prohibited items. It must be the only country in the world where a badly drawn map is deemed more dangerous than a stash of class As.

The Chinese issue has shaped this region since 1962 and is the prism through which the Indian government and people view this far-flung frontier state. But Chinese expansionism isn't the only conflict that has riven this far-off corner of the world in recent decades. Since Independence, guerrilla armies and liberation fronts have sprung up all over the Northeast, each of them fighting for autonomy from an India that feels geographically, culturally and religiously separate. Caught in the cross-currents of communism, the Vietnam War, the Cold War and the chaos of East Pakistan and Bangladesh, this Hydra-headed struggle for independence has been further agitated by frequent outside interference. The US backed Naga rebels between the 1950s and 1970s, with CIA agents operating in the area being easily mistaken for missionaries, and Pakistan and China have consistently funded and trained various groups. It's been a long and bitter battle that few outsiders have heard of, yet one that has claimed the lives of an estimated 200,000 Naga – killed with eye-watering savagery by soldiers of the Indian Army. Today the violence is a fraction of what it was in the 1950s, '60s and '70s, but numerous guerrilla factions still exist and the dream of independence from India still fuels numerous rebel groups throughout the Seven Sisters.

All this has meant that this disputed frontier territory – which was named Arunachal Pradesh, 'the land of the dawn-lit mountains', in 1987 – has remained uniquely isolated, a hidden land that time and the outside world forgot.

*

Fate, once again, had dealt me a lucky card. In October 2013, on the very day I emailed the manuscript of my previous book, *A Short Ride in the Jungle*, to my publisher, I received a call from the BBC. A few days later I landed in post-Diwali Delhi, a city choked with fog and filth, to spend a week finding stories and characters for a documentary on Azadpur Mandi, one of the world's biggest fruit and vegetable markets. Traipsing through rotting vegetable matter discussing the inner workings of the Indian carrot trade wasn't the most glamorous TV job I've done. But it did mean I met Abhra.

An ebullient Bengali with a ready laugh, Abhra is behind many of the documentaries about India you see on Western TV screens. Fixer extraordinaire, he's the man the BBC, Channel 4, Discovery and National Geographic go to if they want to film on the subcontinent. He arranges filming permits, hires local crews, deals with the muddling world of Indian bureaucracy, arranges transport and sniffs out locations, stories, ideas and characters from Manali to Mumbai. He smuggled Simon Reeve across the border to Burma to meet insurgents in his *Tropic of Cancer* series; took Gordon Ramsay to meet a Naga chief in *Great Escapes*; helped Michael Palin up the Himalayas and arranged for the *Human Planet* team to meet mahouts and their elephants in the jungles of Arunachal Pradesh. Blessed with the rare ability to find anything and get on with anyone, be they politicians or rubbish pickers, Abhra could charm the pants off Putin. His nickname isn't Abhra-cadabra for nothing.

Abhra also happens to be one of the few outsiders to have travelled extensively in the Seven Sisters. Until then, I'd been only vaguely aware of these anomalous states, bolted onto the eastern shoulder of India like a hasty afterthought. But over lengthy gin-fuelled dinners in the same Delhi restaurant, eyes twinkling behind thick black-rimmed spectacles, he fired my imagination with tales of unmapped wilderness, shamans with magical powers, sacred valleys, matrilineal tribes, yeti sightings and bizarre rumours of human sacrifice. Even more intriguing was that these little-known states, connected to the rest of the subcontinent by a twenty-mile strip between Bangladesh and Nepal, contained disputed frontier territory and were a hotbed of insurgent groups, wildlife poaching and cross-border drug trafficking. I had to go.

I returned to England with lungs full of Delhi smog and a brain buzzing with intrigue. But ideas, like dough, need time to rise, ferment and take form. The Northeast was too large, too disparate, to tackle as one haphazard journey: I needed a focus. For several months I let the idea roll about my mind, prodding it, kneading it, stirring it with sprinklings of research. And the more I did so, the more Arunachal rose to the fore. The most inaccessible, culturally diverse and little known of the Seven Sisters, here was a place hidden in the shadows and wrinkles at the edge of the map; a far-off land that spoke of magic and mystery, gods and monsters and the glorious wild. With the exception of the late Mark Shand, whose 2002 book, *River Dog*, told of his journey down the Brahmaputra, almost nothing has been written about Arunachal since the 1940s. And even Shand, who travelled through just a small eastern section of the state, only scratched the surface. I am not of the curmudgeonly caste that moans about there being nothing left to explore; exploration is a state of mind. But in a world that has largely been mapped, clicked, blogged about, uploaded and tramped across, it seemed unbelievable that such a place still exists. Arunachal it was.

Although the Indian government has cautiously been allowing foreigners into Arunachal Pradesh since 1998, travel there remains tightly controlled. Those who wish to go must apply for a thirty-day permit and travel in groups of two or more, with a guide, and only to stated areas. All this sounded deeply dull. I'd need longer than thirty days to explore the Portugal-sized state, and I definitely didn't want to see it through the window of a minibus full of German lepidopterists. Luckily I knew just the man who could inveigle his way around these tiresome restrictions.

Six months after our meeting in Delhi, I dialled Abhra's mobile number: there was that familiar laugh at the end of the line, his cheerfulness infectious even from 5,000 miles away. Of course he could arrange a longer permit, he chuckled. He knew just the man. And yes, his new travel company, Native Route, would be delighted to help me with contacts and logistics. I trusted Abhra implicitly. With him on board I knew my idea was possible.

While Abhra worked his magic on the guide and permit situation, I turned to the happy conundrums of when, where and how. Maps of this part of the world are both scarce and inaccurate – even London's Royal Society for Asian Affairs, whose drawers bulge with yellowed, musty old maps of the Empire, had a paucity of relevant cartography. Every other corner of Asia was represented, but not this part of India; it really was a forgotten land, a blank space in the popular imagination. Instead I turned to Google Earth, poring over jade forests and snowy ridges, my eyes greedily following the contours from which rivers purled and plummeted and great peaks soared. I befuddled myself with weather charts and rainfall statistics, rooted out contacts and delved into obscure, out-of-print books by long-dead explorers. The deeper I dug, the more excited I became. With India's BJP Prime Minister Narendra Modi's efforts to bring India's eighty million tribal people into the religious mainstream, border tensions with China and the rush for resources to feed, water, power and supply India's exploding population, this long-ignored state seemed on the cusp of exponential change. It could not have been a better time to write about it.

Abhra, meanwhile, had been working his charms to good effect, pulling the creaky strings of Indian bureaucracy to secure me the promise of a two-month permit. As for whether I'd have to travel with a guide, that remained a blurred point and something even the law was unclear on. While Abhra's influence meant I'd be able to avoid the spectre of any sort of guided tour, and essentially travel independently, the sensitivity of the border area, overspill of insurgent activity from Assam and Nagaland, and regularity of police and army checkpoints meant I couldn't entirely dispense with guides. Initially resistant to this, I conceded that either I accepted this situation or didn't go at all, the thought of which was by now unbearable.

I'd soon hatched a plan to loop and wiggle from one end of the lozenge-shaped state to the other, travelling roughly 3,000 miles from the humid jungles of the Patkai Hills bordering Burma in the east, to the *gompa*-clad Himalayan heights of Tawang in the west. It was a journey that would take me through dark, primal jungles, thickly forested hills, remote valleys and to places that few, if any, Westerners had visited. It wouldn't be easy. Arunachal is carved into a series of steep, forbidding valleys by the great tributaries of the Brahmaputra – among them the Lohit, Dibang, Siang, Subansiri and Kameng – which pour down from their sources high on the Himalayan plateau. Since these make it impossible to traverse the state in a straight line from east to west, I'd be forced to travel up and down each valley. Given these difficulties, I would travel by a combination of means – a motorbike that Abhra agreed to find for me, plus foot, boat and public transport.

Deciding when to do this was even more problematic. Northeast India's climate and terrain have been the nemesis of many a would-be conqueror and explorer. Not only is it the wettest place on earth, hammered by monsoon rains from April until October, but either side of this annual deluge stalks the ferocious Himalayan winter. During a military campaign in Assam 300 years ago, Mullah Darvish of Herat wrote:

'Its roads are frightful as the path leading to the Nook of Death . . . its forests are full of violence . . . its rivers are beyond limit . . .'

In 1926, Frank Kingdon-Ward said of the region: 'The frivolous might say there are two seasons; eight months wet, and four months damned wet.'

Being of a reptilian disposition, I dislike the cold and had no wish to battle my way through blizzards and white-outs. But nor did I fancy being washed away by floods and landslides or trekking through humid jungles dripping with rain and pit vipers.

To complicate things further, Arunachal ranges from

Himalayan summits of over 7,000 metres to the near-sea-level plains of Assam, and is home to almost every climatic zone on earth. In late spring and summer it would be beautiful in the higher-altitude areas but wet, sticky and malarial in the lower jungles. In winter these jungles would be cool, dry and appealingly free of snakes and leeches, but the higher passes would still be cloaked in snow. Autumn was the obvious time to go, but it was already late summer and I wouldn't be ready in time. It was a temporal catch-22.

In the end, factors outside of my control delayed my departure date by more than a year. But on 1 February 2016, almost two and a half years since I'd first met Abhra, I dragged my bulging holdall off the baggage reclaim at Guwahati airport and walked out into the mist of the Assamese winter.

2

ALL I NEED IS A HERO

Abhra was busy creeping after snow leopards in Himachal Pradesh for the BBC's *Planet Earth II*, so I was met at the airport by Manash, his business partner. Blessed with the almond-eyed good looks typical of the tall, paler-skinned Assamese, Manash was to be my Man in Assam. An Enfield-riding, rock 'n' roll-loving fount of knowledge and resourcefulness, he was to prove an indispensable addition to Mission Arunachal.

As Manash steered his Scorpio 4WD through Guwahati's honking, polluted streets, the Rolling Stones and Led Zeppelin crackling out of the stereo, I took in the passing bedlam of Northeast India's largest city. An exploding metropolis of over a million people sprawled along the southern banks of the Brahmaputra, it was India in all its Technicolor madness, a riot of barging cars, darting auto-rickshaws, wandering cows, dirt and noise. Bangladeshis pedalled between the traffic on dilapidated bicycle rickshaws. A man stood urinating onto the dusty verge. Women squatted beside piles of burning rubbish. People stared. It was hard to imagine it had once been known as Pragjyotishpura, the 'light of the East', the city where Lord Brahma first created the stars. One of the nation's fastest-growing cities, it was seeping inexorably into the surrounding hills, the bloating peripheries frequently pushing leopards into its concrete alleys.

Speeding under lines of the tall, slender betel palms, which give it the modern name Guwahati, 'market of betel nuts', I remembered that to love India you have to hurl yourself at it feet first – embrace the chaos, the oddities, the unexpected, the frustrations, the failures. If you don't, it will probably drive you mad. And besides, the India I was heading for wasn't India as we know it; it was another world entirely.

The following few days passed in a whirlwind of mechanics, paperwork, shopping, packing and pujas. I first met my motorbike down a rutted alleyway the next morning. A 150cc Hero Impulse that Manash had picked up for 39,000 rupees (about £390), it stood at the back of a mechanic's cluttered shed, a plain thing but perfectly suited for the task. Light, simple and designed for off-road use, I was glad to have chosen it over a beautiful but brutish Royal Enfield. A crowd assembled as I swung my leg over the saddle and tapped it into first gear for a spin. But it had been six months since I'd been on a bike and nerves and unfamiliarity sent me careering down the alleyway, narrowly missing an oncoming rickshaw and almost knocking an old woman to an early grave. Thankfully I'd calmed myself and the wayward Hero by the time I returned to the gawping crowd, and I glided to a stop with limbs and pride intact.

For the rest of the day we threaded through a maze of choked streets, scouring the city for all-terrain tyres, Manash weaving expertly through the traffic ahead of me on his old black Enfield. It wasn't long before I felt accustomed to the Hero and the familiar irregularities of Asian traffic. My last journey, a solo exploration of Indochina's Ho Chi Minh Trail, had begun in the cacophonous streets of Hanoi, a city whose roads were even more frenzied. Here cars pushed and barged and beeped, rickshaws cut you up and no one cared a jot about those pointless white lines on the tarmac. But at least there were no women staggering across the road under back-breaking yokes of fruit and vegetables, or swarms of mopeds, or streams of gossiping girls bicycling nonchalantly through the clamorous mass of man and machine. Compared to Hanoi, Guwahati's traffic was verging on sane.

We passed markets where trays of live fish flapped and gasped at the roadside, zipped down side streets, and dived into boy racer shops bustling with gelled heads and gold chains. When the tyres eluded us I bought the Hero a Sex Pistols sticker instead, the closest thing I could find to a Union Jack. In the fusty offices of an insurance company, where plump workers typed idly under Krishna calendars, Manash encouraged the woman with 400 rupees, around four pounds, to insure my bike. Had he not, it would have taken a week, instead of an hour, for her to do the job.

It was dusk before we found the right tyres, and two thin, grubby boys squatted barefoot in the street to fit them by the light of a mobile phone torch. I crouched on the pavement beside them, keen to see how it was done, only to be distracted by a pathetic, limping beggar who appeared beside me, babbling and holding out his hands for money. It was impossible not to feel sorry for him, so I handed over some notes and watched him hobble away, a poor pitiful creature, the sort you sadly see so many of in India.

Occasionally our errands would take us along the banks of the Brahmaputra, where couples sat on benches under palms and fishermen poled narrow wooden boats into shore. Vast, still and perpetually foggy at this time of year, the river looked placid and benign, but under that silken surface eddied knots of lethal currents and the gift of life and death. The only male among India's major rivers, the 'son of Brahma' is the fluvial spine of Northeast India, its lifeblood, destroyer and shifting serpentine heart. By the time it reaches Guwahati, its waters have travelled a thousand miles from their source beneath Mount Kailash, flowing east through Tibet as the Yarlung Tsangpo, thundering south through Arunachal Pradesh as the Siang, and then emerging onto the plains as the Brahmaputra. South of Guwahati it becomes the capricious Jamuna of Bangladesh, then the Padma and, finally, as it merges with Mother Ganges and flows into the Bay of Bengal, the mighty Meghna. A frequent companion over the coming months, never would it look the same.

The one thing we couldn't find in this entire heaving city was a top box. Setting off on a journey through some of the wettest mountains on earth without a lockable, waterproof box on the bike was unthinkable. But such a thing apparently didn't exist in Guwahati.

'Come on, Manash, this is India; there's always a solution. There must be *someone* who can make me a top box,' I said one evening.

'I'm damn sure there is too,' he replied, a determined look in his eye. Manash, I'd learnt, was not a man accustomed to giving up.

Besides working with Abhra, Manash was also involved in project-managing a slew of government-funded solar power installations in remote Assamese villages, part of Modi's drive to bring electricity to 400 million rural Indians. The fabrication work for these projects was done at a local factory and, within minutes, Manash had made a few calls and arranged for them to make me a top box the next day.

'It's not going to be the top box of your dreams,' he warned, with a wry smile. 'It's going to be an Indian-style top box. But it should be OK.'

At 10 a.m. we arrived at a cavernous warehouse on the industrial fringes of the city. Steel girders lay stacked on the dirt floor and blade-thin workers, their backs shiny with sweat, stood and stared as I walked in.

'You Britishers are very stronger [sic], mentally and physically,' said Probir, the factory owner, as we sat drinking tea in his beige, air-conditioned office. On the dirt track outside the warehouse, three of his men bent over the back of the Hero to measure it up. The measurements had to be precise; a millimetre out and the new box's bolts wouldn't fit into the pre-existing rack at the back of the bike. The men furrowed their brows and chewed the ends of pencils with *paan*-stained mouths. They squinted. They conferred. They measured their hands against the rack and scribbled vital digits on a scrap of paper. No one thought to use a new-fangled device such as a ruler or measuring tape. Why bother when hands and eyes would do?

Probir wobbled his head from side to side in the classic Indian manner that variously means: Yes, OK, I understand, Hello, Maybe or You're welcome. 'We will do the needful.'

The top box, he said, would be ready that evening.

In the meantime, there was one more thing I had to do before I left Guwahati. No journey in India could possibly start without a puja, a ritual to invoke the blessings of the deities and ask for good luck on the road ahead, especially for a wildly superstitious traveller such as me. Where better to do this than at one of the country's most ancient and powerful monuments to the divine feminine – Kamakhya, Guwahati's Shakti temple to the mother goddess.

The late-afternoon sun glowed through the mist as we climbed the marble steps to the temple. A begging torso, his head the only protrusion from a grossly malformed body, solicited the passing crowd for rupees. Sadhus with matted locks and dirty orange robes squatted under a banyan tree. Lines of stalls offered gaudy Shiva figurines, garlands of orange marigolds, incense, coconuts and butter lamps. And at the top, under a stone gateway guarded by a pair of muscular granite hounds, skulked a pack of priests, scarlet-robed and vulpine-eyed, who scanned the approaching crowd. There was big money to be made from the superstitious, particularly at somewhere as famous as Kamakhya.

Manash, wise to the rapacity of the temple's holy men, had called his family *panda*, or priest, in advance and, just as the pack prepared to pounce, a bony old man with a comb-over and rheumy, bespectacled eyes materialized before us, a plastic bag of offerings clutched beneath the folds of his faded navy shawl. Under the glare of the jilted priests, we took off our shoes and walked barefoot into the temple compound.

Beyond the gates, crowds of devotees milled around the sprawling, squat stone building. Bells rang. Priests chanted. Families took selfies in front of the ridged beehive dome. Pigeons flapped around stone effigies. Throngs of sari-clad women rubbed ringed fingers on the worn feet of elephant-headed gods, adding to the slick of 500 years of grease and vermilion. And among it all strutted, butted, nibbled, grabbed and chewed numerous fat stinking billy goats.

I'd expected goats, but bloody, headless carcasses, not live, well-fed pets, their coats smeared reverently red. For Kamakhya is a sacrificial temple, a place whose courtyards have oozed with blood for more than a thousand years. Hindu mythology, never one to shy away from a ripping yarn, relates how the temple's origins lie in the marriage of Lord Shiva, one of the most powerful gods in the dizzying Hindu pantheon, to a beautiful goddess called Sati. But Sati's haughty father didn't approve of his daughter marrying a dreadlocked ascetic who spent most of his time meditating at the top of Mount Kailash, and excluded her from the family. Shamed and furious, Sati went into deep meditation, burst into flames and died.

Mad with grief and hellbent on destruction, Shiva rampaged through the universe with Sati's lifeless body on his head. The other gods tried mantras, chanting, jokes and dance to soothe him, but nothing worked. Eventually Lord Vishnu mounted his eagle, Garuda, and flew up to Mount Kailash, flinging his discus at Sati's body and slicing it into fifty-one pieces. The place where each piece fell to earth became a site of worship of the divine mother: of these, the most powerful was where Sati's *yoni*, or vagina, had fallen, a hilltop over-looking the Brahmaputra River west of modern Guwahati. From then on Kamakhya, as the site was soon known, became a powerful centre of worship of the divine feminine.

No one knows how old Kamakhya is, but by the tenth century it was already an important centre of sacrifice, mysticism and sorcery. And it wasn't just wild boar, alligators, lions and rhino whose heads thudded from the chopping block. Humans, specifically men, were frequently offered too. After the original, pre-Aryan temple was destroyed by Muslim invaders in 1498, its reconstruction was celebrated with the decapitation of 140 human 'volunteers' whose severed heads were presented to the goddess on bronze platters. In need of particular divine favour, one seventeenth-century ruler offered the goddess the heads of 700, apparently willing, devotees.

There are whispers that human sacrifice hasn't entirely disappeared from these parts. Possessed of a mind drawn to the edges of things, this was one of the many mysterious subjects that had initially attracted me to write about this forgotten corner of the subcontinent. Incredulous when I'd first heard tell of it in Delhi two years previously, a subsequent trawl through the internet turned up a series of disturbingly recent Indian media reports involving Tantrik priests, superstitious villagers and decapitated bodies. In 2013 a fifty-year-old woman from Mumbai had been killed in a Tantrik ritual. Uttar Pradesh had suffered a spate of alleged sacrifices in 2006, the illiterate villagers apparently goaded by travelling priests promising bountiful harvests and untold wealth. And there were persistent rumours that children were secretly sacrificed to ensure the successful completion of large-scale construction projects.

Only hours after arriving in India I'd found myself sitting in the dimly lit corner of a restaurant, being told with surety that human sacrifice still took place.

The journalist lowered his voice and looked furtively around us. 'It's best no one overhears this conversation.' He paused to light another cigarette before continuing, his leather jacket creaking as he lifted the flame to his mouth. 'It's not just for big construction projects, it happens here too. Every summer a Tantrik fertility festival is held at an important local temple and it's said that in the middle of the night, in a closely guarded ceremony, a child is sacrificed. Rich men pay priests a lot of money to do it, believing it will bring them even greater wealth.'

I was agape. 'But who are the children?'

'I don't know, but they're sold to the priests for around fifty thousand rupees [roughly £500]. I can't tell you any more, but I've heard about it too many times for it not to be true.'

Whether it was true or not, what *was* certain was that in 2012 a plastic bag containing a man's severed head and pieces of paper inscribed with Hindu mantras had been found on the road to the temple.

Nowadays, although humans are off the public menu, people still travel from all corners of India to make furred and feathered offerings to the goddess. When travel writer Mark Shand visited in the 1990s, he met a family who had made a 'four-month, 2,000-mile journey from the south, hauling a young buffalo all the way'. Goats, buffaloes, chickens, ducks – generally male – are slaughtered here daily, usually, I learnt, in the early morning. The goat I'd later approach for a cuddle was one of the lucky ones, given instead as a live offering to the bloodthirsty deity. No wonder he was so happy to munch on my marigolds.

Probir was true to his word and that night my bespoke, handmade top box was complete. There was just one problem – the paint wasn't dry. In their eagerness to 'do the needful', the steel box had been sprayed a dashing powder blue, with the sort of paint that takes days to dry. By 9 p.m. it was still woefully wet. Undeterred, Probir disappeared into the dark bowels of the warehouse and returned with a plugless hairdryer. Cramming the wires directly into a wall socket, we crouched hopefully around the box, blasting it with a hairdryer that had all the power of a gerbil's fart. An hour later we gathered around the Hero to fit the perfect, powder-blue box. Except it wasn't quite as perfect now; it was smudged, smeared with oily fingerprints and gummed with dust. The paint hadn't been as dry as we thought, but by then it was too late, and perfectionism had been blunted by a desire to go home.

There was one other small problem: only two of the four bolts were in the right place. A tape measure might have been useful after all. We clustered around, tools and sticky box in hand, sawing and drilling, our efforts attracting a crowd of curious passers-by. It was almost midnight by the time Probir had bodged and drilled everything into place, grinning triumphantly at the completion of his 'Number One Indian Quality Top Box'. I drove away, my smudged, fingerprinted, bodged box held on by three bolts, rattling in the night air. The whole episode was a perfect microcosm of all the maddening brilliance of modern India.

It was time to leave. Not only did my permit for Arunachal Pradesh start in a week, but Guwahati was in danger of turning me into a spoilt, overfed memsahib. For four days Manash (or Manny, as I now jokingly called him) had collected me each morning from his and Abhra's soon-to-be office, an empty house in a gated city centre compound I temporarily called home. He'd fed me. He'd driven me to every seething corner of the city, hunting down tyres, top boxes and temples. He'd bribed fat insurance brokers. He'd even bought me a key ring for good luck.

But it wasn't just Manny's generosity that was to blame. Of my own volition I'd also stuffed myself with spicy fish curries, sticky rice wrapped in bamboo and smashed, smoky brinjal at the best Assamese restaurants, been taken to dinner by local journalists and fed an ever-increasing number of breakfasts by kindly, inquisitive neighbours. The latter had started with one elderly man popping his woolly-hatted head around the front door with a 'You are hailing from?' and an invitation to his house. Soon the popping heads had multiplied to three. Not wanting to cause offence, I'd accepted all their invitations – at this rate I'd soon be hitting double-figure breakfasts. This was supposed to be a rufty-tufty adventure through the wilds of India, for goodness sake. I needed to cut the apron strings and stride boldly forth.

After all the months of planning, excitement and

apprehension, I awoke with only mildly simmering nerves. Rolling up my sleeping bag and shoe-horning the last of my belongings into my rucksack and faithful old panniers, I watched my mind as a sailor watches a surging sea, expecting a tidal bore of emotion to sweep over the horizon and swamp me at any minute. But it never came. I remembered the jaw-clenching, teeth-chattering nerves of that morning in Hanoi three years previously and thought how, just like each person, each journey has its own personality, its own set of fears and desires.

In a quiet christening ceremony, I sprinkled my steed with a pot of silver glitter packed specially for this purpose, and asked it to look after me in those unknown hills, the still-sticky top box perfectly holding the iridescent dust in place. By the time I heard the throaty single-cylinder thud of Manash's Enfield approaching at 9 a.m., I was packed and ready for lift-off, the sparkling Hero looking like a packhorse under its virgin load.

Oh, the headache of packing for this expedition! How do you cram everything you need for a journey that's going to be blisteringly hot, shiveringly cold, undoubtedly wet and extremely remote onto one small motorcycle? It was a question that had caused me some consternation. I was travelling by both motorbike and foot, so needed to be fairly self-sufficient, but I also had to travel as light as possible. Extremes of temperature necessitated bulky gear such as a proper sleeping bag, down jacket and body bag-style water-proofs. Remoteness meant spanners, spare inner tubes, a tyre pump, a medical kit and emergency food supplies. Recording the journey in words and pictures required a laptop, diaries, chargers, a hard drive and camera kit. Superstition called for my teddy bear – a small squishy anteater a dear friend had given me long ago – and a clutch of lucky talismans. Then there were water filters, a mosquito net, dry bags, a roll mat, a rucksack for trekking, four empty notebooks, copies of Mark Shand's *River Dog* and Ursula Graham Bower's *The Hidden Land*, and the absolutely essential travel yoga mat. Nothing could be superfluous.

I'd ride in waterproof trekking trousers, abrasion-resistant Kevlar leggings, a lightweight motorcycle jacket and walking boots, and take one warm fleece and two shirts, both of which had to pass the boob test. They couldn't show a suspicion of cleavage, nor could they present a fleshy view to passing opportunists when I bent down.

'Aren't you worried?' my boyfriend Marley's mother had asked the week before I left.

'About what?'

'About getting raped, of course. It happens all the time in India.'

I wasn't worried, I told her quite truthfully – attitudes to women are very different in the tribal Northeast. But I was still a woman travelling alone and, wherever in the world that was, the less I flashed my pearly white flesh, the better. Not that I'm blessed with a fabulously heaving bosom but, well, some people get excited by anything.

Without further ado I pulled on my open-face helmet, swung my leg into the narrow gap between panniers, ruck-sack and tank bag, fired up the Hero and wobbled through the compound gates behind Manash's bike.

I was immediately cast into the midst of a shifting,

sharp-edged metallic sea. Lorries beeped. Brakes squealed. Cars pushed. Rickshaws nosed through impossible gaps. Pedestrians dashed. Unused to the weight of my luggage, I lurched unsteadily after Manash, beeping furiously, intent on both staying upright and not losing sight of his khaki fleece as it led me through the surging tide. On the outskirts of town, at the junction with the main road east, we pulled over and I hugged him goodbye, waving at him in my wing mirror until he dwindled to a dot. Manash had been so incredibly generous with his knowledge and time and I was sorry to leave him behind.

My plan was to cross into Arunachal Pradesh at Jagan, a small town in the lee of the Patkai Hills, near the point where India, Burma and Tibet collide. From there I would wiggle anti-clockwise through the state, ending two months later in the far northwestern corner of Tawang. Barring some gross meteorological malfunction, this meant I'd be ahead of the monsoon rains. I'd also be less likely to succumb to malaria, drowning or the legions of poisonous snakes and blind, blood-sucking leeches that are the scourge of Arunachal's summers.

But first I had to cross 500 miles of Assam, a state that was as populous as its neighbour was not. A fecund finger of grass, jungle and wetland probing its way east along the course of the Brahmaputra, its thirty million inhabitants are hemmed into an area the size of Scotland by the Naga Hills to the south and the Himalayas to the north. Forced into compactness by this savage geography, its people are trapped like insects at the bottom of a leaky bucket, at the mercy of the mighty river. Rich in coal, oil, timber and tea, Assam had been the furthest point of Raj rule – an anomalous, multi-ethnic sliver of India thrusting between the Tibetan plateau and the jungles of Southeast Asia. Since 1947, many of its 240 ethnic groups have fought for independence from India, forming splintered liberation armies with lengthy names such as the National Democratic Front of Bodoland and the Karbi People's Liberation Tigers. Most famous of all is the United Liberation Front of Assam, ULFA, who have fought an often-violent battle since the 1970s, maintaining that: 'An independent Assam is our basic fundamental birthright.' So far an estimated 30,000 people have died in this fight for Assam's sovereignty.

That morning it felt like half of the state was heading east on Assam's main artery, Highway 37. Auto-rickshaws trundled the wrong way down the dual carriageway under teetering piles of bricks, sacks, bananas and humans. Trucks belched black diesel fumes, the words 'HORN PLEASE' and 'HORN DO' painted merrily across their ends. Lorries made U-turns without warning. Chuntering red Tata taxis pulled out in front of me, only to stop seconds later to disgorge passengers onto the verge. Scrawny, sun-wizened men pulled handcarts into oncoming traffic. It was typical of the cavalier disregard for life that seems to characterize Asian driving. Certainly no one was paying the faintest bit of notice to the 'Let's take safety seriously' road signs, least of all the assorted, wandering menagerie of skeletal cows, mangy dogs, imbecilic goats, chickens and waddling geese.

On top of this was the small matter of the 2016 South Asian Games, the cycling events of which were being sweated out on the concrete of Highway 37 that day. Without warning, all the eastbound traffic was funnelled to the other side of the carriageway and I found myself riding through a corridor of cheering, brightly clad spectators, paunchy policemen and haphazardly erected bamboo fencing. Pumping and panting in the opposite direction was a straggling peloton of cyclists, finalists in the men's 40km individual time trial. One of them, a Pakistani, was closely followed by a moped, on the back of which perched a lady in an emerald-green sari riding side saddle, imperially upright, clutching a spare bicycle wheel. Behind came the follow cars, their official stickers pasted wonkily onto the doors as if stuck on late the previous night after too much whisky. If Basil Fawlty had organized the Olympics, I imagine they'd look a bit like this. Soon the clamour passed and I was back on the eastbound carriageway, bemused by the surrealism of it all.

Beyond stretched the dull, tabular landscape of the plains, their visage not improved by winter and a clinging fog. Rice paddies, so green and vibrant in the growing season, lay brown and empty. Rubbish sprouted from the verge like weeds. The tall, slender chimneys of countless brick kilns spewed black smoke into the haze and, for miles at a time, tea estates fanned uniformly from the road, the precious bushes dusty and drooping with pollution. I'd read that Assam's tea estates were experiencing a decline in productivity, and it wasn't hard to see why.

By mid-afternoon, when the highway narrowed to two lethal lanes, gently undulating hills had sprung from the surrounding plains and adobe and bamboo-hutted villages sat clustered amidst the paddies on raised islets. During the monsoon these villages become islands, the paddies an ocean, their owners poling across them in dugout canoes. Here great grey storks lumbered over my head, patches of jungle darkened the tarmac and yellow signs warned of elephants crossing. 'We're a long way from Kansas,' I said out loud to the bike, stopping to take a photograph of one such sign. As I zipped my camera into my tank bag, two young men on a moped skidded to a halt beside me, all stonewashed jeans and hair gel, with a 'Madam, one selfie?' It was a question I would soon be used to.

3

Tea and Unicorns

It would be sacrilege to drive through Assam and not visit Kaziranga, India's Serengeti. The world-famous wildlife reserve is home to two-thirds of the global population of the greater one-horned rhinoceros, or *Rhinoceros unicornis*, over a hundred Bengal tigers, 1,300 Asian elephants and more species of bird than you can shake a twitcher at. It's also home to Manju Barua, naturalist, musician, botanist, Sanskrit scholar and authority on cricket, elephants, Shakespeare and the Beatles. Described by Mark Shand as 'the Fidel Castro of Assam', Manju had been a close friend of the late author, acting as his oft-exacerbated boat fixer in *River Dog*. It was at his charming but faded resort, Wild Grass, that Shand's canine companion Bhaiti had ended his days. Intrigued to meet Manju, and see if any of Bhaiti's curly-tailed descendants still roamed the grounds, I turned at dusk down the palm-lined track to Wild Grass.

A bear of a man in his youth, age had shrunk Manju, but he was still a splendid character. All silver beard and obsidian eyes and mischief, he had the air of someone who had just played a marvellous practical joke and was waiting for his victim to find out. Well into his sixties, Manju liked to play the doddery old man, but beneath the crumpled brown balaclava, tweed scarf and protestations about his age were an undiminished intellect and hearing capable of picking up a gnat's squeak on Mars. As we discussed Henry IV and the English Civil War over a pot of tea and slightly curling cucumber sandwiches, he tuned in to passing conversations: flinging orders at idling staff here, picking up comments from chattering guests there.

Pausing as three nearby Canadian women remarked on the quality of lunch, he stroked his beard with a silver-ringed hand and chuckled. 'The cooks were on form today, then, you were lucky. They're not always on form, rather like the Indian cricket team.'

He was like a benevolent, ageing headmaster, his staff a rabble of devoted but unruly children. You couldn't help but like him.

Sadly none of Bhaiti's descendants were anywhere to be seen, so I had to make do with rhino-spotting instead, setting off from Wild Grass as daylight flooded the plains. Most people go on elephant safaris at Kaziranga, but I didn't fancy the idea – something about clambering aboard one of these noble beasts for my own silly pleasure didn't sit right with me. A jeep held no such guilt. For two hours the open-topped Gypsy bumped along sandy tracks through forest and grassland, my eagle-eyed guide excitedly pointing out feathery blobs at the top of distant trees. My favourite was the 'greater pissing eagle', the product of the Assamese tendency to muddle the pronunciation of certain consonants.

By the limpid, lacustrine waters of the Brahmaputra we stopped to admire a family of moat otters curled up on a sandbank, their lithe bodies entwined like oiled rope. The river here was several miles wide, and on the far bank we could just make out the shimmering grey forms of a herd of wild elephants. From a nearby copse came a sound like the bursts of a chainsaw – male rhinos bellowing as they locked horns over some hot rhino totty.

The one rhino we saw was a mammoth male, big as a van, his huge articulated backside just ten metres from the jeep. Myopic, cerebrally challenged and given to charging when startled, rhinos can be extremely dangerous, one-tonne battering rams fitted with three-inch incisors perfect for popping off human heads. The driver was careful not to get too close. Already this year three forest guards had been seriously injured by charging rhinos.

These prehistoric-looking pachyderms have every reason to be wary of us humans. When Marco Polo came across these curious creatures in the thirteenth century, with their 'hair of a buffalo . . . feet like an elephant' and 'single large black horn in the middle of the forehead', he thought he'd stumbled upon the legendary unicorn. But by the time Lady Curzon, wife of the then viceroy, came to see the 'three-toed, one-horned beast' here in 1902, hunting and poaching had driven them to the brink of extinction and there were only twelve left.

But since Kaziranga was established as a wildlife reserve in

1908, the *Rhinoceros unicornis* have staged a Lazarus-like come-back: 3,400 individuals now roam the grasslands of Northeast India and Nepal, 2,400 of them in Kaziranga. But it's a precarious existence. The Northeast is hit by extraordinarily heavy rains every summer and, shortly after I returned home from my 2016 journey, that summer's monsoon displaced 1.6 million people in Assam and drowned twenty-one of Kaziranga's precious rhinos, along with countless other wild animals.

There's also the issue of poaching. Rhino horn – a substance made from the same compound as hair and toenails – is believed by the Vietnamese and Chinese to have miraculous curative properties and currently has a street value of up to $100,000 per kilo. That's more than gold. Used for centuries as a cure for fever, gout, devil possession, impotence and a host of other ailments, in 2005 a rumour swept through Vietnam that it had cured a top politician of terminal cancer. Prices sky-rocketed, the poachers dusted off their rifles and the mutilated carcasses multiplied. In 2005 only one rhino was poached in Kaziranga. By 2015 the number had risen to twenty-three. If Kaziranga's army of forest guards wasn't tooled up with .303 rifles and a controversial shoot-to-kill anti-poaching policy, the numbers would be far higher. When I met Uttam Saikia (a local journalist turned anti-poaching super-sleuth) a few days later, he told me one suspected poacher had been killed by guards already this year.

Of course the situation isn't simple. Most of the poachers are from Nagaland, a state riven by decades of fighting for independence from India, where rhino horn, drugs and arms all mix in a nefarious cross-border flow with Burma and China. But the trigger-pullers are guided to their prey by local men from the dirt-poor tribal villages that border the park. Rhinos might be the state symbol and pride of Assam but, while the reserve gets rich on conservation funding and tourism revenue, the villagers have no roads, no running water, no jobs and little hope. It's not hard to see how the young men are easily swayed when pushy outsiders offer them 15,000 rupees (around £150) to lead them to 'just one' rhino. It's exactly the same in South Africa, where impoverished villagers peer through razor wire at safari lodges that cost more per night than they earn in a decade. What's one rhino to them when their children are starving?

The scarcer rhinos become, and the more the price of horn rises, the higher the demand seems to be. Among the new breed of Vietnamese super-rich, a gritty shot of ground-up rhino horn is the ultimate 'look how disgustingly rich I am' status symbol – the equivalent of a mountain of coke at a 1980s pool party. Unless these bragging billionaires find a better way to flaunt their wealth than downing powdered toenail, it's hard to see how Marco Polo's unicorn will survive.

The irony of this is that Kaziranga is probably the safest place in the world to be a wild tiger, an animal even more endangered than the greater one-horned rhino. It takes ten minutes to shoot a rhino, hack off its horn with an axe and leg it out of the park. Shooting, skinning and deboning a tiger is a much messier business. Kaziranga, home to the highest density of tigers in the world, loses very few to poaching.

To my disappointment, though, I didn't so much as catch a whiff of tiger scat, although everyone around Kaziranga had a tiger story to tell. Those dratted Canadians, having admired their lunch, had also been lucky enough to admire the striped derrière of a large male as it padded along the sandy track in front of their jeep that very morning. A local teenage boy recounted how a snarling tiger had leapt out of the long grass and grabbed their mount's trunk on a recent elephant safari.

'The elephant shook its trunk and ran very fastly.' He shuddered at the memory.

And a stilted, tribal village on the edge of the Brahmaputra had lost a cow to an old hungry female only days before, one of 150 taken from local farmers each year.

'Be back before sunset,' the staff warned me, when I set out for a late-afternoon walk near that very spot, the sun already a crimson orb in the haze. The most dangerous wildlife we have in England are angry badgers; taking one's evening stroll in tiger country adds a certain frisson to the experience. I imagined orange stripes in every clump of whispering grass, had a minor seizure when a cow bellowed nearby, and was glad for the four trotting curs that joined me. As desperate as I was to see a tiger at some point during my travels, I'd prefer it wasn't the last thing I saw.

In the village, life carried on as normal: children shouted, dogs barked, geese honked, and bony men yelled at bony cows as they beat and drove them home. They'd lived cheek by jowl with claw, fang, horn and tusk for countless millennia; it was as normal for them as having a cup of chai. For the first of many times over the next few months, I thought how lily-livered we are in England; how removed from the real wild our mollycoddled, sanitized, urban existences have become. Maybe it would do us good to throw the odd tiger into the mix.

*

At 9 a.m. Manju's staff lined up outside his red-brick house to, in Manju's words, 'bray and squeak' their way through that day's rendition of the Assamese national anthem. Afterwards a middle-aged English couple, the three Canadians, Manju and all twenty staff gathered on the steps outside reception to watch the Brave British Biker set off in a glorious spurt of dust and brio. But a poor night's sleep had left me feeling as twitchy as a rabbit's nose and nothing seemed to be going smoothly that morning. The bungees didn't want to stretch over my luggage. The top box wouldn't close properly. Sweat ran in sticky rivulets down my spine, even though it wasn't even fifteen degrees. Wedging my features into my best fearless smile, I swung my leg over the saddle, turned the key in the ignition, gave a triumphant wave, pulled the throttle and ... fell over, tumbling hands-first into the dirt. It wasn't the exit I'd hoped for.

I dusted myself down and, on the second attempt, rode away from Wild Grass, this time keeping the rubber side down. Maybe it was just the lack of a good night's sleep, but my ignominious fall had brought about a sudden, unwelcome sense of apprehension: all at once the thought of two months travelling alone in those inhospitable mountains yawned ahead of me like a bottomless chasm and my brain churned with anxiety. I'd been so calm when I set off yesterday, but now I felt like a quivering mess.

Locked in this internal struggle I rode east under a flinty sky, shivering with cold and uncertainty, the clouds tumescent with approaching rain. The traffic was just as merciless, the goats just as dim, but all of it appeared distant beyond the fog of my doubting mind. At Nimati Ghat a colourful, disorderly throng of cars, motorbikes and foot passengers pushed and revved and jostled to board the green tub that would take us forty minutes across the Brahmaputra to Majuli Island, three wiry men lifting the Hero onto the very last space on the clanking metal deck. Scores of men in grubby dhotis swarmed along the steep, crumbling banks, shoring up the monsoon defences with rocks and sandbags before the river raged again.

Majuli, once the world's largest river island, is another one of Assam's 'must-sees'. But sleep again proved elusive and, the next day, I looked listlessly around the famous Kamalabari Vaishnavite monastery, with its bizarrely identical, feminine-looking monks, and dawdled through an unremarkable landscape of beige paddies dotted with grazing cattle, their attendant egrets and lesser adjutant storks, who picked their way around pools of water like snooty old duchesses looking for lost pearls. When the owner of the guesthouse where I was staying took me to a mask-making studio, I felt trapped and irritated, as if my long-dreamt-of journey had morphed into some dull guided tour.

I didn't want to be on Majuli, in Assam, hearing how masks were made and looking politely around monks' cells. I wanted to be puffing up hillsides, tramping through the jungle, splashing through rivers and drinking moonshine in villages miles from the nearest road. Assam, with its traffic and crowds and rubbish and pollution, was part of the problem. I felt disengaged. If I could just get beyond this, into Arunachal, into the guts of the adventure, then I'd be OK. Sod the Ahom ruins and 'must-see' tea estates that, in a fit of 'shoulds', I'd planned to visit – I'd reach Arunachal as soon as I could.

In Jorhat I unwittingly sniffed out the worst hotel in town, a dismal place with spluttering brown water, scuttling cockroaches and damp, stained walls. Whoever had named it the Paradise Hotel had either been blind, an optimist, or both. But at least it was cheap.

'Is it really like paradise?' I asked the man on the desk, taking in the dark concrete staircase and bare light bulbs.

'We think so,' came the sincere reply.

Manash, who by chance was installing solar panels in a nearby village, came to visit for the evening.

'This is the wrong Paradise Hotel,' he laughed. 'There's a much better one around the corner.'

But by then my belongings were strewn about the room and I was too idle to move.

Jorhat was once the tea capital of Assam, the centre of a booming industry that began in the 1830s. Until then all our tea had come from China, but, as relations between Britain and the Celestials cooled in the lead-up to the Opium Wars, the British were forced to look elsewhere. Local tribes such as the Singpho had cultivated and drunk tea for centuries, but it was only when a Scottish trader called Robert Bruce was given Assamese tea by a Singpho king in 1823 that the notion of an Indian tea trade was born. Although Bruce died the following year, by January 1839 the first chests of Assamese tea were being sold at auction in London. By 1900 more than a million acres of virgin jungle had been cleared by the British in Northeast India and Ceylon to make way for the black gold.

Jorhat's Gymkhana Club, founded in 1876, soon became a favoured haunt of the cognac-quaffing tea planters. A pastiche of refined British society in the midst of the malarial jungle, there was lawn tennis, a swimming pool, horse racing, polo, billiards, ballroom dancing, champagne and six-course banquets, where turbaned butlers served jungle fowl alongside Scottish salmon. Crystal glasses clinked beneath sporting prints, hunting trophies snarled from the panelled walls, and *punkah wallahs* cooled the memsahibs as they gossiped over tea. The first aeroplane ever to land in Assam touched down here in 1928 and the club's golf course was only the third to be built in the world. Nehru gave a rousing speech in its sprung ballroom in 1937, pleading with world leaders to back the movement for Independence. Prince Philip visited in 1960. Few places in Assam can boast such a grand colonial pedigree.

I'd heard that the Gymkhana Club was still standing, a relic of the Raj where the modern generation of Indian planters sip chota pegs of whisky in wood-panelled rooms. A sucker for a bit of faded romance, and convinced they'd have gin, I suggested to Manash that we pop in for a snifter. But when we walked down its rutted tree-lined avenue at dusk we found a sorry shadow of the formerly grand establishment. The ballroom was deserted, the ivories of its grand piano tuneless and mouldering; the tiled swimming pool was filled with leaves and brackish water; the eight tennis courts were overgrown and the polo fields long gone. On the walls hung stained sepia photographs of burra sahibs with pipes, pith helmets and pressed linen suits, their wives in bonnets and starched white dresses – a 1907 golfing party, an Edwardian luncheon by the polo pitches. A handful of cane chairs sat empty in the bar, the shelves that had once held bottles of Kimmel, Bristol Cream and Haut Sauternes now offering just Johnnie Walker and Royal Stag. There was definitely no Gordon's. The whole place reeked of neglect and disrepair.

A noticeboard pinned with the January 2016 Bulletin – a single A4 sheet listing that month's prizes – was the only evidence anyone still came here. Underneath the awards for Best Dressed Lady, Best Dressed Gentleman and Best Dancing Couple was the prize for the Most Energetic Dancer, won by a Mrs Gayatri Goswami. I imagined a stately woman flinging herself around the empty ballroom to sparse applause.

The only living relic was a diminutive, elderly Naga who peered at us over the mahogany bar, his small, watery eyes framed by gold-rimmed spectacles. Above him a British Airways poster showed cricketers on an English village green. When we asked for two shots of Johnnie Walker Black Label he shuffled off to fetch the bottle, barely able to reach the shelf. The first Naga I'd met, he looked completely different to the Assamese, more like the sort of character you might find mixing potions in a Chinese apothecary. He'd been the bar manager here since 1962, he told Manash in Assamese, as we leant on the bar to drink our whisky. He'd fled here from Nagaland after two years in prison for fighting with the Naga National Council and had been lucky to escape with his life. When he arrived, the club had only three Indian members, the rest were British, and there was still dancing in the ballroom every day. In those days a man travelled from Calcutta once a year to tune the piano, but since he'd died in the 1970s no one else had come and, by 1974, the last of the English had gone. Gripped by his story and the atmosphere of the place, I asked him how he felt to see it now.

He raised one hand and put his bent, arthritic fingers to his mouth to intimate eating.

'When I arrived the English ate with silver knives and forks. Now people eat with their hands. Things change.'

Few buildings I've been in have felt so haunted by the ghosts of a vanished age.

Manash, ever resourceful, made up for the lack of Gordon's at the club by hunting down a bottle of Tango-flavoured gin in one of the numerous wine shops in Jorhat. Its label read, ominously I thought, 'for sale in Assam only', and I doubted the medical-grade alcohol had ever encountered a juniper berry. But beggars can't be choosers. We sat on the hard wooden beds in Manash's dismal room in Paradise to drink it, and he told me about the village he was working in – one of many in Upper Assam that Modi's solar power initiatives was bringing electricity to. It sounded pretty wild. Not only had a man been killed by a tiger while collecting firewood in the forest just the previous day, there'd also been a recent accusation of witchcraft.

'It's common in Assam,' he said, in response to my surprise. 'It's nearly always about some village rivalry or jealousy over property.'

In Europe, witch-hunting has long been consigned to the history books, a ghastly medieval phenomenon that saw as many as a million men and women accused of bizarre supernatural offences before being tortured and hanged or burnt at the stake. But in Assam witch-hunting has remained part of the fabric of village life. In 1837 J. M'Cosh wrote: 'The Assamese are by the inhabitants of most provinces looked upon as enchanters ... the women ... are believed to be all enchantresses.'

And it seems such beliefs still prevail: nearly ninety people have been beheaded, stabbed or burnt alive in witch-hunting incidents since 2010, with another sixty injured. A woman had been beheaded by a superstitious mob from her village just months earlier, and in 2014 gold-medal-winning javelin thrower Debjani Bora was tied up and severely beaten after being branded a *dain*, or witch, in her village near Kaziranga. Witch-hunting was only officially banned in Assam in August 2015, when the government passed the Assam Witch Hunting (Prohibition, Prevention and Protection) Bill, stating seven years' imprisonment and a five-lakh rupee (around £5,000) fine for calling or identifying a witch – significantly less than the fine for publishing an inaccurate map.

I studied the European witch-hunts as part of my history degree at Edinburgh, and what was happening in Assam (and Jharkhand, Orissa and several other Indian states) was eerily similar, just five hundred years later. It was violence motivated by ignorance, illiteracy, fear and superstition, where illnesses and the unexplained were often blamed on black magic. You wouldn't want to be a rich, propertied widow in rural Assam when a jealous neighbour fell foul to a mysterious illness.

The next morning, the road from Jorhat to the border of Arunachal became increasingly dangerous – a violent swathe through the calm of endless tea estates, where man and animal gambled recklessly with life, as if frantically trying to reach somewhere before Assam ran out. Vehicles of all kinds veered, swerved, honked, sped, dashed, cut up and overtook head-on. Men leant over the steering wheels of their tiny Tata cars, absentmindedly picking their noses and talking animatedly on mobiles as they drove me into the verge. Truck drivers roared up behind me, so close I could have polished their bumpers. Long convoys of Ashok Leyland army lorries – bored soldiers staring out of their open backs – sent the traffic behind them into even greater paroxysms of impatience. Sandy-coloured cows lay on the tarmac idly chewing their cud, impervious to the stream that swerved and beeped around them. I felt like Mel Gibson in the final scene of *Gallipoli*, sprinting across the sand to Jean-Michel Jarre's *Oxygène*, waiting for that stray bullet to hit me.

But by far the worst culprits were the demented bus drivers of the Assam State Transport Corporation, who screamed past in their red barouches, honking and listing, scattering everything in their path. Woe betide any valiant fool with a notion to hold onto their sliver of road – it was move or die. On several occasions I was sent veering onto the dirt verge, my wheels bumping along ruts made by previous escapees, shaking my fist pointlessly at the disappearing bus.

Until now I'd been fairly sanguine about the driving here. This is India, I'd told myself. Just accept it. But as I swerved, tooted and braked through the crazed traffic of Upper Assam, I became fired by a bellyful of righteous indignation, furious that my fate should rest on nose-picking nonchalance and bovine stupidity. I shook my fist, swore liberally at my assailants and stuck my tongue out (again pointlessly) at one lunatic driver who sped past inches from my panniers. I even swore at several cows, goats and dogs, all of whom seemed afflicted by the same incautiousness as their countrymen. Amidst my rantings I considered how, when it comes to driving, the whole of India seems in the grip of a collective madness, where perfectly reasonable men transform into murderous psychopaths at the merest grip of a steering wheel. The only thing you can say is that the driving is predictably awful: expect the worst and it will probably happen. Of all the dangers I'd imagined on this journey, I'd omitted to consider the very real one of death on an Assamese road. I was craving the wilderness ahead.

4

WHERE'S JOHN?

In Dibrugarh I picked my way along the banks of the Brahmaputra, between piles of rubbish and stinking turds, realizing too late that I'd wandered into the communal loo of the neighbouring slum. I'd wanted to see the river here; not only were our ways about to part, but few other places in Assam were such potent reminders of its power. Meaning 'fort on the banks of the river', the town was built by the British in the nineteenth century as a last line of defence against the bothersome hill tribes, and remained the most important trading centre in Assam for seventy-five years. But in August 1950, one of the century's most violent earthquakes changed the course of the Brahmaputra and sent its waters crashing through the town, obliterating three-quarters of it. The Great Earthquake, as it became known, shook the region with the force of 10,000 atom bombs, causing catastrophic landslides and wiping out whole communities. Today India's 'city of tea' is still a teeming hub for the local tea, oil and coal industries, but the river remains a threat: more of the town is carried away each year and some believe that if erosion continues at the current rate, Dibrugarh may vanish altogether.

But now the river looked benign, a beast in hibernation, its waters drawn back beyond a wide expanse of grey sand. People fished in shallow inlets and cattle wallahs had erected flimsy bamboo shelters on the flats, the greyness and little figures reminiscent of an L. S. Lowry. Keen to avoid the unpleasant scenario of walking back to my hotel smeared in human excrement, I walked gingerly down the steep bank to the sand, pursued by a rag-tag mob of screeching children. They surged and giggled around me, bundling into shyly grinning groups as I took their photos, then yelling with delight when I showed them the screen. One of them was a hauntingly beautiful girl, a tiny thing in a dirty yellow dress with huge, melancholy, kohl-ringed eyes. I wondered if beauty amidst such poverty could ever lead anywhere but a brothel.

Soon the infant rabble was leading me noisily into the darkness of the riverside slum, through rough passageways of bamboo and rusting metal, stopping at a narrow doorway where a young woman in a pink headscarf beckoned me in for coffee. By now the horde had swelled to twenty, half of whom poured into the one-roomed hovel in a frenzy of anticipation. The smallest home I've ever been in, the hut consisted of four bamboo walls, a hard wooden bed, a single kerosene lamp and a wood fire sunk into the earthen floor. A few scraps of clothing hung from nails on the walls. It was a third of the size of my ten-pounds-a-night room at Dibrugarh's generously titled Royal Palace hotel, yet somehow the young woman, her husband, one of the rabble and the baby she dandled on her slim hip existed here.

It was akin to a Dickensian scene: the woman – her gold earrings and nose-ring glinting in the darkness – squatting to boil a pan over the fire as eleven grubby, curious faces assessed me in the gloom. Perched on the bed, a crush of children on the floor at my feet, I communicated in smiles and sign language, hammily acting out riding a motorbike and being from England, 'far far away' – all the time more surprised faces appearing outside the door. When the pan had boiled we all sipped sugary powdered coffee from small china cups and I wished I had something to give them in return. They were Bangladeshi migrants who lived at the mercy of the river, their meagre dwellings frequently flooded and washed away. They had so little, but were so generous towards me, and so full of smiles.

Beyond Dibrugarh, Assam is chiselled to a point by the hills of Nagaland, Burma and Arunachal Pradesh. Here I rode slowly through a string of plastic-strewn towns where ragged old men sat on broken pavements and a grey pall hung over everything. Webs of electrical wires sagged disconsolately over the roadside; jerry-built shop fronts leant drunkenly on each other in wonky, rusting rows; women sat on their haunches selling hillocks of dusty vegetables; creaky old bicycles bulged with silver milk churns; cows chewed plastic bags; rickshaws clattered; men stared. Bored faces gazed out of tiny shops stuffed with packets of biscuits, strings of shampoo sachets, soap, cigarettes and cheap Chinese clothes. Behind hand-painted signs for 'lodging and fooding', figures hunched over plastic tables devouring plates of rice and dhal.

The faces that looked at me as I passed were a mixture of pale, dark, tribal and Oriental; a legacy of both Assam's position at the crossroads of South and Southeast Asia and the Raj's brutal programme of imported labour. A vast workforce was needed to power the Empire's new tea, coal and oil trades, but the locals quite wisely shunned the poorly paid, back-breaking work.

'They are perfectly indifferent to providing for their future want,' wrote J. M'Cosh of the Assamese in 1837. 'They are idle and indolent ... childish and timid ... they have the greatest aversion to hire their services; and it becomes a necessity to catch workmen like wild animals, and keep a constant watch on them to prevent their running away.'

Instead the British passed the 1863 Transport of Native Labourers Act and imported hundreds of thousands of indentured labourers, known as 'coolies', from Bihar, Orissa and beyond. Rape, flogging and torture of these male, female and child labourers was shamefully common, and those who tolerated the wet, cruel, malarial conditions were branded 'Class 1 junglies' by their British overlords. It would be putting it mildly to say that Britain's dealings in Assam are not a part of our history to be proud of.

Through all of these disorderly settlements ran the railway, built by the Assam Railways & Trading Company in the late nineteenth century to carry Upper Assam's largesse west.

Wild elephants took umbrage at the construction of these iron roads, regularly pulling down the telegraph poles that lined the tracks. But man won in the end. At Dibrugarh the bales of tea, barrels of oil and mountains of coal were loaded onto steamers and taken down the Brahmaputra, the Empire getting fat on the toil of bonded labour. Today this remote corner of India still produces a quarter of the world's tea, thirty per cent of the country's oil and huge quantities of coal, as well as holding forty per cent of the nation's water. All this natural wealth, and the sight of it trundling west towards Delhi, has added fuel to the fires of discontent that have raged in Assam since Independence: one of the United Liberation Front of Assam's main arguments being that an independent Assam would profit from its own resources, rather than seeing the wealth leak out to the rest of India.

In Chabua, where Assam's first tea garden was opened in 1837, a convoy of army trucks carrying heavy artillery clogged the road outside the town's air base, and Indian Air Force fighter jets roared over oil fields. One of the seven bases in Upper Assam hurriedly built by the Allies to airlift supplies to China in the Second World War, it was bombed in October 1942 by a hundred Japanese fighters. Today it is part of India's bristling defence against the Chinese, its sentries snapping to salutes under a sign that reads: 'Defending the Eastern Skies'. A later sign proudly welcomed me to 'Digboi: the birthplace of Indian oil'. Here Italian engineers commissioned to build the railway from Dibrugarh to Margherita had noticed a sticky black substance on their elephants' feet and, when the Englishman in charge had exhorted the men to 'Dig boy! Dig!' in search of more, the name stuck.

At Margherita the jungle-clad slopes of the Patkai range reared up to the south, their dark imprints in the mist a welcome respite after the plains. Originally called Ma-Kum, meaning 'abode of the tribes', before it was renamed after their Queen Consort by those same Italian engineers, the town lies just a few miles from the border with Arunachal's Changlang district and less than twenty miles from Burma. Here I was met by thirty-year-old journalist Manash Gogoi, a self-confessed 'fatty' with an expanding waistline and a kindly face, his almond-shaped eyes typical of Assamese looks. As his mother served us steaming bowls of rice, dhal and fried fish in their cool, concrete kitchen, we discussed how, from colonial-era scraps over tea to the guerrilla fighting that still limped on in the surrounding hills, this far corner of Assam had long been an unlikely hub of political ambition; all the while the family's overfed vegetarian spaniel howling pitifully every time one of those infernal buses screamed past. I knew how it felt.

Afterwards, one of Manash's friends appeared, wielding the sort of TV camera that hasn't been seen in England since Moira Stuart presented the *Six O'Clock News*. And before I knew it a large microphone had been shoved under my nose, the camera was flashing red and Manash was interviewing me for the local news.

'I love Assam. Its people are very kind,' I responded politely, before his mother ceremoniously placed a *gamosa*, a traditional Assamese white and red cloth, around my neck.

My visit there coincided with Saraswati Puja – a celebration of the goddess of knowledge, music, arts, wisdom and learning – and the streets were brimming with people in their finery. Women flitted through the traffic in fantastically coloured saris – jade, daffodil yellow, magenta, vermilion, turquoise – looking, amidst all the dust and rubbish, like misplaced birds of paradise. Young men loitered and played with their smartphones, swaggering in their tightest pairs of stonewashed jeans. Crowds milled around temporary roadside shrines.

In honour of Saraswati and the attainment of knowledge, the hottest ticket in town was the coal museum, a bizarre homage to the rich carbon seam that runs through here along the base of the Patkai. Manash insisted I pay a visit and we gawped around it, trailed by the darting cameraman and a twittering crowd. There were glass cabinets stacked with different varieties of bricks, a boat engine, a pile of old type-writers, random collections of coal-mining ephemera and, outside, a lurid green, fifty-foot plastic T. Rex. But by far the most photographed exhibit of the day was the lone Westerner.

'Please, Madam, one click,' they said, sidling over with banks of smartphones.

'Your good country?' asked young men, slipping their arms around my shoulders.

'One selfie?' ventured shy teenage girls, their pretty faces slathered in make-up.

I smiled sweetly as they clicked and posed and sidled, understanding, for a few hours, how awful fame must be. After more photo-mobbing outside, I bravely ran away to the nearest hotel and closed the door on India, lying on the hard bed drinking the last of the Tango-flavoured gin while watching a badly dubbed, theatrically breathless Hindi version of Bear Grylls on TV. It much improved him.

Stifled by Assam's crowds, that night I dreamt of the entire subcontinent coming loose from its tectonic moorings and sinking into the Indian Ocean under the sheer weight of humanity and its waste.

Five miles beyond Margherita was Ledo, a small un-noteworthy town choked by the dust of its open-cast colliery. Heaps of coal lined the railway sidings and Terex earthmovers crawled over wrecked and blackened hillsides. Behind rose the wild hills of Changlang and Tirap, a slender finger of Arunachal Pradesh jabbing its way between Assam and Burma. Stopping in the main street to take in the usual melee of clattering rickshaws, ambling cows and crude shop fronts, it was hard to believe that this town was once the fulcrum of one of the most futile and forgotten campaigns of the Second World War.

By mid-1942, Singapore, Malaysia and Burma had fallen to Japan, and the Imperial Army was now advancing rapidly towards Northeast India, their sights fixed on Delhi. Fleeing through the jungles of northern Burma ahead of them was a desperate column of 600,000 refugees, dying in their tens of thousands from starvation, disease and the merciless strafing of Japanese fighter planes.

Japan had to be stopped and China – our only surviving ally in the East – kept in the war at all costs. Their surrender would not only free up a million Japanese troops to fight the Allies in the Pacific, but would put paid to Roosevelt's vision of Chiang Kai-shek as the anchor of a post-war, non-communist Asia. At the helm of these efforts was Joseph Stilwell, the blunt, acerbic US commander of the

China-Burma-India (CBI) theatre. Better known as 'Vinegar Joe', Stilwell's sole task was to keep the duplicitous Chiang Kai-shek on side by supplying his floundering regime with enough fuel and weapons to fight the Japanese. It didn't help that Stilwell loathed the 'crazy little bastard' he dubbed 'Peanut', recognizing him for the crooked, self-aggrandising despot that he was.

There were two ways to keep China supplied: by air or by land. Neither was easy. The air route involved flying over 'the Hump' of the eastern Himalayas, where abominable weather and poor equipment regularly flung the transport planes against the mountainsides like toys. The land option meant building a road through Japanese-occupied Burma.

Amidst disagreement and warring egos, Roosevelt gave the go-ahead for the latter. In December 1942, 15,000 American soldiers and tens of thousands of coolies began work on the Stilwell Road, a 465-mile supply route that would connect Assam with China. Beginning in the small settlement of Ledo, the proposed road would cut southeast over the Pangsau Pass – soon known as 'Hell Pass' – through the tiger-infested Burmese jungles and on to Kunming. Churchill damned the project from the outset, predicting it would be 'an immense, laborious task, unlikely to be finished until the need for it has passed', and he was quickly proved right: the road was a gross failure, a Sisyphean endeavour costing thousands of lives and billions of dollars.

Conditions were hellish. The men worked sixteen-hour days in humidity so intense it rotted the fatigues off their bodies, and they built much of the road by hand or with outdated, unreliable equipment. Leeches left them covered in oozing sores. Bamboo lice infested hair, beards and groins. Scrub typhus meant a brief but agonizing death. Ninety-eight per cent of the soldiers contracted malaria and many suffered more than a dozen bouts during their tour. Dysentery was *de rigueur*. Cobras slithered through the muddy jungle camps. Tigers attacked at will. Enemy snipers lurked in the sylvan gloom. Monsoon rains destroyed bridges, buried men in mudslides and swept them away in flash floods. And their reward at the end of each ghastly day was another can of Spam and gibbons screeching from dusk till dawn, depriving the exhausted troops of proper sleep.

As one popular ditty said:

> Long may you live
> And when you die
> You'll find hell
> Cooler than the CBI.

Unsurprisingly troops and coolies died in their thousands. Of those who survived, many took solace in 'gunga' and opium (the British often substituting the latter for the coolies' wages). Others simply went mad. No wonder the mocking soldiers renamed CBI 'Confusion Beyond Imagination'.

Seventy per cent of the US conscripts toiling in this jungle hell were African American. The highest concentration of black troops in the entire war, they were deemed by the US Army to be too stupid, idle and cowardly to do any more than crush rocks, load trucks and wash their white officers' underpants. An official US Army document of 1939 titled 'Command of Negro Troops' stated: 'These men are so limited in their ability that there is no use trying to make good soldiers out of them.' The same document warned white troops to 'stay completely away from them' during training.

Another US colonel wrote: 'The average Negro is naturally cowardly' and 'lacks the courage and intelligence' for conflict.

The only positive – and entirely absurd – beliefs about black soldiers were that they had better night vision than Caucasians and were more resistant to malaria, thus making them ideal for jungle warfare. German and Japanese prisoners of war were treated, fed and housed better than America's black conscripts. It's no surprise many black soldiers came to despise their white superiors.

One of these wretched GIs was 21-year-old Herman Perry, a handsome fellow from Atlanta who arrived in Margherita on 7 September 1943. Six months later, an exhausted, diseased, embittered Perry shot dead a hated white officer and fled into the wilderness of Burma's eastern Patkais. Idolized by his fellow black conscripts for his phenomenal ability to dodge bullets, tigers and the military police, Perry ended up settling in a Naga village, marrying the chief's fourteen-year-old daughter and fathering a child. Months later, after one of the biggest manhunts of the Second World War, the 'Jungle King' was finally captured and, after a sham of a trial, hanged by the US Army at Ledo. All in the name of supplying a dictator far more interested in filling his own coffers and fighting Mao Zedong's communists than in aiding the Allied cause.

The Stilwell Road officially opened on 20 May 1945,

twelve days after Germany's surrender. As a United Press story wrote in 1946: 'There can be no better example of the terrific waste of war.'

Manash Gogoi and his friends had known little about the road and nothing of Perry. And the crowd of men who encircled the Hero in Ledo were far more interested in 'one click', my 'good country', and how much the bike had cost than anything to do with Stilwell's Ozymandias.

Riding on slowly, eyes stinging from the coal dust, I scanned the turbid outline of the hills and thought of Perry and the months he had spent evading capture there. Now these border jungles harboured a very different sort of fugitive: groups of disillusioned young men with AK-56s and desperate dreams of a sovereign Naga state. Despite a peace deal being signed in August 2015 between Modi and the National Socialist Council of Nagaland, the struggle wasn't over for some. And while the army sought to flush the militants out of this southernmost corner of Arunachal Pradesh, the area was sadly off-limits to outsiders.

The troubles weren't solely confined to Tirap and Changlang. Two days later the Indian Army and Assam Police launched a joint combat operation in a village near Margherita, killing three Naga militants and one ULFA rebel and recovering a stash of rifles, IEDs and ammunition.

Riding east out of Ledo on the old Stilwell Road, I soon came to the military post of Lekhapani, where a large, modern sign at the roadside read: 'Stilwell Road: Rejuvenate our lifeline, Revitalize our relationship, Reach out beyond our borders', above a map of the original route. Here soldiers from the Assam Rifles walked along the tarmac in full battle dress and pickups loaded with troops roared past, mounted machine guns at the ready.

Wanting to follow the infamous road for a little longer, at Jagan I forked right towards Burma's Pangsau Pass, and instantly found myself transported to another land. I was still in Assam, just, but the traffic and crowds had vanished and instead I was twisting along a deserted, winding road through a tunnel of jade foliage. Real jungle at last! That familiar matted weave of soaring trunks, bamboo thickets, giant ferns and elephant grass.

A lone man padded barefoot along the cracked tarmac, square-ended *dao* – the machete-type knives ubiquitous in tribal Northeast India – and lengths of freshly cut bamboo slung over a slender shoulder. Through the trees nearby I glimpsed the thatched roofs of a tribal village. Giddy from the thrill of this new world I rode straight through a military checkpoint, the soldiers barely looking up as I buzzed under an arch saying 'Welcome to Arunachal Pradesh'. With my Assam plates and visor down they must have mistaken me for a local. The same happened at a second checkpoint and I continued, slightly warily, repeating my Irish granny's mantra of, 'Do nothing, say nothing till the police arrive.' For all the armed presence and permit rules, it was perplexing no one had stopped me.

Halfway to the Burmese border I parked outside the locked and rusting metal gates of Jairampur's Second World War cemetery, clambering over a low, spiked fence into a pathetically neglected graveyard. Its disrepair synonymous with the forgotten status of the CBI theatre, a peeling sign was the only clue as to who lay beneath the cracked and mossy stones. It read:

> These graves bear silent testimony to those soldiers, unlisted men and labourers who ventured to virgin jungle and blistering heat and laid down their lives in the line of duty during the Second World War, whilst part of the all forces against the Imperial Japanese Army.

What a contrast to the polished and perfectly manicured American cemeteries of Omaha Beach or Lorraine. Just like the road they had slaved on, the men buried here had died and been forgotten.

The snoozing soldiers must have realized too late that I was foreign, for when I turned back towards Jagan I was stopped at both checkpoints. The two young recruits at the first one didn't ask for my passport, but they were terribly concerned about John. Since it's impossible to apply for a permit for a single person to visit Arunachal Pradesh, Abhra's contact had added a mysterious Englishman called John Carter to my application. For all I knew John was fictitious. But as far as the soldiers were concerned John was real, and John had absconded without permission.

'Where John?' they kept asking, pointing to his name on the permit.

'Not here,' I replied hesitantly, unsure whether admitting to travelling alone could land me in the nearest clink.

They looked around the bike mistrustfully and glanced up the empty road, as if checking I hadn't secreted John in a pannier, or hidden him behind a nearby bush. Only when they were satisfied I wasn't holding poor John hostage did they allow me to go on.

At the next checkpoint the soldier was ushered away by a plain-clothes gentleman in Ray-Bans and a leather jacket who was evidently 'The Boss'. But after a brief cross-examination about the whereabouts of John, he again waved me on.

'How many foreigners do you get through here?' I asked, before I left.

He looked confused, so I tried again. 'When you last see English person here?'

'No, no!' he laughed. 'You first Britisher I see. I only see on TV before.'

The main checkpoint to this part of Arunachal Pradesh was east of Jagan, on a broken road that dwindled to dirt. Here a hatchet-faced policewoman, ample bust straining at her khaki shirt, marched out of the hut as I approached, three gangly soldiers trotting at her bossy heels. At the same moment, a passing 4WD stopped abruptly and a Chinese-looking man in a shirt and a purple silk sarong jumped out and strode towards me. For a nanosecond my mind tallied up any transgressions that could warrant my arrest: I was travelling alone; I'd strayed too near the Burmese border; I didn't have a guide; I'd jumped two checkpoints. But my anxious reverie was broken by the man's voice.

'Are you Antonia?' he asked.

I nodded.

He held out a hand and smiled. 'I Phupla.'

Phupla – Singpho prince, conservationist and guide – was the unofficial king of Miao, the next town, and my one contact in this eastern corner of the state. We'd been in touch by email but hadn't planned to meet here, and he was hours late for a Singpho festival when he'd spotted the white woman on a bike. Yet his timing couldn't have been better.

'Why doesn't she have a guide?' the policewoman grumbled to him. 'Why is she travelling alone? Where is John?' (Even I was beginning to wonder as to the whereabouts of John by now.)

Only thanks to Phupla's influence, and assurances that I'd be staying at his camp in Miao, was I allowed through.

'No one comes here on a bike, not even Indians – and all the way from Guwahati!' laughed Phupla. 'The guards didn't know what to do with you.'

After three confusing checkpoints, the rules regarding foreigners, solo travel and Arunachal Pradesh were murkier than ever, with contacts and chance appearing more important than any official laws. I'd been lucky today, but would it be the same next time?

A few miles later I stopped, switching off the engine to savour my surroundings and acknowledge my arrival in Arunachal Pradesh. Just as on the road to Jairampur, it was as if I'd crossed into another country, the clamour of the subcontinent dissolving into the peace of the Asian countryside. Gone were the crowds, the traffic, the noise and pollution. In their place birds trilled, butterflies flopped and betel palms rustled gently in the breeze. As I rode on, the faces that looked up from pruning tea bushes and planting paddies bore the flat-nosed, high-cheekboned features of the Tibeto-Burman tribes.

An hour later I reached Miao, stopping to photograph the

'Welcome to Miao' archway, its peeling yellow paint decorated with fire-breathing dragons, Singpho shields and a
hornbill flying through a rising sun.

I'd arrived. Now it was time for the adventure to truly
begin.

5

Into the Wild

My journey had really begun almost two years earlier, late one summer's night on the M5 near Tewkesbury. It was the first panic attack I'd had in ten years, but I recognized it immediately. Blurred vision. Breath coming in rapid rasping gasps. Dry throat. Shaking. A wildly beating heart. Worst of all, that terrifying conviction that either death or irreversible insanity was imminent. Veering off the motorway at the next junction, I stopped at a 24-hour BP petrol station and called Marley, hyperventilating so badly I could barely talk. It was midnight but, like a true knight in shining armour, he jumped on his motorbike and sped to my rescue. In retrospect the hour I spent distracting myself in the petrol station by talking to Dave, the diabetic septuagenarian shelf-stacker, about his numerous woes was darkly comic. As was the brief, sleepless night Marley and I spent in the nearby Premier Inn – the pale, miserable night receptionist checking us in with a look that suggested we weren't the first couple to arrive in different vehicles in the dead of night, asking for a reduced rate. But at the time it wasn't funny at all.

The next one hit me, a little inconveniently, halfway through giving a talk to 150 people at a travel festival a few weeks later. Trembling and gulping for breath, I somehow reached the end without vomiting, fainting or dashing head-long through the door. Another one struck a month later, the morning I was due to give another talk. And so on throughout that autumn. Needing simply to press STOP, I postponed my plans for Arunachal Pradesh and instead went to visit some friends in Thailand the following February.

But in Thailand I unravelled faster than a dieter's resolve in a cake shop. I had planned to visit friends in Pattaya, go motorcycling around Chiang Mai and idle on a beach some-where. But instead I spent most of it cowering at my friends' house, bedevilled by panic attacks, gripped by insomnia, wrestling my mind away from what felt like the cliff edge of insanity. I was supposedly a fearless traveller, a strong, independent woman, someone who relished tramping alone through remote regions. But here I was cringing beside a nice, safe pool in Thailand.

When I *did* attempt to leave my friends' house, the first of many panic attacks hit me on a ferry crossing from the mainland. A full-blown batshit assault on my already fragile neurons, it convinced me that I was either about to die of a heart attack or inexplicably hurl myself overboard into the churning, turquoise waters of the Gulf of Thailand. I felt about as stable as francium. Fear of imminent death has a wonderful way of blunting your inhibitions: I knew I had to talk to someone, anyone. Turning around in my seat, I scanned the cliques of tanned, chattering backpackers behind me, my eyes alighting on a pair of clean-cut thirty-something men.

I walked over and plonked myself in an empty seat beside them. 'Erm, hi, this sounds a bit odd, but I'm having a panic attack. Do you mind if I come and talk to you?'

'Sure, of course. My name's Roland,' said the elder of the two, proffering a hand. 'I'm a psychiatrist from Berlin. Why don't we take a walk?'

But while Roland's soothing tones provided temporary relief to my addled mind, things soon went wrong again, and after two weeks of vile emotional torment I flew back to England, three weeks earlier than planned.

The next few months were a mess. I couldn't be alone, couldn't work and cancelled talks, the corset of fear ever tightening around me. Forget Arunachal Pradesh, I wasn't able to go to London alone for the night. The apogee was a particularly bad weekend in May when, for a second time, I ended up talking gibberish to the staff at a BP service station in Wiltshire. I emailed BP Customer Care afterwards to commend their employees on their dealings with passing lunatics. The reply came back:

'We hope that you will continue to enjoy many more happy visits to BP service stations in the future.'

Desperate to be rid of this canker, I tried a range of cures.

'Get a stone,' said the white, middle-aged shaman, when I called her on FaceTime at her west London home. 'Blow on it every time you feel anxious and, when the stone is full, bury it in your garden and find another one.'

'Put the raisin to your ear, and really *listen* to it,' urged the matronly teacher at a mindfulness course.

'Try these pills,' said my charming South African doctor.

'Focus on the air as it enters and exits your nostrils,' soothed Andy on my Headspace app.

I dutifully blew on stones, listened to raisins, practised daily yoga and meditation, took pills and saw a therapist, treating getting better like an exam I couldn't fail.

In the midst of all this I received an email from my agent saying I'd been offered a publishing deal for this book. It was what I'd *so* wanted. But instead of greeting the email with cartwheels around the kitchen, I felt a gnawing uncertainty. It was July, and I knew I'd never be able to leave for Arunachal in October, as originally planned. I couldn't go anywhere by myself at the moment, let alone fly to the other side of the world.

'I don't think I can do it,' I said miserably to Marley. 'I'm going to have to turn it down.'

'You're not going to turn it down,' he replied. 'You're going to get better, I know it. Just sign it and see what happens.'

So I signed the contract and decided to put Arunachal Pradesh out of my mind for the next few months and just focus on recovering my sanity.

I know. It all sounds completely bonkers. And it was. To someone who's never had a panic attack it must sound ludicrously melodramatic. But I'm by no means alone. Panic disorder affects roughly two per cent of the British and American population. Charles Darwin was a sufferer. So were

Sir Laurence Olivier, Sigmund Freud, Alfred, Lord Tennyson, Charlotte Brontë, Nikola Tesla and Edvard Munch – the latter's iconic painting *The Scream* a visual representation of one of his attacks. They can hit you at any time, and for no apparent reason, like a storm in a seemingly clear sky; a stab of real and present fear fired by the same receptors that told our ancestors to run from a sabre-toothed tiger. You shake, go numb, can't breathe properly and are in no doubt of your own looming extinction or soon-to-be-issued one-way ticket to the nearest asylum.

My derailment was, in retrospect, unsurprising. I'd been pushing myself too hard for too long: working in television, writing a book, writing articles, giving talks. I worked before I went to work. I worked during my lunchbreaks at work. I worked at weekends. I worked in the evenings. Push. Push. Push. With no respite. I'd forgotten why I was pushing so hard, or what it was I was so desperately striving for, but I'd had my foot on the accelerator for so long it had stuck. My life had become a joyless, ensnaring game of Tetris, the blocks held in place by worry and pressure and endless calculations about time and when and how. I was a travel writer, for goodness sake. This was supposed to be fun. But it wasn't. It was a military operation, with me as the cajoling brigadier. I'd hit burnout.

Slowly, however, I recovered. By late summer I was able to go away without Marley for a night. By the autumn I was giving talks again, speaking, at the end of October, to an audience of 750 at the Royal Geographical Society – only a handful of people there knowing what it really meant for me to stand up in front of that crowd and be OK. It was only then, after months of burying all thoughts of it, that I again considered Arunachal Pradesh. I still desperately wanted to go, but was I capable, after everything that had happened? There was only one way to confront my lingering demons, and that was to commit to going in the spring, to throw a grappling hook over the lip of the abyss and see if it held. If it all went pathetically wrong at least I'd have tried. The alternative was to sit at home wondering, bitter, afraid, dependent on Marley, a shell of my former self. Anything was better than that.

So in spite of my silent conviction, to the very last, that the expedition wouldn't happen, I'd boarded the plane to Delhi, reached Guwahati and ridden the first few hundred miles. And, to my great relief, the grappling hook had held.

Miao sits at the edge of the seething jungle, the final port before an ocean of emerald wilderness. Beyond yawn Namdapha, India's third-largest national park, and the violent forests of Burma's Kachin state. Originally dominated by the Buddhist Singpho, the town was now home to an ever-expanding population of migrants and refugees, driven to this wild corner of India by politics and poverty. In the bazaar, Lisu women squatted behind piles of red chillies, ginger, garlic, coriander and tiny purple aubergines, calloused feet poking out from the hems of brightly woven sarongs; Bangladeshi tailors pedalled at antique Singer sewing machines; Bihari men stood at stalls crammed with tawdry Chinese tat; Tibetans sold momos in shacks strung with prayer flags. With all these peoples had come their beliefs, stamped on the streets and alleyways in wood and stone. Candles flickered around chipped deities in little Hindu shrines, crosses stood outside the wooden churches of the heavily Christianized Lisu and, in the main Buddhist temple, Nepali boys darted between the pillars, laughing and shouting, 'How are you I am fine,' in shrill staccato voices.

I rested here for a few days in the quiet of Phupla's camp, an oasis of thatched huts near the stony banks of the Noa-Dihing, where vented bulbuls bickered in silk-cotton trees and fruit bats gorged on plums in the eaves of my hut. The only guest, I was given the full memsahib treatment by his merry trio of staff: Sanjay, a blithe Nepali teenager whose high voice filled the camp with Hindi ballads from first light; Dorje, a shy Tibetan boy, and Bijay, the young Manipuri cook. They sang and whistled and chopped and cooked from dawn until dark, regularly appearing outside my hut with trays of tea and biscuits. If I needed anything from town Sanjay would insist on riding pillion, clinging on as we splashed across the river and bumped up the stony hill, springing off at the end with a 'Perfect journey, Madam', and an approving wobble of the head.

Their *pièce de résistance* was supper, which Sanjay would announce with a beaming 'Dinner ready, Ma'am', at seven on the dot, and Dorje would reverently serve, covering the small dining room table with dish after wonderful dish. There I'd sit like the Queen at a tasting banquet, mopping up spicy fish curry and chana masala with fresh, doughy chapattis and forkfuls of fluffy rice, washed down with warm Kingfisher beer bought from one of the numerous wine shops in town.

Phupla, now dressed in jeans and a polo shirt, appeared at the camp each morning and we'd sit in the weak sunshine

talking and drinking *phalap*, bitter Singpho tea. A brisk, efficient man of around forty, with receding hair, pale skin and an
inquiring gaze, he had the air of a kindly Oriental potentate.
Sharp as a tack, he'd been 'topping' at his Catholic college in
Shillong, yet he wore his intelligence lightly, his conversation
broken by bursts of laughter. He had never met a lone female
traveller before – certainly not one on a motorbike – and he
studied me in the way one might scrutinize an unknown creature you'd found under your bed. The few tourists he dealt
with were generally Indian birdwatchers and groups of Dutch
trekkers. He questioned me about my age, marital status and
why I travelled alone, steepling his fingers and going 'hmmm'
at my answers, as if completing a mental questionnaire.

His father had been a Singpho king, a great hunter who
shot sambar with a homemade muzzle loader and was
employed to catch wild elephants for the government in the
1970's. *Mela shikar*, a practice officially outlawed in India in
1981, involved the lassoing of wild elephants from the back
of a domesticated one, a *koonki*. Smeared in elephant dung
to disguise their smell, the mahouts would ride their koonki
into the middle of the wild herd, stopping undetected next
to the victim of their choice. Being short-sighted creatures
that rarely look up, the unfortunate beast wouldn't know a
thing until the jute lasso slid over its neck. Ironically it was
the elephants' instinctive reaction to protect their trunks by
pulling them up into their mouths that allowed the lasso to
tighten. It took a brave man to catch wild elephants, and many
a mahout was gored or trampled to death.

There were still cases of illegal mela shikar, said Phupla –
'elephant boys' from the Singpho and Khampti tribes catching

young animals that strayed into their villages. Trained elephants were worth between seven and fourteen lakh rupees, around £7,000–14,000, a fortune here by any standards.

The Political Officer, Major John Butler, perhaps irritable after an evening of fitting his windows, dismissed the Singpho as a 'rude and treacherous people' whose 'excessive laziness, immoderate addiction to opium and general uncertainty of character' made them 'anything but good subjects'. But Phupla was anything but this. Generous with his time and knowledge, he had time for everyone.

'I have many friends,' he said. 'That's what I learn in life – friends are important, not money.'

Butler had been right about one thing, though, and that was the opium, which Phupla bemoaned as the scourge of Miao. But it wasn't just good old-fashioned opium the masses were getting high on; it was 'brown sugar' now too, brought here by unscrupulous dealers from Dibrugarh and cut with 'rat poison and God knows what'. Around twenty-five per cent of Miao's young men were addicts, said Phupla sadly, and people were dying all the time. But the government was doing little to help and, when he had set up a detox camp for local addicts, there was no official support.

'I'm worried about you travelling alone,' he warned. 'There are so many addicts here, you might get robbed.'

After a few days of being in Miao, Phupla reminded me I had to register with the police. At the police station, a run-down collection of buildings around a weed-strewn courtyard, I was questioned by a brusque, bosomy Singpho policewoman with petulant red lips and a dangling .303 Lee Enfield. Miao wasn't marked on my permit, she intimated in halting English, stabbing my list of permitted places with a long scarlet fingernail. She followed this with: 'Who accompanying you?' and 'Where John?' Two more men were summoned – *Miami Vice* types with pleather jackets and slicked-back hair – and we sat in a cell-like room stacked with dusty ledgers while they studied my permit. I mentioned Phupla and pointed out that Namdapha *was* on my permit, and after a few tense minutes they pushed a register across the table and asked me to sign it. It was like learning by Braille, trying to understand the permit regulations here.

In the afternoons I explored the packed earth alleyways of Miao, where Chakma women sat on the porches of their bamboo houses weaving bolts of red, fuchsia and indigo cotton. Asked into one house by a charming, pretty teenage girl, I sat on a low stool on the swept earthen floor while she made me milky ginger tea on a stove made from dried mud and cow dung. Delighted to use the English she'd learnt at the 'most big and beautiful' school in Miao, she told me about her people. They were a Buddhist minority from the Chittagong Hill Tracts of Bangladesh, she said, and had been coming to Arunachal Pradesh since the 1960s, when religious discrimination and the construction of a hydroelectric dam had rendered them homeless. Now there were 100,000 of them here, fighting a long battle to be given official refugee status and recognized as Indian citizens.

When her father, a carpenter, came home, he pulled up a stool beside me, took my hands in his and asked his daughter to translate. How glad he was to meet me, he said, and although he was black and I was white we were all the same – all just human beings. The girl wanted to be a bank manager when she grew up, so she could look after her parents when they were old. As with the Bangladeshis in Dibrugarh, I left feeling humbled by their kindness and resilience.

The very few tourists who come to Miao are on their way to Namdapha, a largely unexplored wilderness of alpine meadows, Himalayan peaks and tangled forests jutting 200,000 hectares into the easternmost nook of India. It's not an easy place to visit. Apart from a single mud-clotted track winding some hundred miles from Miao to the Burmese border, there are no proper roads, very few trails and immense tracts of uncharted land. The forests are so dense that even conservationists who spend weeks sloshing through the dripping jungle rarely glimpse anything of the tigers, snow leopards, leopards, clouded leopards, hoolock gibbons, red pandas or hundred other species of mammal that live here (not to mention nearly 500 species of bird and a thousand types of plant). Encounters with snakes and leeches are far more common. There are about one million snake bites a year in India, 45,000 of them fatal, and few areas have more snakes than the jungles of this, the Northeastern frontier.

'You're lucky the snakes are still hibernating,' said Phupla. 'A bite from most of the snakes around here means you need to say your last wishes and tell your relatives goodbye.'

There was the added risk of insurgents. Researchers conducting a tiger census in 2012 had been shot at by militants and had all their camera traps stolen by poachers. But I wanted to have a taste of Namdapha, and to do so I'd need both a permit and a guide. Phupla applied for my permit in Miao, dashing off at 11.45 one morning to catch the park office before its staff went home for their three-hour lunch.

'When you Britishers left all Indians became lazy,' said Phupla with a chuckle.

My guide would be Japang Pangsa, Namdapha's head mahout, a man I'd been told about over email by a leading Indian conservationist. A dying breed, these mahouts held a strange allure, jungle knights aboard their giant steeds. But there was another reason I was itching to meet Japang. He was a Wancho Naga from the Patkai Hills, the very area Herman Perry had fled to. Of all the Naga's roughly seventy sub-tribes they were one of the least known, and had once enjoyed a reputation for being among the most terrifying.

Read anything about Northeast India and you'll soon be entranced by tales of the terrible Naga. Inveterate headhunters, until as recently as the 1990s there was nothing a lusty Naga warrior adored more than returning from a raid on a nearby village with a bloody basket of freshly taken heads. Heads, they believed, were the dwelling place of the soul and hence receptacles of great power: the more of these grisly, staring prizes a village had dangling from their 'head tree', the greater fertility and good fortune they'd enjoy. Best of all were the heads of women and children but essentially any old noggin would do. The men brave enough to conduct such raids wore little brass heads around their necks, one for each victim. One can only imagine the inconvenience of having the Naga next door. In 1837 a Scottish tea planter observed that 'they are the wildest and most barbarous of the hill-tribes, looked upon with dread and horrour [sic] by their neighbours'.

No one knows where these paleo-Mongoloid peoples came from, or when they arrived in these hills. But their myths and headhunting ways are closely connected with those of tribes in Borneo, Sarawak and the Philippines. It's possible they were all part of the same diaspora that walked and paddled south from Mongolia, Tibet or Yunnan sometime around the tenth century. Although they had no written script until very recently, ancient Naga folktales talk of great sea journeys, and their obscure origins only add to their mystique.

Aware of their unsavoury habits, the British initially left the Naga tribes to their own devices, but when Assam planters kept finding headless coolies among their tea bushes they couldn't let it slide, and there followed several decades of bloody skirmishes. Gunpowder didn't always win against dao, and in one nasty incident in 1875 Wancho Naga tribesmen ambushed and decapitated eighty British soldiers, legging it with the head of the commander, Lieutenant Holcombe. Holcombe's head wasn't found until 1925, when another British Political Officer found it occupying pride of place on the head tree in a nearby Naga village.

British attempts to outlaw headhunting failed abysmally; it was simply too important to Naga society. Verrier Elwin, a British anthropologist and passionate advocate of tribal rights, who became Nehru's tribal advisor in 1954, wonderfully summed up their passion for taking heads.

'If you talk to a Naga on such tedious topics as theology or economics ... he quickly slips away to have a refreshing rice beer. Open the question of head-hunting and his eyes light up and a torrent of exciting and improper information pours from his lips.'

When they weren't boiling heads in pots of chillies their shamans were said to engage in a spot of therianthropy, turning themselves into tigers and leopards to roam the jungles in search of prey.

Incredibly, by 1914, relations between the British and their uppity subjects had improved to the point where around 5,000 Naga fought with the Allied Labour Corps on the Western Front. The Germans were appalled, some even complaining to their High Command about having to fight 'savages'. But they proved a welcome novelty among the British troops. A copy of the *Illustrated War News* from 1917 describes them as 'wild looking little fellows who ... in their native hills do a little head-hunting when the humour takes them ... but here in France they are quite good tempered and jolly'. Needless to say, the 'jolly' Naga were bitterly disappointed when they were ordered not to take German heads, and to settle for just helmets instead.

Thirty years later they fought for the British again, acting as scouts and trackers for the Allies in the jungles of the Indo-Burmese border. Not interested in cash, they were paid in trinkets such as matches, buttons and safety pins. This time the rules were looser and many a Japanese head ended up decorated with grass and buffalo horns, hanging from a head tree.

Dawn had broken on another sultry day when Japang arrived. I'd pictured a gnarled old warrior with skin like knotted teak, his scraggy neck hung with rows of little brass heads – a man who'd lassoed wild elephants and wrestled the odd tiger. But the individual who stood in front of me was a vision in grey nylon – a small, stocky fellow with rounded features, a pot belly and closely cropped hair. No more than forty, his unlined skin was conker brown and his eyes round and hazel.

Painfully shy, he knew only fragmentary English and spoke it with a furrowed brow and flickering downward glances. Only his shot-putter's thighs, straining at his grey nylon trousers, and calloused toes, rough from a lifetime of digging into the back of leathery elephantine ears, betrayed him as a mahout.

Japang was the master of seven working elephants, leviathans that could crush him in a moment or snap him in two with their trunks. And he was a Wancho Naga, the descendant of men who had hunted human heads. But he'd never ridden pillion with a woman before, and a foreign one at that, and apprehension squirmed in every nerve and muscle. He threw his leg gingerly over the seat, flattened himself against the top box and clutched his small rucksack to his chest. But the rough track to the park was blind to his plight. It shunted him into me at every bump, cracked his bare head on the back of my helmet and pressed him awkwardly close to female flesh. He wriggled, he tensed, he shuffled backwards, the epitome of cringing discomfort. But as soon as he'd restored the gap between us another bump would cruelly shoot him forwards again. Given a choice, I'm sure he would rather have been on the back of a wild tusker in musth. Now probably wasn't the time to tell him that, apart from my short forays into town with Singing Sanjay, it was the first time I'd taken anyone pillion. I was every bit as nervous as he was.

At the park gate, where a rusting green 'Project Tiger' sign reminded visitors that this was a designated tiger reserve bolstered by millions of rupees of government funds, I signed a register in a wooden hut. Beyond, the track wound along the lip of a ridge that plunged on the left to the wide, pebbly plain of the Noa-Dihing and soared on the right in a sheer wall of greenery. Near the river, stilted Chakma houses sat neatly amidst a patchwork of brown paddies and tufts of palms. From here it looked idyllic: the mist-cloaked hills, the fertile plain, the palms, the quietly grazing cattle. But life for the Chakma was hard, and the river a mercurial neighbour. Only two months later the water would come roaring through here, bursting its banks and flooding two nearby villages.

I wanted to meet Japang's elephantine charges but all of them, bar one female, were deep in Namdapha on logging duties and ranger patrol. The female was having a day off, munching her way through the undergrowth somewhere in the vicinity of the collection of dilapidated concrete huts that served as the park's elephant station. Elephants, despite their size, can melt into the forest and, for an hour, I followed Japang into the humid gloom, his dao cracking at bamboo and slashing through shrubs that wiggled with leeches blindly seeking our blood. The few that were around now were nothing compared to the plague of the summer months. Piles of fly-swarmed elephant dung and the odd broken branch indicated we were close, but there were no five-tonne pachyderms to be seen. Then Japang, sniffing the air like a keening hound, stopped and pointed to a slope above us where, just five metres away, a wrinkled grey bottom was poking out of a thicket of bamboo. Had I been on my own, I'd have walked straight past it.

Elephants are insufferably greedy and Kanchi, the 21-year-old female, was not amused at being disturbed from her morning's gluttony.

Japang stood at the bottom of the slope, enticing her with a handful of ferns. '*Lo! Lo! Lo!*' he commanded, which I presumed meant 'come here'.

A minute or two later she slid down the slope with a snapping of branches and a rattling of leg chains, turning her bottom towards Japang and letting out an enormous, noisy pee. Only when she'd finished did she swivel around to face us, her expression a resigned: 'Yes? And what do *you* want?'

He patted her rough forehead tenderly and commanded her to greet me with her trunk. '*Salaam! Salaam!*' he ordered.

But that cunning proboscis was far more interested in the food in Japang's pockets than in saying hello to me. Armed with 100,000 muscles and a sense of smell sixteen times more powerful than a dog's, an elephant's trunk can winkle a sweet out of your pocket or lift a tonne of logs. In South Africa I'd seen elephants trained to track poachers, hunting them for miles through the bush after the briefest smell of an abandoned camp. Now, with a surgeon's precision, Kanchi probed and sniffed Japang, flapping her ears intently as she hunted down the goods. When he produced a bag of salt and placed handfuls in her trunk, she blinked and blew contentedly as she swung it into her mouth. I stood beside her, awed, looking into her amber eyes, wondering how such intelligent giants have allowed man to tame them. Only the previous evening Phupla had told me a story about an old Assamese mahout he knew. Once, during the monsoon, the Forest Department's elephants were helping to evacuate villagers across a swollen river. One mahout became so drunk on rice beer that on the way home he slid off his elephant for a pee and passed out drunk on the ground. Rather than leave him, the elephant wrapped its unconscious master in its trunk and carried him many miles home, depositing him at the door of his hut.

We left the bike at a forest camp and spent the rest of the

day squelching along a muddy track between matted escarpments of foliage. Everywhere the jungle harried at the road, threatening it with the soft teeth of giant ferns, the caress of bamboo, the sigh of banana palms and a guard of slender orange trunks that surged towards the canopy. A brilliant naturalist, Japang could identify every shriek, warble and trill that erupted from the trees around us: the distinctive triple call of the blue-throated barbet, the hoarse chattering of a courting rufous woodpecker, the shrieks of a yellow-necked woodpecker, the melodious call of a laughingthrush. Much more exciting, though, were the prints of a big cat, padding along the track for several miles beside us.

Japang squatted down for a closer look. 'Common leopard, yesterday,' he said with assurance.

The trees were so thick here that we wouldn't have known if the leopard was just metres away, licking his paws at the prospect of an English *hors d'oeuvre*. Later we saw the much smaller prints of a fishing cat, daintily picking its way through the mud.

Namdapha is supposedly the only park in the world that is home to four species of big cat – leopard, snow leopard, clouded leopard and tiger. But there was little chance of seeing tiger prints. The reserve and its grandly named Tiger Strike Force are a farce. Everyone knows there are no tigers left here – or only a handful at best. They've been poached to oblivion, their skins, teeth, claws and bones sold to Burmese middlemen for six lakh rupees, roughly £6,000. The Strike Force are a shambolic bunch of sixty underpaid Tangsa, Singpho and Lisu men with eight guns between them, four of which actually work. (Although since my visit I hear that more guns have been purchased.) Of the four rangers employed to cover the 200,000 hectares, one of them never leaves the office in Miao. When I asked a local conservationist if it was possible to go on an anti-poaching patrol they laughed and said, 'There is no such thing.' The poachers can effectively hunt at will, and they know it.

The disappearance of Namdapha's tigers is largely blamed on the Lisu, a Kachin people first discovered on Indian soil by an Assam Rifles border patrol in 1961. They've been drifting across from Burma ever since, clearing the jungle for wet rice cultivation and cardamom plantations and hunting the forests to silence. The fact that Namdapha is a protected wilderness means little to them: not recognized as Indian citizens until 2015, these skilled hunters have few job opportunities or possible sources of income. Cordoned off by Burma on one side and the Himalayas on the other, they have nowhere else to go. Arunachal's unforgiving terrain has always been a last resort, a place where vanquished, fleeing tribal peoples have perched on mountainsides or hewn homes out of the jungle. And now it's no different. With India's population rising faster than almost anywhere else on earth (India is due to become the world's most populous country by 2022) and parts of Burma riven by conflict, minority peoples with nowhere else to go are being squeezed into these blank spaces on the map.

That night I stayed at the run-down forest camp where I'd left my bike, on a bluff above the Noa-Dihing, in a creaking hut whose floorboards scuttled with cockroaches. It was run by a booze-sodden Assamese whose breath could have pickled gherkins. The lake of empty rum bottles behind the kitchen betrayed the fact it wasn't a one-off. The only other guests were a couple of Danish birders, lean, intense and swathed in swishing shells of Gore-Tex, their necks hung with lenses the width of dinner plates. Over supper their conversation rarely strayed beyond ornithological matters. If a tiger had danced the tango in front of them they wouldn't have cared – they couldn't tick it off on their spreadsheet or tell their twitcher friends. It was birds, birds, birds.

Tired of talking birds I retired early to my hut, tucking my holey mosquito net under the thin mattress and huddling under a pile of musty blankets to keep warm. At some point it began to rain, the drumming on the metal roof drowning out the roar of the river below, and several times in the night I awoke, turning on my head torch to find cockroaches hurrying across the bed, retreating from the sudden light. Repulsed, I pulled the blankets over my head and fell back into a fitful sleep.

6

OPIUM COUNTRY

Daylight dispensed with the cockroaches but in their place arrived an unwelcome brigade of the collywobbles. They scaled the ramparts of my rational defence, slung out Calm and Reason and replaced them with Fear and Doubt. With well-practised efficiency they pulled ropes around my chest, polluted my mind with negative thoughts and unleashed a river of nerves. And all because Japang was needed on elephant duty and I had to return to Miao alone. It was only twenty miles but the overnight rain had cloaked the hills in fog and churned the track to a soupy mire. There was no phone reception, few people and, if yesterday's prints were anything to go by, the odd cat with very big teeth. I didn't have a satellite phone or any sort of emergency beacon – if anything went wrong I really was on my own. This was what

I'd wanted; to shed all the 'what if' paraphernalia of the paranoid modern traveller, choosing instead to trust in humanity and the universe, and in my own ability to cope. But now I wasn't quite so sure. I couldn't help recalling Cambodia's Mondulkiri Death Highway, a road I'd had to tackle during my journey down the Ho Chi Minh Trail that had come uncomfortably close to living up to its name.

With the Danish couple long gone – they strode off at dawn with their guide they couldn't remember the name of – I ate my greasy omelette and chapatti alone and stewed with resented anxiety. *Pull yourself together*, I reprimanded myself. *It's only twenty bloody miles.* More than anything I resented the person I felt I'd become. Where was the girl who'd ridden the Ho Chi Minh Trail alone? I wanted her, not this quivering wimp.

Determined not to show Japang my feelings, I thanked him, pressed some notes into his hand and swung my leg over the bike. When he shyly asked for a selfie I pulled my mouth into a smile then rode off with a wave, hoping I wouldn't go arse over tit until I was at least around the corner.

What had been a challenging road yesterday was now a vile slippery sludge. I slid and paddled and splashed and ground, my legs shin deep in mud. *Keep going, keep going, keep going*, I urged myself through gritted teeth, churning slowly on. An hour later I reached the elephant station and the worst was over. I hadn't fallen off, or died, or been eaten by a leopard, or any of the ridiculous things Fear insisted would happen. The collywobbles beat a hasty retreat: nerves became elation; fear became joy.

This was the point of adventure, I reflected: to remove

the coddling net of certainty and lob a few grenades of risk into your life; to face your fears and carry on despite them; to realize, every time you overcome these real and imagined obstacles, that you're a little bit stronger than you thought you were. I was still learning to trust myself after the previous year; trust that I wasn't going to come screamingly unravelled in the forest. This morning's victory over Fear was a vital step forward.

I was heading next for Wakro, a small town in the neighbouring Lohit district in the southern part of the Mishmi Hills. Described by Verrier Elwin as 'the most formidable in the whole of India', the hills surrounding the Lohit and Dibang Valleys were renowned for their terrible climate and extreme inaccessibility. Because of this, and their proximity to Tibet, they attracted more early explorers than anywhere else in the Northeast – soldiers, surveyors and missionaries wanting to pit their egos against the wilderness and proselytize the local tribes. Perhaps embittered by failure, their reports of the Digaru, Miju and Idu Mishmi tribes – the hardy Tibeto-Burman inhabitants of the region – were unanimously vile. Lieutenant Burton, the earliest known European visitor to the area, reported in 1825 that the locals were 'very averse to strangers'. They were 'excessively filthy', grumbled explorer William Robinson in 1841; as 'rude looking as could be imagined', snubbed Lieutenant Wilcox, a surveyor, in 1827. Major John Butler, never one for complimenting the locals, dismissed them as a 'very wild roaming race of people, capable of the most remorseless reprisals and massacres'. Another visitor scorned them as 'deceitful and bloodthirsty devils'.

They didn't only kill each other. In 1854, while travelling into the hills with crosses, a flute, a sextant and a medicine chest, two French missionaries, Fathers Krick and Bourri, were brutally dispatched by a Mishmi chief.

A century later, opinions had shifted little. In 1926 Frank Kingdon-Ward wrote that he'd seldom 'come across a tribe so uncouth and unsophisticated' as these 'almost naked savages'. The sanguine Elwin, writing several decades afterwards, was alone in his praise of the Mishmi. To him they were 'beautiful, cultured and hospitable' with 'quite wonderful coiffures'. Good old Elwin, the English vicar's son who forsook his faith and culture to live among the tribal people of the Northeast.

'You can't go alone,' said Phupla, sitting in a plastic chair marshalling Sanjay as he packed boxes of noodles and loo roll for a group of birders from Mumbai. I'd be riding fifty miles northeast along a skein of trails that weren't on any maps, into the opium-addled Mishmi Hills. If a desperate addict didn't leap out of the trees and rob me, I'd certainly get lost. My map of Arunachal – the best available in England – was largely fiction, he added, casting it aside dismissively. The towns were misspelt, the roads in the wrong place. Nor would the offline mapping application on my smartphone be of any help, since the area I'd be riding through was an ominous white blank. Then there was the question of what the police would do if they found a stray foreigner riding alone.

Phupla, in all his princely wisdom, was right in one respect. If it hadn't been for the strapping Chakma youth he recruited, along with his bike, to guide me, I might have vanished without trace. A moon-faced boy with shades, gelled hair and denim shorts, Karan led me along a convolution of foot tracks, weaving between bamboo houses and paddies until we reached the wide, stony corridor of the Noa-Dihing. We crossed this alluvial hinterland for miles, twisting between grey boulders, thudding over rocks, splashing through streams and crunching through drifts of silvery sand. Impassable during the rains, now the foaming remnants of the river were forded by a pair of flimsy, slatted bamboo bridges that swayed and cracked ominously under our wheels. It was tricky riding but Karan, on a shiny new 125cc sports bike entirely unsuitable for off-roading, led with aplomb.

North of the river, a broken tarmac road snaked through two Chakma villages. Here women in red and blue sarongs walked with silver urns of water on their heads, little boys wobbled along on oversized bicycles and naked, pot-bellied urchins squealed excitedly as we passed. Just as in tribal Laos, wrinkled old folk sat outside their huts drawing on bamboo bongs. Only a government school, where girls in blue and white uniforms hurried across a dusty yard with textbooks on their heads, reminded me that this was still India.

Beyond, the road ran due north, decaying amidst the encroaching jungle. Not high on the government's road improvements list, the rough, weedy surface was strewn with fallen leaves, and drooping thickets of bamboo threatened to garrotte the unwary traveller. At some point we crossed into Miju Mishmi territory, an invisible boundary where the Miju gather once a year to sacrifice a chicken and ensure good luck for the community. Now the bamboo huts were longer, lower and surrounded by cactus fences, and the men dragging lengths of bamboo along the road stouter and darker-skinned.

By noon we were nearing Wakro and I bade goodbye to my guide. He'd be back in Miao by sunset.

I was staying at the only lodgings in Wakro, an overpriced 'eco resort' with hard wooden beds, its own organic tea garden and a young Miju manager with dull eyes and slow, deliberate movements. The absent owner, a wealthy Miju, was a contact of Abhra's and, like Phupla, seemed convinced I'd get raped, robbed or lost.

'My manager will look after you,' he'd instructed down the phone from his government office in Assam.

Upon first impressions Wakro was a drowsy, pleasant-seeming town, a fecund oasis in the crook of the misty hills. Long, squat Miju huts and neat concrete bungalows were dotted between dirt alleys, their gardens bursting with yellow mustard flowers, chillies, onions, peppers, banana palms, roses, hibiscus and sweet-smelling verbena. Orange trees grew in neatly planted orchards, tea bushes sprung in emerald rows and flame of the forest bloomed brilliant and red. But Wakro's idyllic veneer hid a poorly kept secret: behind the wooden fences, away from the blind-eyed glances of the law, grew another crop – the opium poppy. Interested to know more about Wakro's favourite product, I asked the manager to introduce me to one of the town's many addicts. With around ninety per cent of the households growing poppies, we didn't have to go far: five minutes later we were taking off our shoes on the wooden steps of a neighbouring longhouse watched by a herd of ragged, curious children.

We walked in, the bamboo slats springing and creaking under our bare feet, and sat cross-legged beside a square, smoking hearth in the middle of the house. Above it, chunks of meat were being smoked on a suspended wooden tray, the slats of which were shiny with grease. Looking around, I felt as if I'd been teleported to another world, one that I thought existed only in the books of Victorian explorers. The main thing was the skulls – rows of them. They hung along one wall, the charred heads of at least fifty animals, tufts of singed fur clinging to the bases of large, conical horns. They were mithun, *Bos frontalis* – the large, semi-wild bovines indigenous to Northeast India, parts of Burma, Yunnan and Bangladesh's Chittagong Hill Tracts. Highly prized by most of the tribes in Arunachal Pradesh, the number of mithun a man owned traditionally signified his wealth, and they were still used as dowries and payment in the settlement of village disputes. Many were sacrificed as offerings to the spirits, and their skulls smoked and hung in the huts of their owners. It was the first I'd seen of them, albeit far from alive. On the other walls hung sheathed daos, baskets made from cane and woven bamboo, and a few grubby items of clothing.

We weren't alone. On the opposite side of the hearth was a sinewy old man in dirty tracksuit bottoms and a traditional Miju red embroidered waistcoat. He lay limply on a thin mat, the small door near his head punching a rare slab of sunlight into the dark, smoky interior and throwing it like a blanket across him. Only when the manager addressed him did he seem to notice our arrival, peeling himself off his mat to sit shakily upright. I could see now that he had short, greying hair, a gentle face and wide-set, watery eyes that looked unsteadily out from behind wire-rimmed spectacles. His right eye, I noticed, as we shook hands, was swivelled stubbornly to the side, giving him the goggly look of an old salmon.

Bizarrely, under his waistcoat, he wore a faded black T-shirt bearing the words: 'London City of Dreams'.

Pouring himself a cup of tea from a blackened kettle, he talked quietly in Miju, the manager translating in turn. His name was Ajidu Chakwa, he said, and he was a priest and tribal elder. He had been an opium addict for forty of his sixty-one years. Like many of the older Miju, he'd originally only used the drug for bartering, trading it for salt, cloth and matches in the market at Sadiya in Assam, four days' walk away. There'd been no roads then, just jungle, and so much wildlife he'd once seen four tigers in a day. Had he shot any? I asked.

'Oh yes,' he replied, looking wistfully into the embers; he was once a great hunter. He'd shot four – all of them in self-defence. The last one had been when out hunting deer seventeen years ago. Sensing something behind him, he'd turned around to see a tiger stalking through the under-growth. It was huge, he said, shaking his head at the memory, the biggest he'd ever seen, and it was coming for him: if he hadn't shot it, it would have killed him. He always ate the tigers he killed; the meat was delicious, tasting like strong beef. Afterwards he'd smell of tiger for ten days and none of his goats would come near him. But he hadn't seen one since that time seventeen years ago.

As he was telling us this, he pulled a small plastic bag from under his pillow and unwrapped it to reveal a ball of sticky black *kani*, opium, and a few strips of brown rag. He usually chewed on the rags – nettle fibres impregnated with the potent poppy sap – but occasionally he smoked the drug too. At this he picked up a small bamboo bong, packed it with a ball of kani and lit it using a glowing ember held in a pair of bamboo tongs. I watched as the opium hit his bloodstream, searching for any visible signs of altered consciousness, but there was no change at all. Decades of addiction will do that.

Now, for research purposes, of course, would have been the perfect moment to have a few puffs on the bong myself. But after my last experience of the drug I thought it a bad idea. Crawling out of the door, puking as I went, wasn't the way I wanted to end this meeting. I'd tried opium years ago in northern Thailand, you see, as a naive backpacker fond of getting high, and had spent the night projectile-vomiting over a veranda while my companions wallowed in semi-comatose bliss. Suspecting it to be a simple case of beginner's bad luck, I gave it another bash the following evening, lying on the bamboo floor while a shrivelled creature dosed me up with his thin silver pipe. Beyond that my memory is blurred, but as I hung over the veranda, my body convulsing in emetic rebellion, I recall wondering whether it was time to dial the emergency helicopter evacuation included on my travel insurance. Thankfully I didn't, although the experience was enough to put me off opiates for life.

But addiction isn't much fun, and maybe I'd had a lucky escape. At the beginning the drug envelops you like a lover's warm embrace, but it soon becomes jealous and demanding, the opioid receptors in your brain insisting on regular and increasing supplies. Ajidu didn't enjoy it anymore, he hadn't for years, he said sorrowfully, blowing pillars of blue smoke out of his nose while taking short sips of tea, but it was too hard to give up. He'd tried a few times, but the shaking, fever, exhaustion, vomiting, diarrhoea and insomnia were too much to bear.

'It's the English's fault,' he said matter-of-factly, poking the smouldering opium with a strip of wire and taking another drag. 'They gave it to us.'

He had a point. Although no one's quite sure where the tribes here first got a taste for the drug – whether it came east from Assam or west from Kachin and Yunnan – the British certainly played a part. Indian-grown opium financed British rule on the subcontinent, its sales to China accounting for twenty per cent of the Raj's revenue and, in turn, underwriting much of the British Empire. Opium generated the cash for Britain to trade throughout the Indian Ocean, and in China the money bought tea and silk.

But it didn't all get packed into tea caddies and shipped across the Bay of Bengal. Knowing the tribal taste for it, canny British Political Officers like Major Butler used it as a pacifying gift, dispensing it to village chiefs on their flag-waving tours. It was bartered more than smoked back then; the virile tribesmen were far too busy slave-raiding, headhunting and meting out clan justice to lounge around in an opium-induced haze. Ironically, with 'civilization' came a surge in production and addiction. A hundred years ago men like Ajidu would have been warrior fit and constantly alert, but nowadays there is no need. Life in this isolated corner of India can be brutish and boring. Food is often in short supply, medical help is far away and employment is scarce. The pipe offers relief from monotony and pain, and the sale of it gives families much-needed income.

After an hour or so Ajidu looked tired and lay down again,

so we decided to leave. But the problem of how to say thank you and goodbye had my British sensibilities all aflutter. For, as well as having no written script, the Miju have no words for hello, please or thank you. Instead they greet people with a 'How is your health?' and take their leave with a perfunctory *tai min*, 'I am going now'. But please and thank you are the pillars of the British lexicon, the very foundations of our stiff-upper-lipped reserve. Without them we feel rudderless and stammering. In the briefest of transactions at the supermarket checkout the average British person says thank you at least six times. We write thank-you letters and cards and send flowers to show our gratitude. Strolling out with a casual 'I'm going now' just didn't seem enough. Instead I repeated *tai min* moronically and threw in at least four thank yous – just in case.

In the small garden behind the house the naked green pods of Ajidu's poppies bore the scars of the recent harvest. They were barely hidden from passers-by, but no one seemed worried. More illegal opium is grown in Arunachal Pradesh than any other part of India, with Lohit and neighbouring Anjaw being the centres of production. But the Indian government does precious little about it: the problem is too big, the area too remote and the resources to deal with it too limited.

That afternoon the manager and I walked along the dried-up bed of the Kamlang River. A troop of monkeys swung invisibly through the trees on the riverbank, branches swishing and bouncing as they went, and birds fluted and babbled in every tree. We passed several furtive-looking boys, catapults in hand, craning their necks towards the canopy in search of feathered prey: incorrigible hunters, there are few wild creatures the Miju won't eat. Hunting, like opium, is officially banned by the government, but few of the tribal people in Arunachal Pradesh take any notice. As far as they are concerned, both opium production and hunting are legitimate traditional practices and they're not going to stop. Whenever I pulled out my *Collins Handguide to the Birds of the Indian Subcontinent* to identify a flash of blue or a nearby call, I'd casually ask the manager if he'd eaten it. There was my friend the blue-throated barbet, the choirboy of the high branches, a gorgeous creature resplendent in jade and azure plumage.

'Miju like eat this bird – he taste very good.'

The looping hoopoe, with his jaunty crest, was another tasty little number. Morbidly interested in seeing the extent of the Miju's culinary tastes, I pointed to a selection of species in the book. Hornbill, hummingbird, bulbul, Himalayan barbet, roller – no bird was too small or too rare; he'd dined on them all. Trying not to look like Disgusted Vegetarian of England I nodded and turned the pages. Who was I to criticize after all? The British hunt foxes and hares, kill badgers and shoot rabbits. As horrified as I was, it wasn't my place to barge in with my wagging-fingered foreign values and tell him it was wrong.

After a disturbed night of dreams about hunting small birds, I packed up the Hero to the glorious accompaniment of the owlish, see-sawing hoots of hoolock gibbons. Despite the protestations of the resort's owner, I'd be riding alone from here, heading east on the only road towards Walong, a Mishmi town near the Tibetan border. Winding through an otherwise impassable tract of the Mishmi Hills, bordering southeastern Tibet and Burma, the road had grown out of an old tribal trading route; the Tibetans coming west with furs, silver coins, musk and rock salt and returning east with cotton, silk and, later, cigarettes. J. P. Mills, a British Political Officer who led a wartime mission to establish British out-posts in the un-administered parts of the North East Frontier Agency, travelled this way in 1943, describing what was then known as the 'Walong promenade' as 'atrociously bad'. Beyond the road, he said, it was 'extremely difficult country in which to move . . . the rivers are too steep to be fordable or navigable . . . and the high, steep trackless ranges which flank them make lateral movement almost impossible.'

He was followed in 1950 by the intrepid Kingdon-Ward, on his way to a ten-month expedition to Tibet, his forty-one Tibetan porters panting up the hills with 'botanical presses, reams of botanical drying paper and several thousand rupees in coin'. It was during this trip that Kingdon-Ward found himself near the epicentre of the Great Earthquake, when it hit on the evening of 15 August. Jumping out of his tent, just across the border in Rima, Tibet, he observed how the 'shaking mountains had a fuzzy outline as if completely out of focus', and that as well as terror he felt an 'incredulous astonishment that these solid-looking hills were in the grip of a force which shook them as a terrier shakes a rat'.

Nowadays the road comes to a dead end before the border and I'd have to return the same way, but it was an area almost no outsiders visited and I wanted to see what was there. I hoped the road was a little less atrocious than in Mills's time.

'You'll be a lady alone on a dangerous mountain road, and in opium country,' the resort owner protested down the phone. 'It'll be dangerous if it rains. Take my manager with you.'

In an attempt to discourage me further he warned me that last year Huawei, a village near Walong, had been cut off for eight months due to landslides. But I didn't want to take the manager with me or be passed from man to man like some breakable foreign object. Although I was riding into increasingly remote and unknown territory, I *wanted* to travel alone. Solo travel is like a drug – it has its risks, but it also has the potential to unlock rare feelings of euphoria. Only when I've been totally alone, miles from anywhere or anyone I know, have I experienced its pure, unbridled joy. I wanted to eschew guides, to embrace the risks and the fears and go solo in this little-known land. I still had no idea if I could legally travel alone in Arunachal Pradesh, or what would happen if the police stopped me, but I wanted to at least try. Like Freddie Mercury, I wanted to break free – although in this case my longing didn't involve a Hoover and suspenders.

When the owner understood I wasn't going to relent he booked me into the Circuit House in Khupa, a day's ride away, and told me to use his name if I ran into any trouble. I wrote it in biro across my hand, thanked the manager and left.

From Wakro it was briefly north to Parshuram Kund, a sacred pool in the Lohit River where Hindus come to wash away their sins. According to legend, the sage Parshuram had thrown his axe at the mountains here, carving a passage for the river. A coachload of devotees arrived as I passed it, nearly running me off the road in their haste for absolution. From here a narrow road wound steeply into the mountains, snaking up their forested flanks in a dizzying series of switchbacks.

Soon the cobalt waters of the Kund were hundreds of metres below, the pilgrims mere specks of colour on the shore. Minutes later they were gone.

It had been sunny in Wakro when I left but now the air thickened to a pale mist and a chill wind shook the trees with urgent gusts. Rain felt imminent. Stopping to put on my fleece, a small voice questioned if riding stubbornly into the mountains alone was really a good idea, but I told it to be quiet and continued. Onwards the road carried me, a ribbon of dirt and broken tarmac twisting and climbing east through a wild profusion of hills, their sheer slopes clothed in dense blankets of greenery and tendrils of ghostly mist. In all directions nature burst forth, rushed and tumbled in a chaos of superabundance, ridge, peak, slope and valley fading from emerald green to bluish grey before dissolving into the haze. Far below, the Lohit – the Brahmaputra's most easterly tributary – surged through its rocky corridor, height and distance taming it to a whispering stream. This was the Arunachal Pradesh I'd dreamt of, a land of wild, formidable mountains and rivers galloping through deep, sylvan gorges. It was a scene that must have changed little since Butler, Mills et al marched this way a hundred years ago.

The Hero, which had only just recovered from its muddy ordeal in Namdapha, was not enjoying the climb. The higher we went, the more it stuttered, grumbling up the inclines in first and second gear. When I feared it was about to throw in the towel altogether the road levelled out and a stone by the roadside announced the Udayak Pass. The altimeter on my phone read 1,640 metres, a molehill by Himalayan standards. A tatty little metal shrine, its allegiance to Shiva marked by a rusty three-pronged trident, stood beside the stone, inside which passing travellers had placed incense and candles. Ever superstitious, I added ten rupees and half a banana to the pile and asked for protection ahead. Maybe it was the gods, or perhaps just a stretch of downhill, but after that the Hero gamely recovered its composure.

Further on I came upon another roadside shrine, its small stone Shiva garlanded with plastic marigolds and smouldering with incense. I stopped beside it and a bony sadhu in brown rags and a turban scuttled over, crablike and acquisitive, muttering mantras as he planted a splodge of brown tikka on my forehead and held his hands together in supplication. I gave him forty rupees and he sat back down on the ground, his work done. I hadn't expected men like him in these largely animist hills.

Bar a handful of 4WD Sumo taxis – the main form of public transport in the Northeast – and a few Mishmi men on motorbikes with guns slung across their backs, I had the road to myself. Occasionally I passed idling gangs of road workers, dark-skinned, dirty men and women with infants strapped to their mother's backs. Squatting, gossiping and lethargically breaking and shifting piles of rocks, they were pictures of ennui. All of them stopped what they were doing, stared and did open-mouthed double-takes as I rode past waving.

But while the Border Roads Organisation's efforts to upgrade the road left a lot to be desired, they'd excelled themselves with signage. YOU ARE NOT BEING CHASED shouted one thoughtful reminder from its block of yellow concrete. BE A MR LATE, NOT A LATE MR urged another. AFTER WHISKY DRIVING RISKY reminded a third. And for all those loquacious female passengers out there: DON'T GOSSIP LET HIM DRIVE.

At Salankam, a collection of ramshackle huts made from bamboo and beaten sheets of rusting metal, I stopped at a Nepali café for chai, rice and dhal. And by late afternoon, when the mist had drawn a veil over all but the nearest slopes, I reached the red and white barrier of the police checkpoint at Khupa.

7

MONSOON COME EARLY

There were many curious things about Khupa, the first being the police. Instead of greeting me with awkward questions, they welcomed me with 'Hello Ma'am's and friendly smiles. There were no questions about John, or guides, or why I was alone. They didn't even ask for my passport. Bamboozled, I signed a register and rode up the hill into the town, convinced the resort owner had made a few well-placed phone calls on my behalf.

Unless you're the Assistant Engineer of the Electrical Sub-Division of the Department of Power, Anjaw District (and breathe), or the Block Development Officer, Anjaw District (phew), or the Assistant Engineer of Water Resources Sub-Division Khupa, Anjaw District (you get the picture), or one of the other mysterious government jobs that exist in every town in Arunachal Pradesh, you're unlikely ever to visit Khupa. Little more than a government administrative centre, the township – if you could call it that – is a charmless jumble of moribund white bungalows, rusted corrugated iron roofs, broken fencing, baggy wires and whirring electricity sub-stations. On a clear day its mountainous location might redeem it but when I arrived the town seemed drab, neglected and curiously short on inhabitants. The only people I saw as I rode slowly up the main street were two Indian men peering through the metal grill of a wine shop. Certainly no foreigners ever came this way. In other parts of Asia you might find aid workers in places like this, dispensing medicines, food and religion from new white Land Cruisers. But as far as I'd seen, there was no foreign aid in Arunachal.

On a stroll out of town that evening I passed groups of Miju women walking to a nearby village, backs bent under bundles of firewood. Some completely blanked me when I smiled and said hello, a few nervously said hello back. All of them looked dumbfounded to see a foreigner walking by, and one older lady overcame her shock to give me a wonderful gap-toothed smile. A few strides later we both turned around at the same time to have a better look at the passing alien, catching each other in the act and breaking into laughter. With no tourists here, and no foreign aid agencies, it's likely I was the first white person many of them had clapped eyes on.

The caretaker at the Circuit House, a long white bungalow built to accommodate visiting government employees, was equally surprised.

'You first foreigner come here,' he announced, opening the door of the VIP suite with a proud flourish.

Inside was a large white room containing a flimsy wooden four-poster bed, a pleather sofa and a plastic chandelier. The spacious bathroom had eleven taps sticking out of the white-tiled walls, not one of which worked.

The caretaker was a plump, hairy-eared Bihari, whose attentiveness knew no bounds. He bustled along the veranda with trays of tea and biscuits. He barged into my room unannounced with extra blankets and a heater. He played me his favourite Hindi pop tunes on his mobile. He hovered at my side as I wrote my diary by torchlight. And, just to make sure he didn't miss anything, he followed me into my room, plopping his fat bottom down on the bed next to me and grinning expectantly. If I'd asked him to trim my nasal hairs he'd have probably said yes. But when I asked him for my room key he looked offended and held it covetously to his chest.

'I keep,' he replied, returning it to the safety of his trouser pocket.

At dinner he stood over me as I ate the rice, dhal and salad he'd made, exhorting me to eat the cucumber ('medicine') and flying slices of tomato towards my mouth.

'Make red,' he said, pointing at my cheeks. 'Which mister like!' he added, nodding encouragingly, his full lips parting into a smile.

This wasn't an ideal situation, I considered, as I went to bed. I was alone in an empty guesthouse, in an odd town, with no phone reception and my only company an extremely friendly gentleman who refused to hand over the key to my bedroom. But, despite the damp handshake and the beaded lip, I felt sure he was harmless, just lonely and lobotomized by boredom, his inappropriateness more a childlike lack of decorum than anything more sinister. The poor man lived alone here, only visiting his wife and children in Assam every few months. No wonder he leapt at the chance of company. I did, however, still sleep with my Leatherman knife under my pillow. Just in case.

At eight o'clock, during one of Khupa's many power cuts, it started to rain. It began gently at first, pitter-pattering politely on the metal roof, but soon quickened to a hammering deluge. All night I lay in the pitch darkness, listening as the skies unleashed their fury upon the mountains, considering my options for the following day. It was too risky to try to make it to Walong; rain like this triggered landslides and the road would likely be blocked. Nor did I fancy a cosy stint in Khupa playing tiddlywinks with the caretaker. My only choice was to try to make it down to Tezu, a town near the border with Assam.

It was still raining in the morning and Khupa looked sodden and desolate. Thick grey cloud lay like smoke on the rooftops, blotting out the hillsides and casting a drear light over the town. *It's only a bit of rain*, I kept telling myself, watching waterfalls pour off the roof into newly formed ponds.

'Monsoon come early . . . unlucky,' said the caretaker, as he waddled into the gloomy dining room with an omelette and two chapatti for my breakfast.

He stood and watched me eat. 'Maybe landslide. If landslide, you come back,' he said, his mouth curling into a hopeful smile.

Spurred on by this final point I set about preparing for the journey ahead, wrapping myself and my luggage in a rustling carapace of Gore-Tex, plastic bags, dry bags and waterproof covers. By the time I'd pulled on my black poncho, tightening the hood until only my nose and eyes peeped out, and fastened my helmet over the top, I looked like Kenny from *South Park* on a late-night visit to a Hamburg fetish club. It was the nearest I could get to a hermetically sealed diving suit, although a wetsuit and snorkel might have been more appropriate. Finally, I heaved my leg over the saddle, kicked away the side stand and rode out into the storm.

The transformation from the previous day was extraordinary. Rivers that had been benign and turquoise were now boiling brown cauldrons with lids of swirling cloud. Waterfalls pounded onto the road where before there had been nothing. Water gouged through the laterite surface in angry little streams. And all the time the rain kept falling, falling, falling – slamming into the earth with such force I couldn't hear my engine. With visibility reduced to almost nil, all I could see was the road and the eerie silhouettes of trees as they loomed out of the fog. Blinded and bedraggled, I hunched over the bars, my poncho slapping and billowing about me, repeating *keep going, keep going, just keep going* through gritted teeth. There wasn't any other choice. In a perverse way I was glad to see the arrival of the rains, to bear witness to their flaying, visceral power. Technically this was just a pre-monsoon taster of things to come; the real thing wasn't due for another six weeks or more. But I'd never ridden in worse conditions.

There were no road workers today, or jeep taxis. Everyone, apart from mad dogs and an Englishwoman, had sensibly stayed at home. Then, about an hour after Khupa, a lone bike appeared in my wing mirror and continued to follow me from a distance of about twenty metres. Unable to make out the rider's features, I wondered if they'd seen me leave town and were waiting for an opportune moment to rob me. But as we rode on instinct told me they were just glad of the company. It wasn't a day for riding alone.

I was glad for their presence when, soon afterwards, my bike lodged in a torrent of mud and gravel on a steep uphill slope. I was knee-deep in filth, and struggling to stay upright, when the mysterious figure suddenly appeared at my side – a drenched young Miju man of no more than twenty – pushing me out of the bog. I couldn't have been more thankful. At Salankam, a few miles on, we stopped for chai and agreed to ride on to Tezu together, where he was at college.

'Critical conditions today,' he said, in faltering English, staring at the rain.

I didn't think it possible, but around noon the deluge intensified, lashing at my eyes through my open visor and blunting the daylight to dusk. We splashed on, barely able to see, weaving between rockfalls and past minor landslides, rounding a corner at one point to find a lorry trapped in a landslide, blocking the entire road. A digger had arrived from somewhere and was clawing at boulders, tree roots and sodden red earth in an attempt to clear a path, but it was several wet hours before we were able to heave and push the bikes over the rocks and mud. The poor Hero wasn't happy by now, its waterlogged engine stalling and stuttering as we wound down towards the plains. *Keep going*, I repeated over and over to us both. By around three o'clock we reached the base of the hills and it was only ten miles to Tezu. We were lucky to make it down. It's funny how when you travel alone help often appears when you most need it. How fortunate I was that fate, or the universe, or whatever you want to call it, had put the young man and me on the same road at the same time.

In Tezu the Miju, Anilso was his name, led me to a small hotel beside the muddy marketplace, where I rode my dripping bike into a passage and squelched up the stairs. I would imagine Jacques Cousteau stayed drier on most days. Soaking clothes, mushy books, soggy porridge sachets and damp packets of pills were soon spread and hung over every surface of my tiny room, dripping onto the stone floor like a pack of wet dogs. As infernally rattly as my top box was, at least it had kept my laptop and camera dry. What I would have done for a hot shower, but the bathroom had only a squat loo, a cold tap and filthy net curtains.

Later I took Anilso out to dinner to say thank you. We sprinted through the shuttered marketplace, leaping over puddles, purple fingers of lightning streaking across the night sky. In a one-room shack where Mijus and Tibetans huddled around wooden tables, we ate hot, greasy, delicious chow mein by torchlight. Afterwards I lay on my hard, narrow bed with a celebratory Kingfisher beer, too tired to write my diary but elated to have made it through the storm and to be here, alone, in this grotty hotel on the far side of the world. As wet and filthy and horrid as today had been, I felt stronger for having endured it.

After breakfast, I pulled on my damp, smelly gear and set off for Roing under a brooding anthracite sky. It should have been two hours there, west along a road that skirted the base of the Mishmi Hills, but a river was too swollen to cross and its bridge only half-constructed, so instead I had to cut south through Assam. It was only now, cast back into the maelstrom of Assamese traffic, that I realized the damage yesterday's rain had done to the poor, brave Hero. Not only was the engine still spluttering and losing power but, much more seriously, my previously sonorous horn had been reduced to a strangled, waterlogged whimper. This was nothing short of disastrous. Many Indians drive with their ears, not their eyes: it's a simple law of effect and cause, and is probably taught by driving schools – 'no horning, no seeing'. Several people aptly demonstrated my new invisibility by wandering into the road right in front of me, causing us all moments of near-underpant-staining terror. After that I rode along yelling *BEEEP BEEEP!* like a demented human claxon, animals and people scattering in wide-eyed alarm before my wheels. From the sideways looks they gave me as they lunged towards the verge, I suspect even the goats thought me certifiable.

At the checkpoint back into Arunachal Pradesh a fat police-man was sprawled in a yellow plastic chair, lost in a thorough inspection of his earwax. An obese goat nibbled at one of the chair legs. Leaping up when he saw me, he hurried into the adjoining police station, returning a minute later at the heels of an older gentleman in a tight cream kurta.

The older man wrote the Hero's details in a ledger, his admirable belly resting on the edge of the wooden table. When he'd finished, he reached into a drawer and brought out a plate of sugary biscuits. 'Refreshments, Madam?' he said, with a formal wobble of the head.

I thanked him and took two.

'It's our duty to look after you, Madam,' he added, returning them to the drawer.

Soon afterwards I was in Roing, a small town at the base of the Mishmi Hills, where the final shudders of the eastern Himalayas slide into the plains of Assam.

Roing is home to the Idu Mishmi people: tough, hill-dwelling animists whose population spreads from here up the Dibang Valley to the border with Tibet. In the absence of a written script no one really knows where the Idu came from. Their history has been told around fires since time immemorial, warping into a blur of fantastical folktales and obscured memories. They probably migrated south from China, either from northern Yunnan or somewhere near Mongolia, around 800 years ago, coming through Tibet and over the Himalayas into this jagged, empty land. But no one can be sure. What is certain is that this fearsomely individualistic warrior race did not impress the Victorians who came to prod around their territory. The British knew them as the Chulikata, or crop-haired Mishmi, on account of their mop-top coiffures (which the British anthropologist Elwin had so liked): Beatle-like fringes, shaved temples and long hair tied into a knot at the back. According to the British these Chulikata were dirty, deceitful savages who roamed the hills 'little encumbered by clothing', raiding and plundering at will. In 1853 a British Political Officer wrote that they were 'more savage and warlike than other Mishmis, and some year ago, were never seen on the plains except as marauders'.

Colonel F. M. Bailey, the British soldier, spy and explorer, who tramped up the Dibang Valley in 1913 in search of the fabled falls of the Brahmaputra, called them 'troublesome and unpleasant'. The Tibetans went as far as to brand them cannibals who feasted on the bride's mother at wedding celebrations. Countless others insulted their character, looks, hygiene and 'primitive' ways. But from the outset I adored the Idu, and few more so than the owner of Roing's Mishmi Hill Camp, the wonderful Jibi Pulu.

Jibi was an impish, middle-aged Idu with a thicket of black hair that sprung determinedly from a high, balding forehead like the crest of a cockatoo. Below this, twinkly bespectacled eyes slanted downwards onto the apples of high cheekbones, and a scant moustache framed a wide, shapely mouth. Wise, kind and quick to laugh, there was something of Yoda about him, and most of his stories began with a sage-like, 'One fine day . . .' It had been on one of these fine days that he'd sat with a beer by the Deopani River and dreamt up the Mishmi Hill Camp – now a handful of thatched bamboo huts and safari-style tents overlooking the river and the mountains beyond.

I'd intended to stay just a day in Roing, servicing the beleaguered Hero and wringing myself dry, but landslides had closed the one road north up the Dibang Valley and, until they were cleared, I was stuck. But there are many worse places to be stranded than among the Idu, a people who believe that anyone who disrespects a guest will die an unpleasant death. Jibi spent much of the next few days driving me around the potholed streets of Roing – his tiny, battered white Maruti Suzuki squeaking and juddering over every bump – depositing me at the smoking hearths of various English-speaking friends and elders. There I'd sit for hours, cross-legged in the half-light of bamboo huts, drinking countless cups of sweet black tea as puckish men entranced me with stories about the

Idu and their culture. Christianity has made fewer inroads among the Idu than the Naga and many other Northeastern tribes, and these middle-aged Idu still inhabited a world of spirits, magic and animal sacrifice. But at the same time these small, nimble mountain men wore jeans and fleeces and were dentists, doctors and English teachers with children at college in Guwahati and Delhi and jeeps parked outside. Their houses were similarly divided: half-modern and concrete, half-Mishmi hut, with televisions and Hindu calendars in one room and mithun skulls hanging near the *engoko* – the square, centralized hearths integral to Mishmi life – in another.

Jibi was similarly caught between worlds. His wife worked away as a government accountant in Lohit district and his two young children spoke more Hindi than Idu. He wore jeans and a khaki shirt and had been educated in Shillong, at the same college as Phupla. But at his parents' house, a hut in the jungle a few miles from Roing, a gaggle of crop-haired old ladies sat beside the fire chattering like starlings, faces etched with wrinkles and dirt-blackened hands knotted like the roots of ancient trees. Beside them sat fantastically attired old men, their long ebony hair tied in knots under wide-brimmed cane helmets and daos slung across the backs of their *etokojo*, black sleeveless jackets woven with horizontal bands of orange and yellow embroidery.

The women smiled and eyed me with friendly curiosity. 'How can we talk to her if she doesn't speak any Idu or Hindu?' asked one of them, laughing.

The Idu all had one thing in common, though. Whoever they were and whatever their age or profession, no one was in a hurry. Everyone had time to sit and talk and tell stories, their

113

handsome, jovial faces lit up by the flickering flames. How very different to the grim-faced, hurrying, screen-addicted masses of our time-poor Western world.

Jibi was apparently related to everyone in Roing, every introduction beginning with a 'This my cousin brother', 'This my cousin brother father', or another such genealogical riddle. This wasn't down to the Pulu clan having notably fruitful loins. While I struggle to name my second cousins or bend my brain around how exactly it is we're related, with a population of only 12,000 and an extremely rigid clan structure, most Idu share the same blood and all of them can reel off their kin to a distance of ten or twelve generations. They have to: in a society bound by taboos, one of the strictest is to do with marriage – an Idu mustn't marry anyone closer than a tenth cousin. Marrying outside the tribe is also a big no-no. Such a restrictive gene pool makes Idu dating a complicated game of Who's Who and has led to many a star-crossed lover.

Jibi was also kind enough to introduce me to *yuchi*, a delicious and deceptively harmless-tasting Idu rice beer. This I discovered, as we drank it around the fire at the camp on my first night, was significantly stronger than a pint of Pilsner. One glass bathed me in a fuzzy afterglow. Two glasses and I was slurring. Three glasses and making it to bed felt like navigating the sinking deck of the *Titanic*. On one of these evenings we were joined by a pair of PhD students who were passing through – a Britisher (to my great surprise) and an Assamese, who were travelling around the Northeast researching border issues. The Assamese, a weighty intellectual called Mirza, took great delight in informing me of the leeches that would soon come out of hibernation.

'The worst are the elephant leeches,' he said, sucking his teeth. 'They can make your foot or leg swell up like an elephant and the bite can easily go septic and kill you.'

The following day Jibi banged on my door at 7.30 a.m. with news that the Big Chief of the Arunachal Pradesh and Upper Assam Police was coming to the camp for breakfast. Soon afterwards, seven impossibly clean white Land Cruisers swept down the track and disgorged a small army of khaki-clad soldiers stiff with assault rifles, jungle boots and identically clipped moustaches. Behind them came a white van, out of which leapt a flock of waiters. They dashed across the grass like anxious penguins, bearing silver dishes, white tablecloths, bottled water and ashtrays, laying everything out in a fervour of activity. Ten minutes later another Land Cruiser sped in and out stepped the chief, all polished belt buckles and epaulettes and shoeshine. More interested in the Hero and who'd ridden it here, he ordered a series of photos: me with the bike, me and him, me and the top box, him with the Hero.

'Our Indian girls need Dutch courage like this – hopefully you'll inspire them,' he surmised.

I left him to his luxuriant spread and retired to my hut to write my diary, interrupted every few minutes by soldiers sidling up with a 'One selfie, Madam?' In India you never know how your day is going to start.

The rain continued all week but at some point news filtered through that the road north was open again. With more rain forecast, and landslides likely, I decided to leave the Hero – who'd been serviced for the grand sum of 200 rupees, or two pounds – with Jibi and travel to Anini, the farthest town up the valley, by Sumo taxi instead. The main form of transport in the Northeast, these tank-like 4WDs ply all the main routes in the state, roaring up the mountains laden with people, animals, food and domestic goods. It would be an interesting deviation from two wheels. Without the bike I'd at least be able to walk south again if further landslides closed the road. It was a week's walk to Roing from the upper reaches of the valley; with the bike I could be stuck there for far longer.

There was one person I hadn't yet managed to meet in Roing and that was Tine Mena, an Idu girl I'd heard about from Abhra. She was away in the mountains collecting medicinal plants and no one knew when she was coming back. But as chance would have it she returned the evening before I left, roaring into the camp on a racy red Yamaha, her long black hair streaming behind her. Thirty years old, and from a remote village halfway up the Dibang Valley, Tine had cheekbones you could swing off and eyes that regularly vanished into a crumple of laughter lines. She was tiny, the top of her head only just reaching my shoulders, but tougher than biltong. In 2011 she'd been one of the first Indian women to conquer Mount Everest, and the first woman from the Northeast, standing on the summit holding the Indian tricolour and a photo of her family in front of their bamboo hut. It was physically easy, she told me; she was an Idu – she'd grown up marching up and down mountains. It was the mental endurance that was tough; keeping going when you hadn't slept properly for days and your body was weakened from altitude.

By even greater chance, it transpired that Tine's clan were about to hold a festival. A private celebration of the main

Idu festival of *reh*, it involved five days of shamanic chanting, animal sacrifice, feasting and drinking – all in the name of bolstering clan ties and garnering the good favour of the spirits. It was taking place in a small village a few hours south of Anini and about a thousand people would be attending, almost ten per cent of the Idu population. Tine wasn't able to go but I must, she said; she'd send a message to a cousin in the village and ask them to look after me. By the time I wriggled into my sleeping bag that night, my head spinning with yuchi and anticipation, we'd concocted a loose plan. I'd take a Sumo tomorrow as far as the village of Etalin, about ten hours north of here, and wait at the Inspection Bungalow there for someone to pick me up. There was no phone reception in the village and Tine didn't yet know how she'd send the message, who this person might be or when they would turn up. I just had to reach Etalin and wait. It all sounded delightfully tenuous.

Dawn was announced by the usual discordant orchestra of cocks crowing, dogs barking and men hoicking and, by six o'clock, I was waiting at the Sumo stand near the market. I'd left half of my luggage with Jibi, so with me was just a rucksack and, in case I found a bike to borrow in Anini, my motorcycle helmet. Most people in Arunachal Pradesh arise at the abominably early hours of four or five in the morning and already shutters were clattering open, women were sweeping their stalls and a squad of paramilitary was jogging down the main street, their boots drumming on the ground. A small crowd milled around the Sumo stand, waiting as luggage was tied onto roof racks by whippet-thin Nepali drivers. Idu teenagers giggled and flirted – the boys sporting the streaked red hair that was all the rage among young tribals here; the girls in tight jeans and SARS-like face masks (the latest fashion too, apparently). Older Idu men in cane hats and etokojo, their daos across their backs, waited silently to leave. At their feet a black piglet squealed and quivered miserably in a bamboo cage, and a basket clucked with chickens. A woman with a shy little boy turned out to be Jibi's cousin, a headmistress travelling to visit her husband in Anini.

Half an hour later a delicate-looking Nepali youth clambered behind the enormous wheel of our Sumo and we were off – nine people squeezed into three rows of seats, plus a pig, chickens, sacks of rice and a television set – winding, bumping and beeping up into the maw of the mountains. Soon we were high above the plains and climbing through a mass of lushly forested hills, the wheel spinning and turning through the Nepali's skilled hands. He was only nineteen but he'd been driving this route for three years already and knew every curve and camber. It was the first clear day in weeks: the steep slopes gleamed with dew and sunshine, and distant ridges melted into a cerulean sky. Far below, the entwining fingers of the Deopani and Dibang rivers shone like shards of silver on the plains. The juncture of hill and plain seemed even more pronounced from here and it was easy to see why the British had drawn a line along the seam. Occasionally we'd pass a village, its buildings encircling the slopes like crowns of thatch and iron. Around these, mithun – the first live ones I'd seen – bucked away from the roadside as we passed; dark brown, muscular beasts with heads like battering rams and those thick, conical horns.

Up, up we went, the air getting colder as we climbed, my

fellow passengers numbed into sleep or silence by the constant jolting. Now the hills swelled in such abundance it was as if a monstrous mole had feverishly nosed its way through the earth's leafy crust, leaving waterfalls of foliage to froth and pour down the precipitous slopes. The little boy was sick out of the window but never cried or complained for a second, and now and then we'd stop briefly at a roadside hut while the driver tied another package to the roof. After a few hours we reached the 2,655-metre Mayodia Pass, rounding a corner into an arena of glittering snow-dusted peaks. Here, at a sorry collection of rusted metal hovels, where lines of washing flapped in the breeze and snow lay on the verge, we stopped for tea and bowls of instant noodles.

At 4 p.m. we reached Etalin, a small settlement on the banks of a roaring green river. Only forty miles from Roing, as the crow flies, it had taken us ten hours to cover the 160 miles by road.

All I had to do now was wait.

8

TRIBAL GATHERING

The Inspection Bungalow, a shabby white building with four dank rooms built to accommodate visiting government employees, was on a hill just off the main road. Not knowing whether I'd be waiting for an hour or two days I took a room from the one-eyed Nepali caretaker and sat on the steps to wait.

Darkness fell, the crickets took up their twilight duties, and still there was no sign of anyone. To pass time I wrote my diary then walked to the nearest wine shop to buy two bottles of suspiciously cheap Royal Stag whisky for my as-yet-unknown hosts. At seven o'clock, a jeep pulled up at the bungalow, but it was only three government engineers passing through for the night. Then, an hour later, as I ate rice and dhal in the dimly lit kitchen, I heard the sound of a car engine approaching and knew it had come for me.

I walked outside as a dashing-looking young Idu man stepped out of his white Scorpio truck. 'Hello, my name Sadhu Mihu. Mr Ajitu Molo sent me,' he said.

In dark-green cords, a floppy khaki hat, green gumboots and a navy down jacket, he could have been dressed for an English country fair. Only his broad Tibetan features and dao, hanging in a bamboo sheath at his side, would have given him away. Who Mr Ajitu Molo was I never did find out, but whether by smoke signals, telepathy or the bush telegraph, Tine's message had clearly found a way through. Ten minutes later, having apologized to the caretaker for leaving so soon, I'd hefted my rucksack into the truck and was being driven into the blackness of the hills by this handsome Idu tribesman. I had no idea where we were going or what lay ahead but, in the short time I'd spent with the Idu, I trusted them instinctively. Wherever Sadhu was taking me, and whatever the next few days held in store, I felt sure it was going to be a marvellous adventure. I hoped my instinct wouldn't let me down.

We drove for an hour down a twisting dirt track, clanking over metal Bailey bridges, a river purling far below. Sadhu, who was a few years younger than me, couldn't have been further from the Victorian depiction of the Idu as ferocious and filthy savages. Gentle and exceedingly polite, he insisted on calling me 'Madam', and was terribly concerned his house wouldn't be up to my standards.

'The guest is god,' he said, as we rounded a corner an hour later and saw the lights of Atunli village sewn into the hills. 'I am honoured to have you here.'

But Sadhu needn't have worried about Madam's standards,

for I would rather have stayed with him than in any five-star hotel. His house – a spacious, three-roomed abode made of wood, bamboo and concrete with a roof of rusting corrugated iron – was the location for the festival warm-up party. Half-drunk whisky bottles and bamboo flagons of rice wine stood around the engoko, and the room was bawdy with the laughter of a roistering, garrulous crowd. Roughly twenty men and women were huddled about the fire, their arms draped affectionately around each other's knees and shoulders, the light of the flames falling upon the brims of cane helmets, bandoliers of bullets, pistols, strings of beads, hooped silver earrings and the tips of elephant-bone knife handles. Almost all of them had the traditional cropped hairstyle so rarely seen in Roing, freshly cut and shaven for the festival. A silent, scrawny Indian boy flitted among them, filling the kettle, pouring cups of tea and adding logs to the fire.

The minute I sat down an old man thrust a glass of whisky into my hand with a mischievous grin. The others, unable to speak any English, eyed me curiously and smiled. Warmed by the whisky and the flames I gazed around me, spellbound by the hubbub of nasal, sing-song voices and the beautiful, elfish faces. It was like attending a gathering of wood sprites. One woman, who must have been about forty-five, had the button nose, rosebud lips and perfectly rounded cheekbones of an exquisitely carved porcelain doll. Even Colonel E. T. Dalton, a British soldier and explorer, had begrudgingly admitted to the Idu women's beauty when writing in 1872.

'Some among them have red lips and ruddy complexions, and I have seen girls that are decidedly good-looking, but their beauty is terribly marred by their peculiar method of cropping the hair.'

The men were small and lithe with bulging calves and fringes falling over handsome, chiselled features. It was a scene that seemed to belong to another age entirely. If you'd para-chuted me in blindfold, not for a second would I have thought this was India. It could have been the Brazilian Amazon, Siberia or a Navajo reservation in Utah. Surely these people were the descendants of those who had walked across Beringia to the Americas 13,000 years ago.

Over the next few hours a stream of villagers drifted in and out – all of them, said Sadhu, coming for a look at the English visitor. Emboldened by alcohol, one middle-aged man with a pistol at his waist and a bandolier of bullets worn across a woven, striped jacket said, 'I luff you,' then burst into peals of laughter.

'He two wives and eight children,' said Sadhu, joining in. 'He romantic. Watch out!'

Around midnight Sadhu showed me to the communal bedroom. I unrolled my sleeping bag on a narrow bed and fell happily unconscious, the sound of voices and laughter drift-ing through the wall. At various points Sadhu, his sister and unidentified others stumbled into the three other beds, and every time I awoke I could hear the sound of men talking and laughing next door. I tried to imagine what subjects would be covered during an all-night Idu bender: who had the biggest mithun; the bear they'd caught on their latest hunting expe-dition; how this season's rice planting was going; whose wife made the best smoked rats. At 6 a.m. most of them were still going, with a few smoking breakfast hits of opium for good measure. Others were passed out under blankets. The silent Indian boy squatted by the fire, handing out plates of rice and meat and cups of sweet, milky chai.

My breath smoked in the chill morning air as Sadhu led me through the village's scattered huts, their rounded thatched roofs reminiscent of the upturned bows of boats. The Talo River roared through a deep gorge somewhere below and on all sides rose the mountains, each one a green fortress guarded by ranks of leafy sentinels. After a few minutes we reached the festival ground, a well-trampled space half the size of a football pitch, surrounded by huts and temporarily erected shelters. At one end was the *khundu*, the sacrificial area, where six male mithun would soon be tied to a wooden post and slaughtered. At the other end was a bamboo platform for butchering the carcasses. The mithun were tethered in a grove of trees just beyond this, chewing their cud in total ignorance of the fate about to befall them.

In a dark hut beside the butchering platform three male shamans, *igu*, sat in a row beside the fireplace, watched by a half-cut crowd. They'd been singing all night, a repetitive, mesmeric chant in a dialect unintelligible to the normal Idu, offering up the mithun to Inni Maselo Jinu, the supreme creator of the Idu, and leading the mithuns' souls to the afterlife. Even in this age of rampant globalization the Idu inhabit a world of spirits, both good and evil, and the igu are powerful mediators between the spheres of the seen and the unseen. Central figures in Idu life, these shamans heal illness, preside over births and deaths and are involved in every aspect of the community. In the middle of the three sat the chief igu, a man of indeterminate age with flawless bronze skin, a particularly fine cane helmet and the top half of a leopard's jawbone sewn into his dao strap. He sang in a strange, contorted voice, his hands moving up and down as he beat and shook out the slow, galloping triple rhythm on a small hand-held instrument that was part drum, part maracas, part bell. The other two repeated him, a line behind, to create a rolling, hypnotic effect. Unlike Amazonian shamans, who use powerful hallucinogens such as ayahuasca, the vine of life, the Idu shamans rely on just chanting, music and the power of their guiding spirits to achieve trance states. The igus can sing for four or five days at a time like this, fuelled by no more than tea and a non-hallucinogenic plant root called kalita, which they believe has the power to ward off evil spirits. When it was time, the chief igu went outside and chanted beside each mithun, brushing their backs with a leafy branch to signify Maselo was ready for them.

Being a pescatarian, I can think of better ways to start my day than a bout of animal sacrifice; even the whiff of a British butcher makes me feel nauseous. But I felt it polite to watch, although I was the only woman who did. Standing about ten metres from the khundu, I looked on as the first mithun was led up, plodding towards his death with the docility of an old Labrador. Nor did he struggle as he was tied to the post, or as three men held him by the tail and another brought a dao down on the back of his muscular neck with a resounding *thwack*. On the second *thwack* the beast fell silently to the ground, the top of his neck split open in a crimson slush of flesh, bone and arteries. The men laughed and dragged him aside by his tail, then went to fetch the next one. Steam rose from the bleeding wound and the village curs gathered expectantly, but the mithun's sides were still heaving and it was twenty minutes before it let out an awful rasping sound, kicked for the last time, and died.

The same happened with the next four. The men hacked and laughed and jibed at each other's ability to kill, and the mithun fell silently to their slow, ghastly deaths. Soon the area around the khundu looked like a bovine Somme and the air steamed with death. But the final mithun saw and smelt the carnage. He guessed what fate awaited him. He fought and bellowed all the way, five men hauling him by a rope, another five yanking at his tail. When they did manage to lash him to the post, a young man hewed at his neck with sickening ineptitude while the others laughed and taunted his inefficiency. I could feel the bile rising in my throat, my stomach churning in revolt. Gagging, I slipped away and vomited behind a tree. I live in the St Werburghs area of Bristol, a wonderfully alternative community where crystal healing and vegetarian shoes are the norm. It was Saturday morning, and in an hour or two the good people of my street would be pouring hemp milk into their tea and making scrambled tofu for breakfast. And here I was kicking off the weekend with a grade-A bloodbath.

I didn't want to judge the Idu: this was their culture, and had been for centuries. They are hardy, self-sufficient, unsentimental people who rear and kill their own meat. They're not soft and mawkish like most of us in the West, whose meat comes ready-wrapped in cellophane. In many ways their method was far more humane than our industrialized systems of rearing and killing animals. Their beasts roam freely in the forest all their lives and know nothing about their death until the very last moment. If I were a mithun, I'd rather this than a short, mechanized life in a cattle-feed lock, deprived of freedom and pumped full of antibiotics. But I wish the killing was more efficient, and the death not so horribly prolonged. No animal deserves to die like that.

Amidst much laughter and jollity, the mithun were immediately sliced, chopped, skinned, dismembered and carried away. Men staggered past with whole heads across their shoulders, the eyes blue and staring with death. Hunks of flank and rump were lashed onto lengths of bamboo and carried to the butchering area. Cane baskets were filled with oozing, slimy intestines. Everywhere men were elbow-deep in blood and shit, one of them so drunk he kept slipping on a slick of intestines and dropping his armfuls of meat. In the midst of it was Sadhu, my gentle, quietly spoken host, squatting as he cut out the tongues and strung them onto sharp threads of bamboo. On the butchering platform a circle of men sat among heads, legs, haunches and piles of flesh, slicing it all up for the pot, their bare feet dark red and sticky with blood. Everything would either be eaten at a feast this afternoon, or divided between all the attendant families of the clan. Nothing would be wasted.

Meanwhile the women stood under shelters stirring great vats of rice and mithun meat, or handing around plastic cups of chai and bamboo flagons of *yu*, a weaker version of the lethal yuchi. Still feeling a little queasy, I joined a crowd of them and self-medicated with a flagon of yu. By noon I'd had several and was communicating in fluent nonsense with a diminutive, puckered old lady who had an uncanny resemblance to E.T. She sucked her toothless gums and chortled at everything, lost in happy senility.

The rest of the day passed in a sunny orgy of drinking, butchery and carousing, an Idu version of Glastonbury, just with more blood and gore. At intervals I'd retreat to Sadhu's house to escape the swarms of tiny, biting dam dum flies that had come in place of the rain. No bigger than a pin-prick, these little blighters are endemic in parts of Arunachal Pradesh and seek out human flesh with the precision of a guided missile. You don't feel a thing when they sink their nasty little proboscis into you, but afterwards the bites swell into madly itching blood-blisters. Already my wrists, hands and neck were dotted with red.

On one of these occasions a group of people were sitting by the fire watching an episode of *India's Got Talent* on television. It seemed impossible to believe that the heavily made-up wannabes on a stage in Delhi 1,600 miles away belonged to the same century as these dao-wielding tribesmen of the Mishmi Hills, let alone swore allegiance to the same flag. Another time, the news was on and Modi was standing on a podium waving to an adoring crowd.

'Your David Cameron is very handsome,' said Sadhu, after telling me how much he liked Modi.

When they weren't glued to *India's Got Talent*, Sadhu's female relatives would try to teach me Idu. I've often noticed how, when you travel alone, among people with whom you share no common language, you are reduced to the position of a child. And so it was here. They pointed at their noses, mouths, ears, the fire, firewood, and so on, repeating slowly and loudly the words, then hooting with laughter as I tried to pronounce them. With no written script, spelling was largely guesswork, but soon the back of my diary was scribbled with Idu words.

At around four, by which time so much yu had been consumed it was a miracle anyone was still vertical, a prodigious feast was served. We sat in rows on the ground while lines of men and women handed out palm-leaf plates, then piled them with armfuls of boiled mithun, greasy chunks of fat and heaps of rice. They served it from baskets as big as oil drums and with hands still dark with blood and filth, the helpings so huge most of it was rolled into the palm leaves or skewered onto strips of bamboo for later. Politely turning down the meat, I settled for just an armful of rice.

'Madam, after fooding?' said an older man, sending a glass of Blender's Pride down the line of greasy revellers.

All this time the shamans had been chanting in their hut, calling up the favour of Inni Maselo Jinu, Nani Intaya, Ela, and the countless other spirits of the Idu world. After nightfall the chief igu did a swift costume change and began to dance – a slow, shuffling movement with his head bowed and his bare feet turned out at angles. Now he wore a richly embroidered red skirt, a headpiece of cowrie shells hung with tufts of yak's tail and a sadly magnificent bandolier of yellowed tigers' teeth, some six inches long. I was surprised to see this. I'd heard the Idu believed the tiger was their brother and didn't hunt or kill them. Behind his back hung a small pair of cymbals that clashed together as he moved. This was followed by a sort of shamanic open-mic session, during which various members of the audience put on the igu's outfit and imitated his moves. At one point a near-unconscious drunk was carried in by two others and deposited on the floor in a blethering heap. There followed much thigh slapping, hectoring and uproarious laughter as he was manhandled into the costume and levered upright, making a valiant attempt to dance.

In life as hard and historically brutal as the Idu's, comedy has always played a crucial role in their society and, looking around me, I saw that every face in the hut was lit up by a wide, joyous smile. Much later, drunk and happy, I walked back to Sadhu's under the first clear sky I'd seen in India, stopping to scratch the belly of a black pig lying in a muddy pen behind the butchering platform. From what I'd heard, tonight would be his last.

Sunday was the day of *ili moo*, the pig sacrifice, but unlike the biddable mithun the four black pigs sensed there was murder afoot. They squealed and ducked and dived in frantic bids to evade capture, and it was half an hour before they'd been wrestled into the mud and trussed by their legs to lengths of bamboo. A large black female with tusks and an upturned snout was the last to be caught, sending several of her assailants headlong into the sludge. By the time all four animals were squealing, shaking and gasping in a row on the butchering platform, the jubilant young men were black with mud and pig shit. The smallest pig, my friend from last night, lay defeated and trembling, his ears twitching as he squealed. Unable to watch their misery any longer I went for a walk along the road, only to return half an hour later at the moment of their horrid demise. I'd been told it was quick, a sharpened bamboo stick straight to the heart. But as men pushed the green sticks into the pigs' chests there erupted a hellish cacophony of squeals and shrieks, and it was minutes before it ended.

Within seconds of their final squeals the pigs were lifted onto burning pyres and men were rubbing the singed hair off their bodies with long wooden poles. Blood bubbled out of their wounds and the fat popped and crackled in the heat. Afterwards they were carried to the butchering platform, where daos sliced through their thick outer layers of fat with the ease of knives through soft butter. In no time, chunks of fat and flesh were being thrown into baskets and the platform was slimy with blood and guts. The speed of the transition from living, breathing animal to lard, blood and bone was shocking. Give me tofu sausages any day.

The only way to recover from the horror of it all was to hit the yu, and by midday I was well on my way to unsteady inebriation. I was by no means the only drunkard in the village: on the platform one man had passed out mid-butchery, head lolling on his chest, legs stretched out between piles of grey fat; in the igu's hut several older men were asleep on their bearskin bags, the floor around them a blitzkrieg of discarded flagons and empty whisky bottles. It was like Stonehenge on solstice morning, apart from here the men chanting were real shamans, not bongo-bashing hippies on acid. Now the chief shaman had been joined by a new igu, an exceptionally good-looking man of about forty. Maybe it was the drink, but as I watched them chant I imagined him being signed by Storm models and sashaying down catwalks in New York and Milan. When someone offered me another flagon of yu, I declined. One more glass and I'd be anyone's.

That afternoon the Idu feasted on lumps of boiled pork and chunks of fat, threading what they couldn't eat onto strips of bamboo. I ate rice. Again. Afterwards some of the revellers began to drift back to their huts and nearby villages, clutching leaves stuffed with mithun, pork and lard, and dark bundles of what looked like sticks. It was only when my friend E.T. pulled out one of these sticks and thrust it towards my face, cackling, that I saw a pair of incisors and a tail and realized they were dried rats. She peeled off a flaky, blackened bit of skin and moved it towards my mouth, grinning. As much as I was open to trying things, dried rat was taking it a little too far, and I recoiled with a poorly disguised grimace.

Despite the horror of the sacrifice my affection for the Idu was undimmed. That night, as I listened to the slow, evocative songs of the igu, an old man passed out snoring across my feet, I felt blissfully content and at home among these exotic, smiling people. Every journey is an exercise in unshackling yourself from the safety and routine of everyday life at one end, and letting go of your fears of the unknown at the other. And on every journey there's a moment when the bonds are loosed, when at once the journey inhabits you, and you inhabit it. Sir Richard Burton described a similar feeling in his diary, as he sailed from Bombay to Africa in 1856, at once 'shaking off with one mighty effort the fetters of Habit, the leaden weight of Routine, the cloak of many Cares and the slavery of Civilization'.

It was a month since I'd left home, and it had taken travelling to this faraway village in the Mishmi Hills, thousands of miles away, to reach this moment of equilibrium. Later, on the way back to Sadhu's, I stopped to gaze at the sparkling vault above, its magnificence and my drunken happiness moving me to tears. On my return Sadhu was already snoring gently in one of the other beds and the house was silent, so I slipped into my sleeping bag and went blissfully to sleep.

The following morning the festival had all but come to an end. A few diehards remained in the igu hut and I told them I was *nga Anini bawe*, going to Anini, the closest thing to an Idu goodbye. They all waved cheerily and wished me *chi pay na ba*, a good journey, and the chief shaman stood up to take my hands in his. He didn't speak a word of English but his round face beamed with kindness and wisdom and I had the odd feeling he could read my very soul. I hoped we'd some-how meet again.

On the drive back to Etalin, Sadhu pointed out the site of a proposed dam on the Talo, one of seventeen planned for the Dibang Valley and 168 agreed for Arunachal Pradesh. Many people I'd spoken to in Roing were strongly opposed to these dams. The deals were rife with corruption and money laun-dering, they told me, and the Dibang Valley's sandy, unstable soil made it unsuitable for such projects. The valley had been the worst-affected area in the 1950 earthquake, the violent tremors unleashing massive landslides and floods that wiped out half of the Idu population, a catastrophe from which their numbers have never recovered. It was madness, they said, to even consider building dams in unstable mountains prone to such seismic activity. The structures would also be built by tens of thousands of labourers from Assam and beyond, many of whom would remain there.

'You'll need a microscope to find us Idu after that,' one man had lamented.

The most controversial project is the proposed 3,000 MW

Dibang Dam, a 288-metre behemoth that will submerge thousands of hectares of virgin, largely unexplored forest and create a 26.7-mile-long reservoir visible from space. Already 300,000 trees are being cleared to make way for its construction. Rejected by Manmohan Singh's government, it was pushed through by Modi within months of his election. Surfing to power on a wave of promises about *achhe din*, or 'good days', Modi's government saw environmental issues as far less important than Progress and Jobs. At the same time, he signed agreements on tens of other controversial dams in the state, curbed well-known environmental activists, cancelled the licences of Greenpeace and 9,000 other foreign-funded NGOs, and softened environmental restrictions on coal-fired power stations. The Dibang Dam, due to be India's largest, was approved on the back of an environmental impact assessment that was labelled farcical by many observers and no study whatsoever of its effect on downstream areas. Smaller hydro-electric projects have already led to rivers in other parts of the state running dry and lifeless, and the Assam Valley, home to around thirty-two million people and a fecundity of flora and fauna, depends on the ebb and flow of the Brahmaputra for its survival. In the absence of studies, it's anyone's guess how badly the dam will affect the already flood-prone region. While many of the 168 'paper dams' will never be more than that, it's no wonder protests against the Dibang project and other major dams planned for Arunachal Pradesh have been widespread.

I was surprised, then, when Sadhu told me he approved of the dam that was to be built just a mile from his village. The construction company had been busy with their propaganda, promising compensation for all affected peoples: pensions for life, new schools and health services, free electricity and skill-development programmes. The glossy brochure he showed me even promised a 'sports complex and gymnasium', as well as streetlights and a bus shelter. (I'd heard that a dam company in Arunachal's Siang Valley was giving opium to the local Adi people in the hope it would quieten any protest.) As far as Sadhu was concerned, the dam would bring the development that the government never had. The road from Roing to Anini only opened in 1990, the one to Atunli in 2006 – and only then because the Indian Army needed a road to their Indo-Tibetan Border Police Force post at Malini, the last village in the valley before the Tibetan border. In 2010 flooding had washed away a bridge on the road and Atunli had been cut off for five months. Electricity only arrived in 2013, although, like the rest of Arunachal, it was patchy and usually went off around 6.30 p.m., when demand in Assam peaked. Sadhu wanted progress and a different life for his children, not the isolated childhood he'd had in a now-abandoned village near Atunli, when it had taken two days for them just to walk to Etalin.

At this, I asked him about his childhood and how different things were now.

'Before the nineteen-eighties our people were very ferocious,' he said seriously, navigating his truck around a sharp corner.

Killings over land and women were common, he told me, but as there were no roads and very little outside influence the police didn't get involved.

'How could a policeman arrest the culprit? They'd have to foot march five days to reach the village,' he added.

Instead the Idu had their own form of governance, a system called *abela*, whereby a respected individual would negotiate a solution between the affected parties. This still took place, said Sadhu: he'd recently settled a dispute between two men in Atunli, one of whom had been having an extra-marital affair with the other's married daughter. The girl's father was given one pig and one lakh rupees, roughly £1,000, by the transgressor and the case was settled. It was typical of how Sadhu's generation of Idu were caught between worlds. Sadhu had a truck, a motorbike, a large cardamom plantation and houses in Roing and Atunli. He played computer games on his mobile to 'time pass'. But he'd had to give his father-in-law a mithun and two pigs to seal his arranged marriage and had settled a village dispute with pigs and money. It's no surprise suicide is becoming increasingly common among young Idu torn between the taboo-laden world of their ancestral society and the tsunami of globalization.

'Madam, I am going to miss you when you leave,' said Sadhu, as he left me in Etalin to wait for a passing Sumo. I'd miss him too. Reh had been the hinge on which my journey had turned, and Sadhu had been a part of that. How fortunate I was to have been there.

9

Secrets of the Tsangpo

Ringed by a stadium of snow-streaked peaks, Anini lies scattered across a bluff at the confluence of the Dri and Mathun rivers. Below it the waters gouge deep corridors through the mountains, and on all sides stretch a rumpus of steep, forested slopes. Only a few thousand people live in this remote town and houses are barnacled across the saddle of the bluff in unruly clusters: some concrete, some bamboo, some scratched together from reeds, polythene and scrap metal. Among them are army barracks and the grey stamp of a helipad, reminders that Anini lies just thirty miles from the border with Tibet. Bored squaddies play cricket in dusty fields and army trucks rumble along winding, broken roads. On the edge of town small boys wander by the roadside, catapults in hand, scanning the trees for small birds to kill.

My plans for Anini were vague. I had nowhere to stay, no contacts and no motorbike, just a notion to trace Colonel Frederick Marshman Bailey's century-old footsteps north from here towards the Tibetan border. In early 1913 Bailey – soldier, spy, explorer, linguist, naturalist and butterfly collector – had oiled his hair, clipped his fine slug of a moustache and set off up the Dibang Valley on an expedition to solve a geographical enigma that had remained a mystery throughout the Victorian era. With him was the surveyor Captain Henry Morshead and a train of reluctant porters, their cane baskets weighed down with specimen cases, canvas tents, theodolites, sacks of coins and bottles of Trumper cologne. In *No Passport to Tibet*, his brilliant account of the expedition, Bailey outlines the mission as follows:

For many years geographers were puzzled to know where the waters of the Tsangpo eventually flowed ... The only way to find out was for someone to follow the Tsangpo River down its course until it became some other recognisable river; but ... the Tsangpo flowed through some of the most mountainous, difficult and inhospitable country in the world. The political obstacles were even more difficult to surmount. The Chinese, having won a precarious hold over Tibet, were keen to prevent any other foreigners from what they regarded as their private preserve ... To the traveller approaching from the direction of India there was a further hazard. In the foothills between the plains of India and the mountain ranges of Tibet lived a number of primitive and savage tribes. Quarrelsome, treacherous

138

and riddled with suspicion, they were continually at war with one another. They regarded strangers as welcome only as possible victims of extortion by pacific or violent means, or as allies from whom they might obtain weapons with which they could massacre their neighbours more efficiently ...

Thwarted by Tibet's isolationism and India's 'savage' tribes and terrain, early British efforts to solve this mystery had often ended in a hail of poisoned arrows. But there was another question that the British were desperate to solve: a mystery that had dogged geographers for much of the previous century. If the Tsangpo and the Brahmaputra were indeed one, then by what fantastic means did the river plunge almost 3,000 metres from where it disappeared off the map in southeastern Tibet, to where it flowed languidly into Assam only 150 miles later? The only answer seemed to be that somewhere in the unmapped borderlands between the two countries was a stupendous falls to rival Livingstone's Victoria. The sooner the British staked their claim to it, the better.

Determined to solve these secrets of the Tsangpo, in 1863 the Great Trigonometrical Survey of India began training a group of local surveyor-spies at their headquarters in Dehra Dun. The Pundits, as they were called, would travel into Tibet disguised as pilgrims and traders, hiding their notes and surveying equipment inside ingeniously adapted Buddhist prayer wheels, caskets and clothing. They were taught to remember information as verses and mantras and to measure distance using rosaries made from one hundred – rather than the usual 108 – prayer beads. Of these brave pioneers, it is the story of Kinthup, an illiterate Sikkimese Pundit's assistant, which is the most remarkable.

Poor old Kinthup; he didn't have much luck. After several unnoteworthy missions he set off again in 1880 as an assistant to a Chinese lama. Their mission, as given to them by Captain Henry Harman of the British Survey of India, was to enter Tibet, travel as far east along the Tsangpo as possible then, on an agreed date, throw 500 marked logs, each a foot long, into the river. If the logs appeared where Captain Harman's men were waiting downstream on the banks of the Brahmaputra, it would establish with certainty that the two rivers were one. It was a simple, but genius, plan.

Sadly the Chinese lama turned out to be a dastardly fellow, a philandering gambler with little dedication to the cause. After a year of travelling, he sold Kinthup to the headman of a remote Tibetan village and fled home to China. But over the course of the following three years Kinthup showed remarkable loyalty and resilience. Escaping from the village, he found refuge in a monastery further east along the Tsangpo and doggedly pursued Harman's mission. He cut, marked and hid the logs in a cave, then found a way to travel to Lhasa to send a message to Harman. In a typically stoic manner it said:

'Sir, the Chinese Lama who was sent with me sold me . . . as a slave and himself fled away . . . On account of this, the journey proved a bad one. However, I, Kinthup, have prepared 500 logs according to the order of Captain Harman and am prepared to throw 50 logs per day into the Tsang-po river . . . from the 5th to the 15th of the tenth Tibetan month of the year called *Chhuluk*.'

Months later, when the appointed date approached, Kinthup returned to where he'd hidden the marked logs, threw them in the river over the course of the ten agreed days then, finally, after four unbelievably difficult years, returned home to Sikkim.

But he didn't receive the hero's welcome he deserved. Captain Harman had died from frostbitten lungs during a surveying expedition to Kanchenjunga, so the letter had never reached him: after all Kinthup's heroism and hardship, the logs had floated unnoticed down the river and out into the Bay of Bengal. Even worse, having dictated his extraordinary story to a scribe at the Survey of India offices, many doubted him, and he eked out the rest of his days as a tailor in Darjeeling, unrecognized for his efforts.

Kinthup's account had mentioned a falls, but it certainly wasn't the colossal cascade of Victorian fantasy. Mystery, romance, adventure, danger, Empire – the idea of such a waterfall lit the tightly corseted Victorian imagination, and by the turn of the century the elusive falls had become the stuff of fantasy, a geographical Holy Grail that the British were jolly well going to find before the Chinese. And when they did plant a Union Jack at the top of these vast falls, they'd build a 'spacious hotel for sightseers and sportsmen' – or so wrote Sir Thomas Holdich, the then president of London's Royal Geographical Society, in 1906. In 1910, after the Chinese invasion of Tibet, the quest took on a renewed intensity. With Chinese flags and troops popping up around Walong and the fringes of the Mishmi Hills, the British dispatched several surveying parties into the uncharted frontier zones. Among these were Bailey and Morshead, the former writing:

As far as the Western world was concerned, [we] were exploring country of which nothing was known, but much was speculated; one of the last remaining secret places of the earth, which might conceal a fall rivalling the Niagra [sic] or Victoria Falls in grandeur.

The indefatigable pair spent ten gruelling months marching 1,680 miles through mountains populated by warring tribes, tigers and a great deal of leeches, the latter so numerous, Bailey writes, that Morshead once counted 150 on his clothes. Morshead, by all accounts an extraordinarily fearless man, stood there 'covered with leeches and with blood oozing out of his boots as oblivious as a small child whose face is smeared with jam'. They were arrested in Tibet, suffered bouts of fever, were abandoned by their porters and were frequently having to convince wary Tibetan villagers that they weren't Chinese, yet remained models of Edwardian stoicism throughout.

By the time they returned to the plains of Assam, the usually immaculate pair weren't quite so well presented. Bailey writes:

I was forced to admit that sartorially Morshead did not look impressive. He looked a tramp, and a rather unsuccessful tramp at that.

But their dishevelment was worthwhile. They hadn't discovered the mythical falls, but their efforts had established that Tibet's Tsangpo and India's Brahmaputra were indeed one river, and they'd closed the unexplored gap to less than fifty miles. As Sir Thomas Holdich said upon their return:

They have succeeded in unravelling a geographical knot
which we geographers in India had looked at with longing
eyes for many a long year.

Both men went on to excel in the First World War, Bailey
surviving the Western Front and Gallipoli, Morshead dis-
tinguishing himself at the Somme and Passchendaele. Sadly
Morshead was murdered in Burma in 1931, although to this
day no one knows by whom, or why.

Having covered much of the same territory as Kinthup,
thirty years earlier, Bailey realized the veracity of the illiterate assistant spy's account. Tracking him down to Darjeeling,
where he was still living in poverty as a tailor, he lobbied the
British government to provide him with a pension. But by
the time they reluctantly agreed to a one-off reward of 1,000
rupees, Kinthup died not long afterwards.

Incredibly it wasn't until 1998, after multiple efforts,
that a team led by British Buddhist scholar and explorer
Ian Baker discovered a 105-foot waterfall in the innermost,
unexplored gorges of the Tsangpo. While the falls weren't
as impressive as their legend had suggested, their discovery
did, as Baker writes, 'put the centuries old question of its
existence to rest'.

My Sumo jolted up the hill into Anini as day faded to another
clear, stelliferous night – at 1,968 metres above sea level,
the air noticeably chillier. The only two 'hotels' were the
Circuit House and the Inspection Bungalow, both technically
reserved for government staff. The woman at the Circuit
House turned me away, even though they had rooms: I hadn't

booked and wasn't a government employee, she said, not even bothering to open the metal gate. The Inspection Bungalow, a mouldering yellow building surrounded by rubbish and weeds, had one room left and, after some persuasion from a motherly fellow passenger in the Sumo, they allowed me to have it. For 300 rupees I had two single wooden beds, a cold concrete floor, curtains as thin as rice paper and a patient congregation of fat, black spiders. A tiny bathroom had a cold tap, a bucket, a squat loo and two more resident spiders, the largest of which lived at eyeball level on the wall beside the loo. It was enough to give one stage fright.

Beside the open fireplace in the gloomy kitchen I found a sulky young Idu man with tattoos and an undercut. He was flinging orders at the cook, not even bothering to look at her, as he flicked his cigarette ash into the flames. The cook, like every domestic help I'd seen in Arunachal Pradesh, was an outsider, a frail-looking girl of no more than fifteen. With her was her younger sister, a waif of about six. The man was the caretaker's son and was studying botany at Guwahati University, he told me in good English, lighting another cigarette. When I asked him if he wanted to be a botanist he just laughed and carried on staring at the flames, my question apparently too stupid to answer. He hardly spoke any Idu; they were an 'extinct' tribe, he sneered. Of all the Idu I'd met, he was the only one I disliked.

Not wishing to linger in his company I ate a few incineratingly spicy mouthfuls of rice and dhal and went to my room to call Jibi in Roing. Using Bailey's account and Google Earth I'd plotted his 1913 route north from Anini up the Mathun Valley towards Tibet, and wanted to see how far I could follow it before the mountains or the military turned me back. To do this I'd need a guide, not only to show me the way but also because the Indian Army wouldn't tolerate a lone foreigner wandering around so close to the border. Who this guide would be, and how I'd find them, I wasn't yet sure. But if anyone could help me find the right person, my friend Jibi could. Half an hour later he called back.

'I find someone,' said the distant voice at the other end of the line with a characteristic chuckle. 'His name Edi Rondo and he young, handsome man. He come Inspection Bungalow seven-thirty tomorrow morning.'

Thanking Jibi profusely, I checked the positions of the largest spiders with my head torch, had a turbo pee, zipped myself into my sleeping bag and pulled it over my head. In the morning the beast beside the loo had vanished but the others hadn't moved a leg.

Edi arrived at 8.30 a.m. which, in the mystifying world of IST, Indian Stretchable Time, almost counts as punctual. A lanky, unusually tall Idu whose short hair was tinted red and shiny with wax, he leapt off his motorbike in a waft of aftershave, greeting me with an enthusiastic handshake and a formal 'Good morning, Ma'am'. At once we sat beside the kitchen fire and set to making plans, Edi speaking in an eager, breathless manner, suffixing each sentence with a typically Indian 'na'. The same age as the caretaker's sullen son, he couldn't have been more different; within no time he'd made a few phone calls, borrowed a motorbike for me and agreed that we'd ride up the Mathun Valley to the end of the tarmac road and see what happened then. Not knowing if we'd be away for one day or five, I put on my thick down jacket and trekking gear and packed my rucksack with the essentials: sleeping bag, toothbrush, water filter bottle, head torch, medical kit, teddy bear, diary, camera and spare pants. The rest I locked into my room at the Inspection Bungalow.

Edi stood watching me as I stalled and juddered down the slope from the bungalow. 'Ma'am, I think we need test drive first, na,' he shouted anxiously after me.

Accustomed to the feel of the Hero, I was having difficulty adjusting to the red 150cc crotch-rocket Edi had borrowed for me. The gears were sticky, the clutch hardly worked and I had to lean over the tank to reach the bars like some poor imitation of Valentino Rossi.

'Oh, I'll be fine,' I shouted back breezily, bunny-hopping out of the gate.

By the time we stopped for a late breakfast at a restaurant next to the army helipad I was vaguely in control, and Edi was too polite to say otherwise.

The restaurant, Anini's best, was a single room with four tables and a huge poster of Lhasa covering one wall. Two young Idu men sat at one table, daos strapped across their backs, shovelling spoonfuls of fried rice into their mouths with one hand and playing computer games on their mobile phones with the other. At another, two teenage girls were slumped over the table, fiddling with their mobiles. We ate chow mein, our voices drowned out by the reverberant thud of helicopters taking off, then stocked up on essentials for the trip: Maggi noodles, 'Good Day' biscuits and two bottles of the finest Royal Stag whisky. At 500 rupees a bottle it was the Rolls-Royce of local blends and even came in its own cardboard box. Just in case we ran out, we bought a bottle of McDowell's No.1 Rum too. Lastly I had to register with the police.

'Where John?' queried the fat, jolly Singpho commander-in-chief, as he copied the details of my permit into a yellowing ledger.

I asked him how many foreigners registered here each year and he paused, tapped his mouth thoughtfully with his index finger and replied: 'Four, maybe five.'

We rode out of town on a rough tarmac road that threaded its way along the side of the hills. It was a drab day and the sky was smeared with hoary clouds, but I was in high spirits, exhilarated to be riding towards the end of the road, to be so near Tibet. Beside me rode Edi, his grey nylon trousers and pointed black shoes more suitable for a day at the office than a tramp across the hills. But he was an Idu – these mountains were in his blood, and he didn't need all the pampering paraphernalia us Western travellers lug around.

Altitude and the cold had shaped the landscape differently here, and the luxuriant emerald jungle of the lower Dibang Valley had morphed into tonsured hills, their bald copper pates ringed by slopes of thick green coniferous curls. Occasionally there'd be a single hut on a hillside, grand in its startling isolation, an ancient warren of footpaths embossed onto the surrounding slopes like lugworm casts on a beach. Below galloped and gurgled the Mathun River, secure in its wooded gorge. If it weren't for the frame of stately white peaks it could have been Scotland in October. After an hour we reached the village of Mipi, where the tarmac road ended.

When Bailey arrived here in March 1913 he found an

enfeebled community of Tibetans, the last of a group of 2,000 pilgrims who'd left eastern Tibet a decade earlier in search of the promised land of Pemako. Many had died crossing the high passes, and those who made it never found the prophesied 'holy mountain of glass' surrounded by fertile valleys. Instead they'd succumbed to disease and been attacked by the Idu, who'd ambushed them, set traps and shot them with poisoned arrows. In 1909, disillusioned and defeated, most of the settlers returned to Tibet. By the time Bailey arrived only the old and infirm were left.

Now Mipi was a tiny Idu settlement, just a few houses and a helipad splayed over a grassy spur above the river, girdled by an arc of trees. I was expecting a large red and white barrier and a checkpoint patrolled by stern-faced, heavily armed soldiers telling me I wasn't allowed any further. But there was no checkpoint, and no soldiers to be seen, just two drunks lolling on a bench outside their hut. Beyond, a footpath climbed down to the river then emerged from the trees on the other side, winding alluringly across the tawny hills towards the snowbound ridge of the Indo-Tibetan border.

'Ma'am, we have choice, na,' said Edi, after talking to the drunks for a few minutes. 'We stop here, or we leave the bikes with these people and walk. There's a village half-day walk away. We could go there, na.'

The two drunks lolled and looked at us.

'Let's go!' I replied, unable to resist the lure of adventure and the pull of those forbidden mountains. It was just after midday; if we walked fast we could reach the village before dark. The drunks might not be models of responsibility but what was the worst that could happen? (Cue a brief mental montage of hot-wiring, joyriding, our bikes disappearing over the edge of mountains, crushed limbs, destroyed helmets, dead chickens ... but all of that was unlikely. Wasn't it?) Ten minutes later we'd wheeled the bikes behind the hut, pocketed the keys, given our helmets to the drunks and told them we'd be back in a few days. Shouldering our rucksacks, we set off down the hill to the river at a brisk, jubilant pace, the men shouting after us: 'Be careful! They're uncivilized people up there.' After similar warnings on his journey, Bailey had written: 'It seems to be universal, the inability of human beings to feel virtuous except when surrounded on all sides by rogues and villains.'

Bailey mentions being in Mipi 'in the middle of March in falling snow', but it was early March now and at least ten degrees. Edi said it had never snowed here in his lifetime. A wooden bridge took us across the river and from there we followed the narrow, winding footpath due north along the valley. We strode across open hillsides, our feet swishing through dry, yellow grass, then dipped through elfish dells where gnarled branches were hung with ragged pennons of moss and giant ferns sprouted from the nooks of twisted trees. Later we looped through lush pockets of jungle thick with bamboo and banana palms and slid across slabs of rock at the bottom of small, gabbling waterfalls. It was like travelling from Scotland to the tropics in the space of a few miles.

Fired by excitement and a desire to reach the village before nightfall, we kept up the momentum, swinging along with bamboo staffs, sweat trickling down our reddening faces. The wind whispered in the trees, water rushed and babbled around us, and our feet and staffs thudded rhythmically on the path. We paused only briefly at clear, fast-flowing nullahs, Edi bending down to scoop water out of the stream with his hands while I refilled my water bottle. And every time we emerged into the open again there were the snowy mountains, ranged like guardians across the northern horizon. It was on the other side of those mountains that Bailey had slipped over the edge of a cliff one afternoon. He was saved, he wrote, 'with the handle of my butterfly net'.

That afternoon I found a huge smile spreading across my face. It didn't matter that I was puffing and sweating after Edi, or that my legs were tiring: I was elated to be walking into the unknown, towards Tibet, my rucksack clanking with whisky and rum. But there was something else, too. It was as if every joyous stride was sloughing off the last remnants of an unwanted skin. I wasn't just walking towards the last Idu houses; I felt as if I was walking away from the past and into a brighter future, one free of batty episodes on Thai ferries and in BP service stations. I realized, in those few hours, that the fears and problems of the past year were just that, the *past*: that I'd been restored to the essence of who I was by the Idu and their hills. It was one of those rare occasions in life when you feel a pure, unrestrained joy to be alive, right here, right now. I wanted to call Marley and say, 'I'm back! I'm back!' and to jump up and down and skip through the grass. But I just kept walking across that magical valley, my whole being suffused with light and happiness.

It was six o'clock, and almost dark, when we reached a single bamboo longhouse on the edge of a forested hill above the Mathun. The Idu don't use the same calendar as us but this time of year is known as *Mu-La*, the time when the fields are cleared for planting, and the bare earth around the hut was smudged with ash and dotted with blackened tree stumps. Four black pigs grunted in a muddy pen and a foxy ginger dog ran towards us barking, then stopped, wagged uncertainly and skulked away, unaccustomed to sweaty white females landing on its doorstep at dusk.

Edi disappeared into the hut, emerging a minute later with a sooty older couple. 'These my fifth cousins, na.'

Elsewhere I would have thought this a startling coincidence, but among the Idu it was perfectly normal.

He nodded towards the pair. 'Their name Kormu and Mishing.'

Kormu's tracksuit was tatty and caked in years of grime, his bare feet black and calloused, the rough hand he held out ingrained with ash and dirt. Filth was embedded in every crease and wrinkle of his face and neck. His short black hair was thick and matted. His wife, Mishing, was tiny and bird-like, her sweatshirt and sarong equally soaked in dirt. They seemed shy and extremely surprised to see us, but they were Idu, and Edi's cousins, so they welcomed us in for the night. A glance at the map on my phone showed we were at 1,700 metres altitude and just twelve miles from Tibet.

I sat by the engoko as the couple talked excitedly to Edi and Mishing poured us cups of watery yu. On the woven bamboo walls around us hung a plastic clock, a calendar, an old Indian National Congress election poster, a few bamboo baskets and a string of grubby clothes. Two wooden shelves held plastic jars of salt and sugar, tins of tea and a selection of pots and pans. The only other resident was a brown cat, which sat sphinxlike by the fire, its brilliant green eyes fixed languidly on the flames.

'They never meet foreign person before,' said Edi, after a few minutes. 'They very surprised to see you here, and very happy.'

In honour of the occasion Mishing hurried down the corridor, returning wearing a clean blue T-shirt and a string of white beads. Kormu just grinned, sat beside the fire and poured himself a large glass of the rum Edi had just given him. When I handed him a bottle of whisky, too, Mishing intercepted it, giggling, and disappeared down the corridor to hide it.

I remember that night as one of the funniest of the entire journey. In my mind's eye I can see the hut clearly – the four of us sitting around the fire in the orange light of the flames, the small, elfin couple with their work-blackened hands. I can hear the clack of mugs, Mishing's girlish laughter and Kormu's rasping chuckle. And I can picture the cunning cat, fat as a spoilt pet, which they alternately beat with the bamboo fire tongs and cuddled in the rough way that small children torment family pets. The cat, its eyes never flinching from the flames, seemed utterly impervious to both. At some point we ate dinner, Mishing boiling rice and bitter greens and Kormu slicing raw, bloody venison on a log with hands so begrimed it was as if the dirt had seeped into the skin itself. With no loo and no running water, this would be a bad place to have diarrhoea. But thankfully I was brought up with chickens clucking around the kitchen, a pack of dogs sleeping beside the Aga and one of my mother's pugs regularly sitting on the kitchen table as we ate. As a result, I'm equipped with a stomach like a steel dustbin.

The more rice beer and rum we drank, the more loquacious Kormu and Mishing became, their initial shyness giving way to a childlike excitement. They laughed freely, showing brown, infrequent teeth that had probably never been nearer a dentist than a strip of cane, a tot of rum and a good yank. They were so happy to meet me, they said, to actually see a foreigner for the first time. They couldn't believe it! The only outsiders who came here were Indian Army patrols who stole their cooking utensils and drank their yu. By the time the rum was half-empty Kormu was a staunch Anglophile. How wonderful the British were! How kind! How beautiful! Everything made by Britain and Bhutan was fantastic quality, unlike the rubbish made by India, China and Nepal. They were sorry they didn't have more to give me, that their house was so simple. But I couldn't have been happier, and told them so repeatedly. Whenever the flames died down Mishing took a length of bamboo from the rack above the engoko and pushed it into the embers, showering us all in a blizzard of grey ashes and giggling.

It was after eleven o'clock when we each lay down on our side of the fire, Mishing fussing around her guests, apologizing it wasn't more comfortable. She watched as I unpacked my orange sleeping bag, falling about laughing at the sight of my teddy bear and patting its head and squeezing it to her chest in the same rough way she cuddled the cat. Kormu did the same. Afterwards they fell asleep under thin blankets, with logs as pillows, and I lay there listening to the crackling embers, the gurgling river and Kormu's drunken mutterings. I can't remember having spent a happier day in my entire life.

My eyes were gummed together and puffy from smoke when I woke at dawn. Mishing was pulling the kettle off the fire and Kormu was still a lump under his blanket. When he emerged, a reluctant caterpillar from its cocoon, he sat up and poured himself a refreshing glass of rum. Over tea and Maggi noodles I asked them if they liked living here and if they considered their surroundings beautiful. There's always fish in the river, said Kormu, and animals to hunt, and it was never too hot or too cold. But they didn't consider it beautiful – it was just where they lived. Life was hard here, he went on, having another restorative tot of rum. There was no road, no electricity, no telephone signal, and they had to clear the jungle and work all day in the fields to survive. Politicians always appeared before the elections and promised them a road and electricity, but of course these never came. Mishing had given birth to eleven children, alone, with no medical help, only five of whom had survived. The others had died of diarrhoea, hepatitis, malaria, fevers. It might have been different if they'd been able to reach a doctor.

'My family is the same,' said Edi, nursing a breakfast cup of yu. 'My parents had eleven children, but there are only five of us now. It's just part of our Idu life, na.'

It's so ironic. We urbanized, overcrowded Westerners dream of these wild places. We travel to the far side of the world to reach them, to *get away*, to gaze at unpolluted night skies, to be free of mobile phones, email, traffic, noise, crowds. For many of us these dwindling pockets of wilderness are earthly paradises, last Shangri-Las, precious fragments of a disappearing world. Yet for the people who live here the wilderness is there to be tilled, planted, fished and hunted. Their lives are about food, water and shelter – the primal aspects of human survival. They want electricity, a road and a mobile phone connection. They don't want to walk for days to buy clothes or reach medical help. There used to be more villages further up the valley but they've been abandoned. Like a tree, whose farthest branches were withering away, Idu society was shrinking to fit the roads. And it wasn't just in the Dibang Valley: between 2001 and 2011 the urban population in Arunachal Pradesh grew by thirty per cent. Kormu and Mishing's remaining five children all lived in towns. We are an accursed race, always wanting what we don't have. If only there was a happy medium.

Before we left they sat on their porch for photos, Kormu clutching the cat to his chest, Mishing with her arms around the foxy dog, a parody of an English family portrait. Edi then took one of the three of us, and Mishing posed with a bunch of mustard flowers and held my hand tightly in hers. When we hugged each other warmly goodbye, I couldn't believe her diminutive, bony frame had survived eleven childbirths. They'd miss me, they said, and asked when I was coming back, then we all waved and shouted *ji pra ji*, stay well, until we were well out of sight. I was sad to say goodbye and leave them, alone, for another solitary day of graft in the fields. What a life they lived.

There was one more house further up the valley, an hour's walk on from there. But it was beside an Indo-Tibetan Border Police camp, and I wasn't sure they'd welcome my presence so close to the frontier. I wouldn't be able to follow Bailey any further. Instead we walked back towards Mipi, swaying across a hanging bamboo bridge to a village we'd passed the previous day, the river rushing ferociously below. Up a steep hill, on the other side, a herd of mithun stood outside a large hut belonging to the *gambura*, the village chief. Of course the chief was Edi's distant cousin too, so after a brief conversation with three stooped old crones outside the door, we went inside, where the gambura, a noble-looking 75-year-old, was sitting beside a smoking fire weaving a small cane basket. He wore a dirty brown suit jacket, black tracksuit bottoms and an olive-green woollen hat, from under which tufts of grey hair stuck out. Around his neck was a string of white beads. Apologizing to Edi for not having any dried rats to offer me, he beckoned for me to sit beside him. I assured him not to worry, that I'd already had breakfast, and offered him our last bottle of whisky instead.

'The English are so kind and beautiful,' he said, delighted at the gift.

On the opposite wall hung the chief's hunting trophies: the horned skulls of tens of takin and serow (a form of goat-like antelope), and the brown jawbones of at least thirty Himalayan black bears. He was too old to hunt now, he said, but until five years ago he'd gone into the mountains for weeks at a time after musk deer. He'd often met Tibetan hunters up there and, although they didn't share any language, they'd shake hands, offer each other tobacco and whisky and camp together in the forests. Given the wild terrain and the unmarked border, neither could tell who had strayed into the wrong country. It was common for Arunachal's Mishmi to wander, accidentally or otherwise, into Tibet. Some were just hunting; others were shamans who'd been invited to do rituals in Mishmi villages across the border, where communist repression had almost wiped out their own. But a few were carrying mobile phones and cameras given to them by the Indian Army to spy on activity and infrastructure on the other side. I heard of one such Mishmi man who was caught by a Chinese border patrol and spent five years in jail there before being allowed home. The chief had never been a spy, he said, but he was afraid of the Chinese, and of another invasion like that of 1962. Although no Chinese troops had come over this part of the border, the Indian Army had turned tail anyway and fled from Anini to Sadiya, in Assam. He hoped it would be different if the Chinese ever invaded again.

As we were talking, one of the mithun broke into the pigs' pen behind the hut, the intrusion eliciting a volley of alarmed porcine squeals. The chief, belying his age, rushed out with a large stick and bellowed at the creature, at which it leapt over the four-foot palisade, tucking its front legs underneath its chest like a prize-winning show jumper.

We left soon after, the chief smoothing down his suit jacket and posing formally for photos outside the hut. I told him how handsome he was and he puffed out his chest like a proud old cockerel while the three old women crowed with laughter.

I walked back to Mipi with aching legs and a joyful heart, smitten by the Idu and their wild, untamed land. Around us, the world seemed equally joyous. Wisps of cloud sailed across an azure sky, the sun shone warm on my face and dragonflies hovered and darted through the undergrowth. Edi seemed infected by the mood, too, springing along behind me with a wide smile, exclaiming, 'What an adventure, Ma'am!' After a few hours we rounded the edge of a hill and there was Mipi on its knoll, its roofs glossy in the sunlight. Half an hour later we were sweating up the steep hill towards the hut, hoping we'd find both the drunks and the bikes where we'd left them.

10

LAST OF THE IGU

The hut was locked and the drunks nowhere to be seen. But the bikes were exactly where we'd left them. Of course they would be: the men might have been plastered, but they were Idu and we were guests, and a motorbike wasn't worth angering the spirits for. Wondering how we were going to retrieve our helmets, we sat in a tired heap by the hut, swatting off persistent swarms of dam dum flies and, before long, two teenage boys appeared on a motorbike, hunting rifles slung across their backs. They unlocked the hut and returned our unblemished helmets, then rode off with a wave, refusing any money for their troubles. What had happened to the drunks we never did find out.

I dawdled my way back to Anini, giddy with contentment, stopping frequently to feast on the view and imprint its

unfettered beauty on my mind. By the time I reached a junction at the edge of town Edi had long ridden ahead of me and
was nowhere to be seen. Confused as to which way to go, and
distracted by a man on a motorbike who'd stopped abruptly to
stare at me, I dropped my bike, swearing as it bashed my left
shin and began to pour petrol into the dust. The man, whose
rifle, leather jacket and black face-mask had been the cause of
my distraction, immediately rushed over to help me, firing a
series of questions at me as he did so.

'Where your guide? Why you alone? Where your permit?'

He was internal security, he explained, once the bike
was upright, and I wasn't allowed to be in Anini without a
guide. But it soon emerged that he was Edi's uncle, and Jibi's
cousin, and related to Tine Mena, and before long we were
chatting about how Jibi was, and my time at reh. Afterwards,
he escorted me back to the Inspection Bungalow through
Anini's confusing tangle of roads, and Edi – who'd ridden
ahead to mend a puncture – was given an avuncular ticking-
off for having left me.

Back in my room at the Inspection Bungalow the spiders
were still there, waiting, and Shelob had returned to her spot
beside the loo. The power had gone out so I filled the bucket
with cold water and washed by candlelight, shivering as the
freezing water splashed my skin. Afterwards the cook and her
sister made me rice and dahl while I warmed myself by the
fire in the kitchen. I tried to communicate in sign language
and the few words of Hindi I knew, but all I could glean was
that they were from Orissa, and the little one was eight. The
one other guest was a dull young IT engineer from Guwahati,
who joined me by the fire, droning on about the importance

of his job at the State Bank of India and how backwards the tribal people of Arunachal Pradesh were. I did my best not to listen.

My brief foray up the Mathun hadn't sated my desire to travel as far as possible towards the forbidden frontier with Tibet. That barricade of mountains held an almost mystical allure, a disputed, unexplored zone where continents collided and illicit hunters shivered around camp fires in dark forests. I'd asked Edi about accompanying some hunters into the mountains as a means of creeping nearer the border, but strict Idu taboos forbid women from even eating wild meat, let alone going on hunting trips. These taboos extend into every aspect of hunting, varying by clan and region. Before men leave home they must sacrifice a chicken for Golo, the spirit of the forest, and avoid certain foods – usually mushrooms, onions and garlic – and when they return they aren't allowed to sleep with their wives for five days, nor eat any food prepared by a woman with her period. Breaking these taboos will anger the *khinyu*, or spirits, and bring misfortune on their family and crops, something most Idu daren't risk. This fear of supernatural retribution has, for hundreds of years, acted as a natural form of conservation. But I was saddened to hear that in the Lower Dibang Valley Christianity was infiltrating Idu society and, consequently, hunting was on the increase. I'm sure Jesus wouldn't have approved.

It was after nine o'clock by the time Edi and I rode northeast out of Anini and up the Dri Valley the following morning. The landscape was the same curious mix of familiar and exotic, both redolent of Glencoe and the Himalayan valley it was. Coppery hills plunged towards the river, their lower slopes verdant with spruce, larch and pine, their ridges marbled with the last of the winter snows. Plum trees blossomed pink next to spumes of banana palms and the skeletal, wintry forms of elder and oak. By the roadside curling green shoots of bracken periscoped up from the brown grass, the vanguard of spring's vivid assault on the land. In the few villages we passed, stilted houses sat amidst gardens yellow with flowering mustard and women walked along the road bent under shoulder-loads of firewood.

After an hour we reached Dembuen, the final village, where the tarmac dissolved to a tantalizing dirt track and a yellow and white stone was painted with the words DEMBUEN END. A lone soldier waved us through a checkpoint beside an otherwise deserted border police barracks, then jogged after us as we rode the last hundred metres of tarmac and stopped the bikes to look longingly up the track. The place didn't exactly look shipshape or in a condition to jump to the subcontinent's defence, should China once again invade, but the soldier's presence made it too risky to try to sneak north from here. Instead Edi suggested we spend the night in Alinye, one of the villages we'd passed through, where there was a guesthouse owned by a shaman.

To my delight and surprise, the man who opened the door of the large hut in Alinye was the chief igu from the reh festival, the man whose chanting and radiating beneficence had made such an impression upon me. He'd swopped his shaman's garb for a blue checked shirt and black trousers but I recognized him immediately; how strange that fate had led me to his doorstep. He beamed at me, held my hands in his and ushered us into the hut, where we sat on the wooden floor near where an old man was watching television and slurping yu from a dirty plastic jug. The shaman sat cross-legged on a bed in front of us, his cane helmet, ceremonial daos and leopard's jawbone hanging like museum pieces from hooks on the wall behind him. And there we remained all afternoon, sitting at his feet like rapt infants, Edi translating as he spoke, his stories igniting my imagination with sparks of magic and the unseen.

His name was Sipa Melo, he began, and he was roughly fifty-five. He looked a decade younger, I thought, his brown skin smooth, his long hair – tied in the traditional Chulikata knot – as black as night. His mother had dreamt about the powers of her unborn child while he was still in the womb, but it wasn't until he was twenty-two that he became an igu and was able to chant and communicate with the spirits. Most of his power came from Inni Maselo Jinu, the supreme creator of the Idu, but, like all igu, he had a number of tutelary spirits whose power he called upon for different rituals, some of whom could be very dangerous. As he was telling me this the television flashed with news images of a snarling leopard that had been caught in central Guwahati, and the old man mumbled something at the screen. It reminded me of what I'd heard about the Idu's relationship with the tiger, and I asked Sipa to explain this.

Many years ago, he began, a natural calamity, *ini la free*, befell the world. The temperature soared, the heat of the sun became intolerable and everything on earth was burnt and destroyed. The only people to survive were a father and daughter, who had protected themselves from the heat by wrapping in layers and layers of banana skins. In order to save humanity they married and soon she gave birth to two sons, one of whom was a tiger. The tiger and the boy grew up happily until one day they had an argument about how to eat a deer they'd caught – the tiger wanted to devour it raw, but the boy wanted to boil it first. After a lengthy row they decided to solve the issue with a race, agreeing that the winner would kill the loser. But during the race the boy cheated, climbing a tree to drop an ants' nest on the tiger as he sped below. The tiger, infested with angry ants, was too itchy to run, and lost the race. The boy killed his vanquished brother with a bow and arrow and the tiger's body floated down the river to the sea, where his bones and teeth were collected by a bird and taken to its nest. A year later, the bones became a tiger again. Ever since then the Idu have believed the tiger is their brother, and that to kill one is tantamount to murdering a fellow human. It's believed by some conservationists that these unique Idu beliefs are a key reason tigers still survive in the Dibang Valley, and have done far more for their conservation than millions of rupees of government funding has achieved in Namdapha and elsewhere.

If the Idu don't kill tigers, what about the bandolier of tigers' teeth that Sipa had been wearing at reh? The *amrahla* protected him against evil spirits, he answered, and had been handed down to him through eight different igu. There were very few remaining these days. The teeth were mainly from tigers which had been found dead, but a few were from ones that had been killed; something that happens only when a tiger has taken too many mithun from a village. In these rare cases a powerful igu must lead the village in the same five-day funeral ritual as they would for a human. This had happened four years previously in the neighbouring village of Angriem Valley, when a tigress had been killed and two of her cubs captured and sent to the zoo in Itanagar, the state capital. But the igu who'd held the ritual for the dead tigress hadn't done it properly, and soon afterwards his house burnt down and he lost everything. When two tigers killed seventy mithun in Sipa's own village a few years ago, his neighbours had come to him begging for help. He chanted for three days, asking the tiger spirits to leave them in peace, and after that the village didn't lose another mithun.

The story made the hairs on the back of my neck stand on end. But this, it seemed, was just one of many magical feats this kindly, quietly spoken man had performed. He continued talking, his eyes sparkling, a smile constantly playing across his features. Four years ago a huge fire had broken out in the village and no one could stop it. It was a clear, sunny day but Sipa called to the spirits to bring rain, and two hours later a storm came and put the fire out. On another occasion, a villager had drowned and Sipa was called to the river to appease the water spirit snake, which is believed to cause all deaths in the river. He waded into the river and pulled out a long black thread, and when he came out of the water he was completely dry.

The room was darkening by the time we unfolded ourselves from the floor to walk to Sipa's guesthouse nearby. As we left I asked him about kalita, the non-hallucinogenic root used by igu, and he led us behind the hut, past three protesting geese, to an empty pigpen. He bent down and plucked a ginger-like, tentacled root out of the eviscerated mud and handed me a bit to taste. It was bitter, slightly spicy and vaguely reminiscent of ginger. Only igu can grow this, he said, and no animals will touch it – indeed the pigs had stripped the mud of everything else, but hadn't laid a snout on the alien-like root. And it wasn't just a powerful weapon against evil spirits. He told me it also had antiseptic properties and was good for treating fever and dysentery.

When Sipa wasn't overcoming tiger spirits, summoning rain and fighting spirit snakes, he also ran a construction business, and had been contracted by the local government to build the guesthouse he now ran. Since Alinye was unlikely to have a tourist boom anytime soon, I couldn't imagine who the bafflingly large white building with its grand metal entrance gates and tiled bathrooms had been built for. At dinner we sat in a dining room large enough for fifty people, while Sipa's wife dashed in and out with delicious plates of vegetable curry, rice, chapatti and dahl. Sipa, whose strict post-reh taboos forbade him from eating garlic, onions, mushrooms or ginger, sat separately and ate just plain rice and boiled vegetables.

While we ate, he told me about another beast the Idu believed to be their brother – the *khepa*, a ten-foot-high gorilla-like creature that we call the yeti. A long time ago, man had become jealous of the khepa's superior intelligence and, after winning a rigged contest (there's a theme here), had made a deal with the khepa that the two would never meet again. To ensure this, an igu performed a ceremony to make the khepa invisible, then banished him to the forest. The Idu still see their footprints, though, and hear their voice in the mountains, and Sipa believed in the khepa's existence as certainly as he believed we were sitting in front of him. Only six months ago, footprints had been seen near Roing – huge bestial imprints two metres apart. Even the local government officials had seen them, he said.

Of course these could have been fanciful exaggerations of otherwise mundane events, a means of livening long winter nights around the fire. But there was something about Sipa, something godlike. It wasn't just his warmth and lightness of spirit, or the fact it was impossible to imagine anger, envy or any hint of malevolence ever darkening his countenance. It was more than that. I felt that Sipa was plugged into a different plane of existence to most of us, that he knew things that were beyond normal understanding. To be in his presence was to peel away the blinding veils of Progress, Civilization and Science, to peer into a shimmering world of magic and the unseen, to believe in a world beyond that which we see. If anyone had the keys to another dimension, he did. I've never met another human being like him.

But Sipa is one of a disappearing breed. The younger generation aren't interested in becoming igu, and there are very few of them left. Sipa had four children, sons and daughters, and none of them wanted to learn the art. Or maybe it worked both ways. Maybe television and mobile phones and modernity were tuning the Idu to a different frequency and severing their contact with the spirit world. After all, it was said that you couldn't choose to become an igu, but that the spirits chose you. Perhaps the spirits were losing interest. When we left the next day, Sipa held my hands in his and thanked me for recording his stories. They needed to be written down, he said, before it was too late.

*

A few days later, at 6 a.m., I was standing outside the Inspection Bungalow in Anini, huddled in my coat, watching as the rising sun dyed the snow peaks a dusky pink and mist rose like steam from the hills. Land of the dawn-lit mountains indeed. A man jogged slowly around a scrubby football pitch below, followed by a pack of barking, gambolling dogs. Minutes later the Sumo I was booked on roared up the hill, a mountain of luggage strapped to the roof. The sisters gave me a handful of oranges for the journey and shyly said goodbye, and Edi – who'd come to see me off – pumped my hand effusively.

'This most definitely some of best days of my life, Ma'am. I'll miss you, na.'

At that I hugged him goodbye, wedged myself and my bags into the last space on the back seat, and we were off.

The driver, a thin, fast-talking Nepali with gelled hair and crudely tattooed forearms, set off as if pursued by the hounds of hell. We tore down the hill from Anini, careering around corners and nosediving into potholes, a wake of dust exploding from our bald tyres. Ten of us were crammed in, but no one spoke. Everyone just looked numbly ahead, slammed against each other like ships in a stormy harbour, the most violent bumps sending my neighbour, a well-groomed young Idu man, bouncing onto my lap. Outside, sunlight raked down the hillsides, peeling back the cover of night, and mist whorled and eddied in the valleys. But my head was being pummelled against the metal doorframe and Hindi power ballads screeched out of the tinny speakers behind my ears, so it was hard to fully appreciate the view. *Oh God, twelve hours of this*, I thought, as the driver yanked us demonically around another bend. But the hours somehow slid by.

At some point we rounded a corner to find the way blocked by a gang of road workers. They milled about, blank-faced and grubby, lethargically moving a pile of rocks from the road. No one complained or harangued them. Instead we all piled out, glad for the respite, and helped move rocks until there was room enough to pass. One of the workers' children, a tiny girl, sat disconsolately on a heap of rubble, playing with an old shoe, her doleful eyes watching as we worked. I wondered if she would ever escape the binding snare of poverty.

At 5 p.m., in a tunnel of forest just twenty miles from Roing, a wheel bearing went, and we all shuffled out to stretch stiff limbs and pee while the driver assessed the situation. The Nepalis who drive these difficult routes are a band of brothers, bonded by the hardships of the job, and soon two other Sumos had stopped to help. The three men squatted beside the front passenger wheel, elbow-deep in oil and grease, smoking and bantering as they worked. There was no sense of annoyance, or impatience. Quite the opposite; they seemed to be enjoying it. I imagined the same happening to a bus in England – the stressed driver, the grumbling passengers, the tutting and time watching, the feeling that this *shouldn't* happen, *we've paid for this, damn it*. Our problem is expectation. We're poisoned by it. We *expect* things to go our way, to arrive on time, to work as they should. But in India the unexpected is the norm, and with that comes an admirable sense of acceptance. We could learn a lot from that.

It was 8 p.m. by the time the Sumo dropped me off at the end of the dark track to Jibi's camp. After ten days of scant washing I stank like a ferret's armpit. In an attempt to rectify this, much of the next day was spent in a rare fever of domesticity: washing myself and my fetid clothes, and scrubbing, drying and repacking my gear. After the dinginess of the Inspection Bungalow my hut by the river felt like the presidential suite at Claridge's. And oh, the delight of a hot bucket wash!

Jibi was away, scouting a nearby river with an English fishing guide, so that evening I went to dinner with Tine, my Everest-conquering friend, arriving to find her hut spilling with people. Pretty Idu girls sat in a giggling row on a bed against the far wall and a crowd of young men were drinking mugs of yuchi around the blazing engoko. Among them sat Tine and a drunken, gesticulating Indian man who was bellowing instructions at a teenage girl standing nervously on the other side of the fire. It wasn't quite the scene I'd expected. When I sat next to Tine she explained that she was helping a film director from Mumbai (the drunk) audition girls for parts in a film about the Idu. The director, it seemed, had underestimated the strength of the local brew.

The auditioning continued, so I struck up conversation with a young Idu man beside me who, unusually for someone of his age, had his long hair cut in the traditional crop-haired fashion. He was trying to keep their culture alive, he said, since too many of his generation were losing their Idu language and values. I told him about my meeting with Sipa and asked him whether he'd ever seen an igu perform magical feats.

'Oh yes.' He nodded. 'I see igu eat hot coals, jump over huge fires and get possessed by spirits and start talking in other languages. And I hear about them flying and crossing wide river by walking on thread. I don't know what going to happen to igu, though, they disappearing. But they are glue that hold our society together. Without them, how can we survive?'

'What about the khepa?' I asked him, intrigued by what Sipa had told me.

'Yes, khepa exist. In April our people hunt a type of frog which khepa like too. People see his footprints by the river, and the remains of his meals.'

At the mention of the word 'khepa', an impish older man on the other side of the fire interjected in rapid Idu. The man, with his glittering eyes and long scar down his right cheek, was hard to forget, and I remembered his face from reh.

'That Tine's father, Buge,' my neighbour said. 'He says he heard the khepa many times in the forest, and seen his shadow in the trees. But he never see him. No one has. It not possible.'

Aha! The famous Buge (pronounced 'Boogay'): a man whose reputation galloped before him. He was a famous hunter, I'd been told, a legend among the Idu. I'd heard he had been attacked by a bear once, and lived to tell the tale. I asked him about this through my neighbour and he chuckled, then began to talk. When he was twenty he'd been out checking rat-traps in the jungle when he'd spotted a family of bears. He hid in the undergrowth, hoping they hadn't seen him, but the mother leapt on him from behind, knocking his rifle out of reach. The enraged beast pinned him down, slashing open his right cheek with her claws and ripping at his arms and chest. But somehow Buge fought back, wrestling the bear with his bare hands until, all of a sudden, it turned tail and ran. He'd healed his cuts using medicinal plants, but bore the scars to this day. I was in awe. It's not often you meet a man who's survived a wrestling match with a bear.

He was around sixty now, but had calves like pistons and the lean, muscular physique of a thirty-year-old athlete. He still went hunting alone for a month or more, sleeping in the forest and navigating by the stars. No wonder he'd fathered a girl who'd climbed Everest. But of all his seventeen children, she was one of only two who had survived.

When I left late that evening, Tine presented me with a beautiful embroidered Idu shawl. She was one of many Idu I was extremely sorry to say goodbye to. But tomorrow I'd ride west to Pasighat and the Upper Siang Valley, where a very different land and people awaited.

PART TWO

TOUCHING TIBET

11

SEARCHING FOR SHANGRI-LA

Around the middle of the eighth century, somewhere in what is now Pakistan, an eight-year-old boy called Padmasambhava was miraculously born of a lotus leaf. But this Guru Rinpoche, or 'precious master', as he became known, was no ordinary lotus-born prodigy. Credited with establishing the earliest form of Buddhism in Tibet, the thunderbolt-wielding Tantric sorcerer spent much of his life performing miracles, subduing the demons of the old religion of Bon and gadding around on the back of a flying tigress. Amidst these marvellous doings, the Rinpoche found time to write numerous arcane texts revealing the locations of sixteen 'beyuls', or hidden lands, secret valleys deep in the Himalayas that would provide sanctuary to believers in future times of difficulty.

These texts – as the author, explorer and Buddhist scholar Ian Baker writes – 'typically opened with apocalyptic prophecies of war and devastation, but shifted into what read at times like a *Fodor's Guide* to a parallel universe'. According to the writings, these hidden lands were said to occupy several planes of existence: at their most basic level they were real, remote valleys visible to normal people, but at the highest plane they were magical realms containing portals to other dimensions, and only visible to enlightened beings.

The most powerful of these beyuls was Pemako. Meaning 'lotus of great bliss', this was said to be an earthly paradise whose geography mirrored the supine body of the Tantric goddess Dorje Phagmo. From head to navel she lay in south-eastern Tibet, from navel downwards in the Upper Siang region of today's Arunachal Pradesh. The Tsangpo, meaning 'great purifier', formed her spine. This Pemako, the Rinpoche wrote, was a magical land where rivers flowed with enchanted water, trees grew edible bark, old men became young again and a dazzling pharmacopeia of magical herbs held the key to eternal bliss. Anyone lucky enough to die here gained the fast-track to enlightenment. At its heart lay a place called Chime Yangsang Ne, 'the innermost secret place of immortality'. If you made it this far you'd live for a thousand years then dissolve into rainbows at the time of your death. Crucially, in a distant age of famine and calamity, Pemako would provide a refuge for the faithful.

But these beyuls couldn't be stumbled upon by any old Tom, Dick or Harry. In order to stop a stampede towards instant enlightenment, the wily Rinpoche added a few obstacles. Firstly, he wrote his texts on cryptic scrolls and hid them in walls of rock, lakes and monasteries all over Tibet. Known as *terma*, or treasure, they could only be found by powerful mystics called *terton*, or treasure seekers, who would be led to them through dreams and visions. Secondly, the Rinpoche made sure Pemako was a perilous place to reach. The beyul, he warned, was guarded by vicious vipers, blood-sucking leeches, witches, demons, man-eating tigers, cannibals armed with poison darts and wrathful protector deities. The latter would bar the way to anyone of impure mind or false intentions by causing nightmares and illness, or by blocking their path with landslides and avalanches. If you wanted to reach Pemako, you had to be worthy of it.

Ever since the Rinpoche concealed these texts Tibetans have struggled across the mountains in search of this sacred land. They fled here from the Mongol hordes in the four-teenth century and, much later, the Chinese. But it was rarely a quest without mishap. An eighteenth-century terton, the Tibetan yogi Lelung Shepe Dorje, vividly described the challenges awaiting pilgrims in *The Delightful True Stories of the Supreme Land of Pemako*, written in 1729.

> In ... Pemako, the supreme of all hidden lands ... there is a constant menace from poisonous snakes, leeches, flies, clawed and long-snouted animals with fangs, dangerous wildmen and vicious savages ... the land is full of mis-chievous spirits [that] ... constantly display magic and miracles – those without courage, or those with lingering doubts ... such people will have difficulty reaching this land and getting through unscathed.

It wasn't just wild-haired Tibetan ascetics and their followers who went in search of these hidden lands. Along with the Buddhist legend of the kingdom of Shambhala, the Rinpoche's writings inspired a motley collection of explorers, geographers, fantasists and spies in the nineteenth and early twentieth centuries. The oddest of these was Heinrich Himmler, *Reichsführer* of the SS, whose conviction that one of these hidden lands was home to a master Aryan race led to seven Nazi-funded expeditions to Tibet in the 1930s. A decade earlier, Gleb Bokii, a Bolshevik cryptographer and one of the heads of the Soviet secret police, led an equally barmy quest, hoping to use Buddhist spiritual techniques to engineer perfect communists. At the same time, that intrepid plant-hunter Frank Kingdon-Ward was traipsing around the eastern Himalayas in search of orchids, Pemako and the still undiscovered 'Falls of Brahmaputra'.

Accompanied by his benefactor, the young Scottish aristocrat Jack, the 5th Earl of Cawdor, and porters carrying Fortnum & Mason hampers stuffed with the finest pâtés, jams and coffee, Kingdon-Ward set off in 1924 (the same year that Mallory and Irvine were on Everest). But their journey was anything but a picnic. In his 1926 book, *The Riddle of the Tsangpo Gorges*, Kingdon-Ward laments:

'Pemako ... from the snowline to the river gorge, is covered with dense forest. Add to this ... a climate which varied from the sub-tropical to the Arctic, the only thing common to the whole region being perpetual rain; snakes and wild animals, giant stinging nettles and myriads of biting and blood-sucking ticks, hornets, flies and leeches, and you have some idea of what the traveller has to contend with.'

Such conditions didn't engender harmony between the two men. Kingdon-Ward, by now a hardened explorer, scoffed at the young earl's insistence on a weekly bath, while Cawdor grew to despise the botanist's ponderous pace.

'If I ever travel again I'll make damn sure it's not with a botanist. They are always stopping to gape at weeds.'

By the end of the expedition Kingdon-Ward and his grumbling patron had found neither paradise nor the falls, and had resorted to using liberal amounts of morphine for their various bites, stings, aches and pains.

A few years later the English novelist James Hilton published *Lost Horizon*, a fantastical novel set in the mythical kingdom of Shangri-La, a secret Himalayan valley inhabited by happy peasants and ageless lamas who had apparently discovered the key to eternal youth. Their leader was a wise and extremely ancient Capuchin monk called Father Perrault, who'd come upon the valley hundreds of years previously while searching for lost communities of Nestorian Christians in Central Asia. Similarly to Guru Rinpoche, he predicted that:

The Dark Ages that are to come will cover the whole earth. There will be neither escape nor sanctuary, save such as are too secret to be found or too humble to be noticed. And Shangri-La may hope to be both of these.

The notion of hidden Himalayan utopias had existed in Tibetan scholarship for centuries, but it was Hilton who introduced the idea into the Western mainstream. His timing couldn't have been better. For a generation who'd experienced the horrors of the Great War and the Depression – and were now sliding towards another cataclysm – Hilton's imagined paradise ignited a potent nostalgia for a vanished age. *Lost Horizon* became an instant bestseller. Untarnished as it was by war, suffering and mechanization, the valley was an escape from the grim reality of the pre-war 1930s, and the name he gave it, Shangri-La, meaning 'snowy mountain pass', was soon synonymous with the notion of heaven on earth, a dreamlike realm of verdant meadows, celestial mountains and eternal bliss. F. D. Roosevelt named his Maryland retreat 'Shangri-La' and now, eight decades on, despite the phrase being flogged to death by hyperbolic tourist boards, grotty hotels and seedy casinos from Bangkok to Bognor, a yen for such an earthly paradise still remains. Now, even more than in the thirties, we dream of such idylls: wildernesses free from the noise and pollution and troubles and wars and people and technology of our overcrowded twenty-first-century world. They don't need to be the Rinpoche's spellbound lands of rainbow waterfalls and mind-expanding magical herbs (although that would be a bonus), they just need to be the antithesis of our hectic, technology-driven modern lives.

But such places are fast disappearing, consumed by soaring human populations and our fathomless greed for land and resources: our forests are vanishing, our rivers are being dammed, our deserts are being encroached upon, our wildlife is being poached, mass tourism is fingering its way into all but the most distant parts of the planet. Could the Indian side of Pemako be a surviving, modern-day Shangri-La, a hidden valley free from the ravages of consumer capitalism? There

Mist, mountains and a river purling below – a typical view in Arunachal Pradesh. This was taken in the Upper Siang region.

Three Idu Mishmi *igu*, or shamans, chant at *reh* festival in the Dibang Valley.

Kormu and Mishing, the lovely Idu Mishmi couple I stayed with near the Dibang Valley's border with Tibet, plus their fat cat and foxy dog.

The charred skulls of sacrificed mithun hang on the bamboo walls of a Miju Mishmi house in Anjaw district.

Sipa Melo, the Idu Mishmi shaman. Note the leopard's jawbone around his neck.

Kabsang, one of my guides in Pemako, and a deaf (but exceedingly cheerful) villager in Tashigong.

The fog-wreathed gompa at Yoldong in Pemako.

Kabsang, Dorje (the King!) and I take a rest outside the main door of Devakotta Monastery in Pemako.

The view from Tashigong. Paradise on earth.

Adi men fixing a hanging bridge over the Siang River outside Tuting. Not a job for anyone suffering from vertigo!

The sun sets over the rice fields of the Apatani Valley in Lower Subansiri district – such a different landscape to anywhere else in the state.

An old Apatani lady who had recently converted to Christianity.

Ursula Graham Bower (left) with two Naga, taken during her wartime stint in the Naga Hills in the early forties. What a lady she was.

My tent in the Nyishi longhouse at Karoi: a source of great entertainment for all the family.

Freddie 'Buzz Boy Pete' Raubinger, a 21-year-old pilot – one of the US airmen killed near Karoi in 1945 (inset). Me, my ebullient guide, Tapir (left), and a local Nyishi man, with one of the C-46's radial engines at the crash site near Karoi (main picture).

Nuns at school in Tawang. On the left is Phurpa, one of my lovely hosts.

Riding towards the snow-bound Sela Pass near Tawang.

Me with my Hero, looking jubilant at the top of the
4,175-metre Sela Pass.

With my Indian fairy godfathers, Abhra (left) and Manash, at the end
in Guwahati.

was only one way to find out, and that was to try to travel there myself – even if there were a few snakes, fanged beasts, witches and blood-sucking insects on the way.

I couldn't go alone, though. Since Pemako is a heavily militarized area on the disputed border with Tibet, I'd have to travel there with a guide. I also wanted to go with someone who knew the Rinpoche's writings and could take me to the beyul's remoter realms. But few Westerners have travelled to the Indian side of Pemako – known as Lower Pemako – and almost none since Frank Kingdon-Ward. The only vaguely recent source I could find was an article on an obscure Buddhist website, which told of an American woman's pilgrimage to a monastery at the heart of Lower Pemako. With her had been a whimsical-sounding local guide called Ata who, with his gold wellington boots, curling moustache and encyclopaedic knowledge of Buddhism and the hidden lands, sounded like just the person I needed.

But finding Ata was easier said than done. The American's pilgrimage had been a decade earlier, and when I contacted her she had no idea how to reach Ata, or where he lived. Abhra forwarded the article to his numerous contacts in Arunachal Pradesh, but none of them recognized the man in the photographs. Our search was made harder by the lack of mobile and internet reception in Tuting and Yingkiong, the two towns at the top of the Siang Valley he was most likely from. To muddle things even more, it seemed Ata wasn't his real name, just a way of saying 'brother' in a local language. After months of searching, Ata remained no more than a ghost in a ten-year-old article.

*

I was readying to leave Jibi's the following morning when a muddy white Nissan X-Trail sped into camp and out jumped Jibi, the English fishing guide and another local man. They were back from their fishing trip a day early.

The Englishman, Bee, was a raffish type with piercing blue eyes and short greying hair. 'Dahling, have you come all this way on that bike?' he said, shaking my hand.

With his tight black jeans and laid-back drawl he had the louche air of a middle-aged rock star. Jibi chuckled and shook my hand, more Yoda-like than ever.

'Babe, this is Tapir,' said Bee, introducing the third man. 'He's the best guide in Arunachal Pradesh.'

Tapir, five-feet tall and built like Fort Knox, was an Adi from the neighbouring Siang Valley. Previously known as the Abor, the Adi had been a particularly persistent thorn in the Raj's side. But Tapir was the clue I'd been waiting for. As we all sat and chatted over tea on a platform overlooking the river, it occurred to me that Tapir just *might* know Ata. I showed him the photo I'd saved on my phone.

A smile of recognition lit his broad features. 'Yes, mem! I know this man. His name Dorje Tenzing. He live in Yingkiong. But he old and very ill; he no go trekking now. But maybe his son take you.'

At this he scribbled down the son's telephone number. Ten minutes later I'd spoken to him and agreed to meet them in Yingkiong in two days' time. What an extraordinary stroke of luck.

I was less lucky with the weather. After all the warnings of downpours and landslides, there'd barely been a drop of rain in Anini. But now, as I squeezed my laptop, tool kit and diaries into my faithful top box, the first fat sploshes fell from a rapidly darkening sky. Minutes later, it was pouring.

Bee frowned with concern as he watched me pull my black poncho over my head and fasten my helmet. 'Be careful, babe, it's easy to get lost on the way to Pasighat.'

'Oh, I'll be fine,' I replied, not entirely convinced of the ability of my substandard navigational skills.

'Well, good luck and maybe I'll see you in Pasighat. Tapir lives in a village nearby and we're going there later.'

Loath as I was to leave my Idu friends it was time to go. I hugged Jibi goodbye and thanked him for all his kindness, then bumped down the rutted main street and out of Roing, turning towards Pasighat just south of town. The rain was falling in torrents now and I sputtered west under charcoal skies, soaked hands gripping the handlebars like claws, poncho flapping and billowing behind me. The tarmac became a smear of orange mud then gave way to a confusing tangle of jungle tracks and the grey, stony Dibang River plain. To the right rose the veiled massif, to the left yawned Assam, but beyond that there was little certainty. There were no signs, almost no other traffic and, in many places, only the faintest indentations in the stones to suggest which way cars had gone.

After an hour I came to a river crossing where a vessel consisting of a few planks and a clattering diesel engine plied a 100-metre stretch of fast-flowing water. A man appeared from a bamboo shack, charged me fifty rupees, and helped push the Hero up a wobbly plank. When another motorbike arrived a few minutes later the ferry belched and strained across the water, and I followed them across the rest of the wide river plain, pelting after the hooded rider on slippery, unmarked paths. At Dambuk, a town halfway to Pasighat, the rider slowed and took off his waterproof hood, and I saw that he was a young Assamese. He was stopping here, he said, but to reach Pasighat I must turn right at the iron gate, cross two bamboo bridges, go through the jungle, go left at the first village and then straight on. Repeating this several times, I thanked him and sped off.

The two bridges were crude structures spanning vicious little torrents in the otherwise dry river basin. Skinny, sly-looking young men popped out of tents to tax me 100 rupees for crossing, and I held my breath as my wheels bumped over the slippery, creaking poles. Further on was the dark, dripping jungle, the trees stooped under the weight of rain, and beyond that an Adi village, the stilted huts distinguishable by their ochre, palm-leafed roofs. Soon afterwards I was riding across a wide, modern bridge over the languid waters of the Brahmaputra, calm after its raging descent from Tibet, the town of Pasighat cradled in the lee of the hills beyond. It was 4 p.m. and it had taken me four hours to cover the sixty miles from Roing.

Pasighat, the regional headquarters of the East Siang district, was established by the British in 1911 as a base for both surveying the upper reaches of the Siang River and controlling the troublesome Abors. When Mark Shand visited in the late 1990s he described it as being like a 'miniature British market town, with leafy promenades and lines of little houses surrounding neat postcard shaped parks'. But it was too dismal to admire parks and promenades, so I rode straight to the Adi homestay I'd been told about, with Pasighat just a passing damp blur.

A neat little place set in a garden lush with flowers, the homestay was half-traditional Adi hut and half-concrete bungalow. Its owners had recently been trained in hospitality as part of a state tourism initiative – training, I suspected, that had been taken straight from an Edwardian book on etiquette. Kalin, the kind but sombre husband, addressed me with the sort of restrained formality one might reserve for a visiting Royal, while his wife – a homely figure aptly called Mum – bustled about the hut in a whirr of culinary activity. And what a cook Mum was! That evening I sat beside the *merum*, a square hearth identical to the Idu's engoko, digging my hands into leaves full of nutty rice, spicy dhal, banana flowers and tender white river fish. Despite my protestations my hosts refused to eat until I'd finished, Mum hovering in the shadows, anxious for my appreciation. Even more delicious was Mum's homemade *apong* – a sweet, viscous, amber nectar distilled from rice and husks.

'Madam, I would like to tell you something,' announced Kalin at one point during the evening, so solemnly I wondered what was coming next. 'We hill people are very grateful to you Britishers. If your people hadn't introduced the Inner Line Permit in 1873 you probably wouldn't be sitting here now in this traditional Adi house. Our culture would have been dominated by mainland Indians a long time ago.

'Look at Meghalaya and Mizoram,' he continued. 'Now they are campaigning to have the Inner Line Permit system too, but it's too late, their tribal cultures are almost lost.'

The Adi weren't always so well disposed towards the British. Meaning 'unruly' or 'disobedient', these Sino-Tibetan animists were understandably loath to bend to the rule of meddling white men: many a Raj soldier, sepoy and coolie was hacked to death by an Abor dao or spent their last hours writhing in agony after being hit by an aconite-tipped arrow. The British, in turn, deplored their uppity subjects. Our dear friend Butler described the Abor as 'large, uncouth, athletic, fierce-looking, dirty fellows', who were 'as void of delicacy as they are of cleanliness'. Similarly, Sir Alexander Mackenzie, in his lengthily titled 1884 *History of the Relations of the Government with the Hill Tribes of the North-East Frontier of Bengal*, labelled them savage, intractable and barbarous. 'They are,' he concluded, 'in all manner insolent and rude beyond all other tribes of this frontier.' But after decades of intermittent raids, counter-raids and squabbling, it was an incident in 1911 that really lit the tinderbox.

In March of that year the British Political Officer Noel Williamson, accompanied by a doctor called Gregorson and forty-seven coolies, marched north from Pasighat on a peaceful mission to trace the course of the Brahmaputra. The two men were dressed in the sort of tweed and puttees one might wear for a day's pheasant shooting in Norfolk, and carried a gramophone, a magic lantern and a medicine chest. But their expedition was scuppered when Abor tribesmen intercepted one of their mail messengers carrying letters back to Pasighat. Being illiterate, the Abor placed great importance on colours and symbols, and when they saw the letters – white envelopes edged in black as a mark of mourning for the recently deceased King Edward VII, and sealed with red wax – they leapt to a fatally wrong conclusion. The envelopes, they concluded, signified the white man, the black edging their soldiers, and the red the government's anger.

Assuming Williamson's peaceful mission to be a trap, the Abor gathered a war party, and within two days Williamson, Gregorson and all but five of the coolies had been hacked and speared to death.

The British were incensed. Six months later a mighty punitive force consisting of 3,000 Ghurkha, Sikh and Assamese troops and 3,500 Naga coolies marched up the Siang, the Naga carrying spears and striding in columns six abreast, their unique two-tone 'he-ha, he-ho' war chant putting the fear of God into the Abor. The expedition also included a botanist, zoologist and surveyor, and the instructions to 'explore and survey as much of the country as possible, visiting, if practicable, the "Pemakoi Falls" and settling the question of the identity of the Tsangpo and Brahmaputra rivers'. (I was tickled to read in a 1912 account of the expedition, *In Abor Jungles*, that the troops' packing list included: '1 pair pyjamas, 1 pair breeches, 6 handkerchief, 1 pillow, or suit of Burberry's Gabardine and a Brandy flask'.)

The Abor loved a good dust-up and had spent months preparing for the British attack they knew was coming. They'd destroyed cane bridges, stockaded their villages with felled trees and moats and booby-trapped the jungle with concealed pits lined with aconite-tipped stakes. But against the British arsenal of hand grenades, light infantry, Maxim machine guns and elephant-drawn Howitzers, they never stood a chance. In late 1912, after a protracted campaign, the Abor chiefs surrendered, waving copies of *The Calcutta Statesman* on a ridge above the Siang as a sign of truce. In the 1940s the Abor renamed themselves the Adi, meaning 'hill men', and, like their old enemies the Naga, proved valuable allies against the Japanese during the Second World War. Considering the Williamson incident had been only thirty years previously, it was a remarkable change of heart.

All night the rain hammered on the roof like a thousand tiny fists. In the morning, when the leaden sky showed no signs of relenting, I decided to wait in Pasighat and hope conditions were better the next day. Kalin was less optimistic. As Mum served me gooey rice chapatti in banana leaves for breakfast, he dolefully predicted the worst.

'Madam, it has been raining in Yingkiong for more than a week.' He frowned in the manner of someone predicting a dire tragedy. 'It will rain tomorrow too.'

When this didn't put me off he tried again. 'Madam, please, the road is very dangerous – take a Sumo instead.'

Bee, the raffish Englishman, was similarly concerned when, lured by my telephone reports of Mum's apong, he came for dinner that evening.

'Darling, I think you need to take alternative transport,' he drawled, sitting on a low stool beside the fire, his long legs folded under him like a grasshopper. 'It's too dangerous for you to ride up there alone in these conditions.'

But my mind was set. I didn't want to leave my Hero behind again and, besides, perhaps Guru Rinpoche was already testing my resolve.

'Everything's difficult in Arunachal Pradesh,' Bee conceded, 'whether you're driving to Yingkiong or trying to have a crap.'

He was right; travel was difficult here, but I'd never expected otherwise. Whatever the weather in the morning,

I'd clad myself from head to toe in Gore-Tex and polythene and ride into those mountains.

At dawn the deluge had at last subsided but the sky still lay like a wadded lid upon the land and further rain looked imminent. Mum handed me a leaf-wrapped packed lunch and bade me an anxious goodbye – then I rode back over the Brahmaputra towards the wall of mountains. They reared ahead of me, a fortress of rock, the formidable outline of their ridges blue against the pewter sky, clouds clinging to their shoulders like ghostly bridal shawls. I was alone, a tiny, insignificant speck, riding towards the serried ranks of an almighty force armed with no more than a 150cc engine and a couple of spanners. Minutes later I was into the maw of the mountains, winding into the mist on a ribbon of new black tarmac.

The tarmac was short-lived, soon giving way to a morass of mud and a turmoil of road construction. Caterpillars clawed at banks of earth and lorries rumbled through the mud, their black-skinned drivers staring down at me from high cabs. Gangs of women shifted piles of soil and, by the roadside, groups of Adi men, women and children picked their way through the sludge, curly-tailed hunting dogs trotting at their heels, all of them turning to stare as I waved and rode past. Slowed to a crawl, I wove between men and machines, struggling to control the fishtailing bike on a surface that was as slippery as an ice rink. A river dashed through a gorge below and the odd thatched village poked between fans of palms and tufts of pink blossom, but I was so intent on keeping upright there was little chance for gawping. I could have stopped more often than I did, but the threat of more rain had given me a bad case of destination fixation, and I was intent on reaching Yingkiong.

When I did pause, it was to admire the villages' terraced paddies, greening with the new season's crop. They flowed down the lower slopes like a giant's steps, their curving, harmonious lines as perfect as if they'd been modelled by a potter's thumb. Amidst the tumult of the hills they brought an unexpected order to the landscape.

At noon, in need of a rest and petrol, I stopped at a roadside shack in Damroh, a large Adi village on a ridge more than halfway to Yingkiong. A white flag with a red sun in the middle fluttered above, the mark of the Adi's sun- and moon-worshipping Donyi-Polo religion and, outside, about ten men were crowded around a carrom board, gambling, the ground at their feet littered with empty cans of beer. Sharp-faced and unsmiling, they ignored my hellos, staring as I poured two bottles of dirty petrol into the bike and sat on a bench to eat Mum's packed lunch of fried rice and sweet potato. Eventually one of them addressed me.

'Where your friends?' He said it in a cold, accusatory manner, as if being alone was somehow sinful and untrustworthy.

'Waiting in Yingkiong,' I lied.

In 1912 Damroh had been a key centre of defence against the British, commanding a fighting force 'five to six thousand strong'. Things were very different now, of course, but it was the only place in Arunachal Pradesh that I felt the slightest twinge of hostility. For a while, as I rode on, I missed my friends the Idu.

After Damroh the road deteriorated again, churned into an

inexecrable, slippery bog by the digging and blasting of more road-building activity. I slid, swore and paddled through the mud at ten miles per hour, barely managing to keep the bike vertical, my hands and arms aching from the strain. By now the mud had almost conquered me: my boots and lower legs were coated brown; the Hero looked as if it had been rolled in a swamp; my luggage was caked and splattered. Perhaps the mud would soon overtake me altogether and drag me down into some fathomless, chthonic mire. But then, at around 3 p.m., I hit tarmac again, and was so overjoyed to be out of the mud that I swung around the corners whooping and waggling my legs in glee. Yingkiong finally appeared in a lush basin in the hills, its huts and buildings scattered amidst ripples of greenery on the edge of the serpentine Siang.

This time I was lucky with the weather. It was only as I parked the bike outside the town's one hotel – a nondescript place with cell-like rooms and intermittent electricity – that the clouds eventually burst.

12

THE KING

The first thing that struck me was his height. I was accustomed to being a head and shoulders taller than people in Arunachal Pradesh, but Dorje Tenzing was a regal-looking Khampa of almost six feet. Undeniably handsome, his high, arched brows sat above searching eyes, an elegant nose and a wide, sculpted mouth. Although visibly older than the Ata of the American's decade-old photos, his short hair was still jet black, his skin unlined and his closely clipped moustache – half-Japanese emperor, half-Victorian explorer – only slightly peppered with grey. A rosary of dark-brown prayer beads hung around his neck, its silver *drilbu*, bells, and namesake *dorje*, double-headed thunderbolt, resting on a neat pot belly.

He spoke in thickly accented English, his voice quiet but commanding. 'I not been Pemako three years,' he sighed, as his apple-cheeked wife served us tea on the half-constructed balcony of his family's Tibetan restaurant. His two sons sat nearby, listening, and beside us a mallard was tied by its leg to a concrete pillar. 'I sixty-two. Last year I nearly dead from heart attack. I have operation in Delhi five months ago to put three stent in my heart.'

'What about now? Would you consider coming with me to Pemako?' I didn't want to give up quite yet.

He sat back in his chair and looked at me sagely, rolling the beads of his rosary between thumb and forefinger. I had the feeling he wasn't sure what to make of me – this lone Englishwoman who'd appeared from nowhere, so keen to find him. 'You want to go trekking or pilgrimage?'

'Pilgrimage,' I replied, after a brief pause. I wanted to find out more about Guru Rinpoche and his hidden land, I explained, and was far more interested in this than simply striding up distant hills.

At this his eyes widened in glad recognition. 'Ah, you know about Guru Rinpoche!' He muttered something and rolled a few more beads, then looked out across the cloud-wreathed hills that encircle Yingkiong. The mallard waggled its tail and pecked at the concrete, and somewhere in the alley below a dog barked.

'OK, I come with you,' he said, turning to me a minute later. 'My son Kabsang too.' He nodded towards one of the sons, a boyish twenty-something with a wispy moustache, short wavy hair and a tattooed dragon poking out of one T-shirt sleeve. 'His English better than me and he good cook.'

Guru Rinpoche must have been on my side. Not only had I found Dorje through a glancing stroke of luck but, against the odds, he'd agreed to be my guide. We made a plan to take a Sumo the 100 miles to Tuting the next morning, pick up porters and provisions there and walk southeast along the Yangsang Chu River Valley, the heart of Lower Pemako, staying in Tibetan villages on the way. It was too early in the year to trek to the higher passes, but we'd aim to reach Devakotta, a sacred mountain on the river that was said to be the dwelling place of the *dakinis*, or female spirits. In his *Guidebook to Pemako*, Guru Rinpoche had written that, 'Those of fortune who merely come to this place will experience spontaneous realization. By practising meditation here one can in this lifetime attain perfect Buddhahood.' It sounded worth a visit.

'One more thing,' said Dorje, as I was about to leave. 'You have permit for Tuting?' I showed him my Protected Area Permit, which listed Tuting as one of the places I was allowed to visit.

'Mmm, maybe problem,' he said, pursing his lips. 'Your permit just say Tuting. For Pemako you need Tuting Sub-Division. Could be problem with army. If anyone ask, you *not* tourist, you Buddhist pilgrim.'

I walked down the alleyway from the restaurant, fingering the red scrap of cotton that had lived in my pocket since the puja at Kamakhya. There was a magic in this journey, I thought, as there so often is when you cast yourself into the winds of fate far away from home: Kamakhya, the boy appearing in the rain on the road from Khupa, the reh festival, meeting Sipa the shaman again, finding the mysterious Ata. Was it coincidence, fate, or something else? I couldn't tell. But I could feel it. I hoped the magic would allow me to reach Pemako.

*

It was one of those dawns when the liminal state seems suggestive of a quantum gap, as if, for a fleeting moment, one might glimpse the shadows of another realm. Luminous wisps of cloud lingered above the town, and earth and sky had spilt their boundaries: hills were half-sunk in white drifts of cloud and roofs appeared to float in the mist. The illusory nature of it all felt like an allegory of Pemako itself. Below this shifting veil, Yingkiong was waking up. Women in saris swept the spittle-stained pavements outside their paan stalls. (I noticed one carefully sweep around a cow pat, not wanting to offend the resident deity, Lakshmi, the Hindu goddess of wealth.) Men brushed their teeth in doorways, hoicking and spitting into the rubbish-clogged gutter. Tibetan and Adi women laid out mounds of garlic, ginger, chillies, aubergines and bananas on squares of cloth in the market.

At the restaurant, where I left the Hero, my helmet and half my luggage, Dorje was taking his heart pills and Kabsang was lifting the quacking mallard into a bamboo basket.

I bent down to look at him, his beady black eyes staring back through the mesh. 'We're not going to eat him, are we?'

'No!' laughed Kabsang. 'I buy him from the market and we make giving-of-life puja with him – meaning he can never be eaten. We're taking him to Tuting to release him there.'

The journey began with the unlikely combination of the mallard, the Siang and a wildly swinging bridge. Since the long-awaited new bridge over the river had yet to be built, everyone travelling by Sumo to Tuting had to first walk across 200 metres of slats and rusted cables known as the Gandhi Suspension Bridge. It was the stuff of vertigo nightmares. Gripping the side wires with one hand, and Ducky's basket in the other, I slid and swayed across, imagining the awful scenario of dropping the poor mallard to its death. Soldiers trotted past in the opposite direction, seemingly unfazed, greeting me with breezy 'Good morning, Ma'am's. It brought to mind Frank Kingdon-Ward's abject fear of heights and snakes, two things in terrifying abundance in these parts. Goodness knows how he survived all those expeditions.

When I did reach the far side, shaky and a little nauseous, we crammed ourselves, our luggage and Ducky into a waiting Sumo and set off. The hours rolled by in the usual blur of Hindi pop and jolting, the narrow road snaking north amidst a wilderness of clouded hills. There were no roofs glinting in the light, or other roads slicing through the green, just an eternity of crumpled earth receding into the supernal mist. Jungle licked at the muddy road and far below curled the Siang, its waters surprisingly green and calm.

The only other traffic consisted of huge convoys of lumbering Ashok Leyland army trucks. We pulled over to let them by, up to sixty at a time, their turbaned Sikh drivers looking down at us as they passed. Soldiers sat on benches in the open backs, staring blankly out, and I noticed as they rumbled by that there wasn't a man among them with a bare upper lip. I wondered if it was an Indian Army requirement to have a moustache – as if it were a standard-issue item along with boots and fatigues. Or if, in a country where moustaches are traditionally a sign of virility, the length of one's whiskers depended on rank. Occasionally, among the uniformly clipped faces of the sepoys and subadars, would be a Rajput, the curling magnificence of his moustache sprouting from his upper lip and cheeks like well-tended topiary.

The Sumo drove into Tuting at three that afternoon. It looked a run-down settlement, and much smaller than I expected, but Dorje was of a different opinion. 'Tuting very sacred place. This where Siang and Yangsang Chu rivers meet; it most secret place of goddess Dorje Phagmo. In Tibetan language "Tu" means "women's private parts" and "Ting" means "deep inside".'

For the second time on this journey I was in the presence of an extremely holy vagina – although I'd never have guessed it. Strings of damp, faded Buddhist prayer flags hung over wooden Tibetan-style houses and groups of soldiers walked along the muddy, potholed streets. An Adi man rode past on a motorbike, a gun across his back. Half the houses looked empty and the signs outside the various government bunga-lows were stained with rust and peeling. By the looks of it, neither the 'Assistant Engineer, Electrical Sub-Division, Dept. of Power, Upper Siang Dist, Tuting', nor the 'Block Dev, officer, CD-Block, Tuting, Upper Siang Dist (AP)' had vis-ited their offices for quite a while. On the main street, if you could call it that, a group of Adi youth loitered around a shop. The views towards the snows of Tibet and the surrounding mountains must have been beautiful on a clear day, but now the whole place was draped in fog and ennui. It didn't matter, though; I was in Pemako with Dorje and Kabsang and, in one day's time, we'd be walking east.

We stayed at a house belonging to Dorje, a large wooden building on a patch of fenced, overgrown land in the centre of the village. Ducky was released immediately, and we watched as he shook his tail, stretched his wings and dabbled among the weeds. Dorje still needed to finish the house, he said, dropping our bags in an empty room, but this was a 'black year' in the Tibetan calendar, and hence inauspicious for building. For now it was little more than a shell consisting of a simple kitchen, two bedrooms and a shrine room – ubiquitous in Tibetan houses – whose altar was laden with candles, incense, silk-bound sutras and images and icons of the Buddha. In the middle was a framed photograph of an old lama.

'That my father,' Dorje said reverently. 'He was very powerful Pemako lama.'

Dorje, it was becoming clear, was far more than just a simple restaurateur. Like many Khampa – a Tibetan people who'd famously led the resistance against the Chinese from 1959 until 1974, their arms, food and training funded by the CIA – he was a Nyingmapa. Meaning 'ancient ones', they were followers of the oldest form of Tibetan Buddhism, the Tantric school established by Guru Rinpoche. Rooted in Bon, the old religion of Tibet, theirs was a faith of magic and mysticism, of rainbow deaths, reincarnation and esoteric rites. The Khampa have been coming to Lower Pemako for about two hundred years and there were now around a thousand of them in the Upper Siang Valley, all descendants of pilgrims who'd come here in search of the Rinpoche's 'lotus of great bliss'. Dorje's own family had travelled here, via Bhutan, around the 1870s, and settled in Tashigong, a village in the Yangsang Chu Valley. It was there that Dorje had grown up.

Dorje had never become a monk, but much of his life had been lived like one. He'd studied Buddhism in Mysore and Kalimpong and had spent years meditating alone in mountain huts. Even now, much of his time was lived in a dreamy, trance-like state, his lips moving silently as he rolled the beads of his rosary and stared into space. Yet, in a strange contradiction that I soon came to know as typical of his nature, he'd also been an Indian National Congress politician.

'I politician for eight years,' he told me, as we ate bowls of *tsampa*, roasted barley flour, on the veranda that evening. 'It my dharma path.'

'Dad's really a lama,' added Kabsang. 'He's more than that, actually – he's the reincarnation of a powerful terton. When he was a politician he used it to help Pemako. He built monasteries, opened pilgrim routes and arranged for the Dalai Lama to come to Tuting.'

'So he's the King of Pemako,' I said, half-jokingly.

Dorje chuckled. 'Yes! I from Tibetan royal family.'

His ancestor, it transpired, had been the brother of the ninth-century Tibetan emperor, Langdarma. The revelation didn't surprise me in the slightest; I could quite imagine him seated on a tiger-skin throne, a thunderbolt in one hand, a ritual dagger in the other.

Walking with him to Tuting's monastery the following day, I could envision this even more lucidly. It should have taken ten minutes to walk there but, by the time we'd beaten a path through his admiring subjects, it had taken more than an hour. Smiling Tibetans rushed up to greet him, clasping his hands and bowing their heads in respect.

Like the Idu, many of the Khampa were aware of their extended familial connections. 'This my cousin brother … this my cousin sister,' Dorje frequently declared, taking his small, rather un-kingly, spotted rucksack off his back to hand them holy sachets of salt he'd bought in Kathmandu. I stood invisibly behind him, waiting for the king to dispense his beneficence before our royal procession inched on.

'I not been here for long time. I have to talk to my people,' he said with childlike immodesty, splashing on through the puddles in his gold wellington boots.

The newly built monastery, when we at last arrived, glimmered like a jewel in the fog, its opulence at odds with the surrounding gloom. Dragons snarled above richly carved doorways, nesting sparrows twittered behind great golden heads and wrathful deities glared down from elaborately painted walls. Among them was a goddess with a thousand arms and sixteen heads, and a recently deceased guru in fashionable dark glasses. His favourite car, a grey Ambassador, was parked in a glass pavilion nearby. Outside, robed monks hurried across the tiled courtyards like flocks of maroon birds. One of these shaven-headed mendicants was Dorje's third son, a tall, willowy eighteen-year-old who'd come here, aged thirteen, of his own accord.

All so different to the Mishmi Hills, it was hard to believe the Idu's lands began only fifty miles to the east of here. Not for the first time on the journey I had the distinct feeling of having crossed an invisible border to another country.

We left the next day at 6.30 a.m., walking through the mist under the ever-present streams of prayer flags. Known as *lung-ta*, or wind horses, they are believed to carry prayers on the wind, but there wasn't a whisper of a breeze today. Ahead of us wefts of cloud obscured the mountains, drifting across their green flanks like smoke. Dorje, nattily attired in khaki, gold wellingtons and his spotted rucksack, ambled through the village, swinging a walking stick and chanting as we went. He was nervous about his heart, he'd admitted, as he swallowed his pills before we left: if anything happened up here, we were a long way from hospital. Kabsang walked beside us and in front were our porters, two wiry Adi teenagers in dirty tracksuits and gumboots, their bamboo baskets packed with food supplies. They were silent and somewhat sullen, but we were lucky to have any at all; most of the men around Tuting were hired by the army for their patrols, and it had taken Kabsang much of the previous day to find anyone. It all felt rather regal, going trekking with a king, a cook and two porters. All that was missing was a gramophone, a case of Gordon's, some table linen and a butterfly net.

On the edge of the village we picked our way over a bank of debris onto a huge, half-built military runway, where Indian construction workers stood around standpipes splashing and gargling, staring unabashedly as we passed. Only ten miles south of the disputed McMahon Line, Tuting had been attacked by a column of invading Chinese in the brief war of 1962. They'd crossed the Kepang La pass and burnt a few villages, then retreated after several weeks. The ease with which they'd crossed the pass had made the Indians twitchy.

'There are six thousand army stationed around here,' said Kabsang, as we walked across the strip of newly laid tarmac. 'The hills around here are full of bunkers. Now Modi wants to match Chinese infrastructure on the other side of the border and this runway is going to take jet fighters and cargo planes.'

The runway was a classic example of how the relationship with China is, and always has been, the driving force behind development in this fragile state. The road here was atrocious and it took two days for seriously ill villagers to reach a decent hospital in Assam, but soon there would be multimillion-dollar fighter jets landing on their doorstep.

Beyond the runway we swayed over a slightly less treacherous suspension bridge, the silken waters of the Siang slipping south below. But I was surprised when we came to a muddy track wide enough for cars. It was the beginnings of a new road that would cut through the heart of Lower Pemako, Kabsang told me, and when it was finished it would link Tuting with all the villages of the Yangsang Chu Valley.

I was shocked. A road? Here? Through the heart of this sacred valley? I was even more surprised when a tractor rumbled around the corner, its trailer weighed down by sacks of cement and three Khampa men who dangled their legs over the edge. A few minutes later we were throwing our rucksacks onto the trailer and clambering on board too. A suspension bridge over the Yangsang Chu had broken, the Nepali driver had told Dorje – we'd have to take the road.

Dorje hauled himself over the edge of the trailer and sat cross-legged on the hard sacks. 'We very lucky tractor come. It Pemako bus.'

I'd imagined a day strolling through the jungle on an ancient, winding footpath. But instead it was spent lurching and clanking along the open wound of the new road, our bottoms grinding like pestles on a mortar of cement sacks. Every so often we'd climb down from our jolting throne to push the sliding, straining tractor through mud whipped by the rains into a cloying orange mousse. Around us, the forest brooded silently. Several times we crawled through small Adi villages where Donyi-Polo flags hung above the stilted huts and squealing piglets and filthy children scampered through the sludge.

Who was I, an outsider, to say that the new road was a Bad Thing, that the people of this valley shouldn't have access to the outside world and medical care? But I couldn't help feeling a certain sadness about it. A road seemed so final, somehow, as if a blade was being thrust through the heart of this Shangri-La. Whether you believed in the Rinpoche's prophecies or not, the valley had remained a rare wilderness, too remote and mountainous to be despoiled by humans. But the road would change things irrevocably. It would bring traffic, and noise, and people, and rubbish. It would bring technology, temptation, poachers. It would be the vein through which the poison of our warped Western ideals would flow into this hidden land. It brought to mind something Wilfred Thesiger had said soon before his death in 2003, when asked by the author Jonathan Glancey where 'the wild places' were. In response, the great explorer had replied: 'Wherever there are no motor cars ... wherever people still walk.'

Dorje and Kabsang's opinions of the road mirrored the generational divide. It was a good thing, thought Kabsang, who'd studied and lived in Delhi for seven years; the people of Pemako needed progress and electricity. Dorje was more reserved.

'Pemako not secret place anymore. It too easy to reach,' he said sadly, as the trailer rattled over another bump.

He went on to tell me that in the nineteenth century there had been a famous Pemako terton called Nang Gay, a dreadlocked yogi guided by visions of Guru Rinpoche.

A reincarnation of one of the Guru's twenty-five disciples, he'd revealed many of the treasures of Pemako, including Devakotta, and predicted that one day a road would be built through this valley. When that happened, he'd said, Pemako would be like a leaking glass, its power slowly seeping out. His prediction felt eerily prescient.

For now, though, Pemako still had its challenges. At lunchtime the tractor stopped and we sat on smooth, grey boulders beside a gurgling river eating bread and cold omelette. It would have been an idyllic spot for a picnic were it not for the accursed dam dum flies that swarmed about us like devilish auras, feasting on any exposed skin.

Dorje waved them away half-heartedly. 'It's a sacrifice for Pemako,' he said seriously. 'Even if you don't want to give blood, you must.'

I'd noticed the faces, necks and hands of the other passengers on the tractor dotted with red bites. By the end of lunch, we were the same.

That night we stayed with a Khampa family in Nyering, a small Tibetan village about ten miles from Tuting. Around twenty wooden houses were scattered over a ridge above the river, simple places behind rough fences with faded prayer flags strung above the roofs. Vegetable patches sprouted green behind each one and stout old women with long black plaits, rosaries and rolling gaits led mithun along the muddy paths. Above the village was a bijou gompa, its gilded roof and fantastically ornate interior at odds with the simplicity of this rural life. From its bluff I could just make out a procession of ridges parading along the valley, each of them tapering to a point near the river's edge. Although beautiful now, on a clear day, with the hills glistening in sunshine and the river sparkling in the valley below, it must have been magical.

Our homestay was typical of these houses. Inside, life centred on the *jathaap*, or fire, not the centralized fireplace of the Idu and Adi, but a low, wood-fired earthen oven moulded onto the back wall. Ingeniously simple, logs were fed into an arch at the front and pans heated over hob-like holes on the top. From here the matriarch, in this case an amazingly youthful forty-year-old mother of ten, ruled her ruddy-cheeked clan; ladling, stirring, chiding and feeding with long-practised efficiency. On the shelves beside her, metal pails glimmered silver against the dark wood. One of these pails was always filled with *chang*, fermented millet beer, a drink as ubiquitous among Tibetans as the dreaded salty tea.

It was always the women who would serve this, ladling it into your mug then standing beside you until you'd had a few sips, then ladling in a bit more, and so on, until you indicated you'd had enough. Often the woman would stand patiently beside someone for minutes, full ladle in hand, waiting for the signal to refill their mug. It was a method, I soon deduced, that was designed to make you quickly and ferociously pissed. Even when you weren't drinking chang you could smell the stuff; its yeasty aroma pervaded every house in Pemako.

Slightly worryingly I'd read that chang was the preferred weapon of certain 'poisoning cults' in Pemako. Female witches – usually from the Monpa tribe – allegedly made a toxin from snake venom, aconite and poisonous mushrooms, put a tiny bit under their fingernail and tapped it into the mug of unwary visitors. As it was believed the poisoner would inherit the good luck of their victim, the higher the status of the visitor, the more desirable their death. Such a fate had apparently befallen the wife of the climber Tenzing Norgay during a pilgrimage to Pemako. After reading this I made a mental note to look out for any suspicious-looking ladies with long witchy fingernails. Being a foreigner, I suspected I'd be seen as a pretty good catch.

But I could see no deviant-looking fingernails in this household. Quite the opposite.

'One of her children is the reincarnation of a famous Pemako lama,' said Kabsang, as the mother ladled us warming mugs of chang by the fire. 'As soon as the child learnt to speak he talked about his past life and family. To confirm his identity he was presented with a selection of rosaries, bells and drums belonging to different lamas. He immediately picked out the ones belonging to the old lama, recognizing them as his own.'

This was a classic technique for recognizing the reincarnations of revered lamas, and had been used to identify His Holiness the 14th Dalai Lama.

'Now the boy is twelve and studying at a monastery in Mysore. Three other children are at a boarding school in Dharamsala, funded by the Dalai Lama.'

Through Kabsang, I asked the mother how she felt about her son being reincarnate.

She shrugged as nonchalantly as if I'd asked her the time. 'It's normal here.'

In England it would be headlines and a documentary, but here it was part of everyday life.

Later I asked Dorje about Pemako's alleged cornucopia of bliss-bestowing herbs. He'd been sitting in the lotus position since we arrived, chanting gently and slipping in and out of meditation, but now his eyes were open. He reminded me of a sleepy owl, the way his eyes drifted open into alertness, aloof yet intensely present.

'Yes, Pemako full of magic plants. For example, very powerful grass grow here called *tsakundu sangpo*. If you eat it, you fly.'

'No need to trek,' laughed Kabsang.

During the time of the terton Nang Gay, there was a goat who ate this grass, Dorje went on to tell me. It spent the rest of its life in deep meditation, producing ringsel – crystal-like pellets said to appear in the cremated ashes of great spiritual masters – when it died. I'd never heard of this phenomenon until now, and certainly not from a meditating ungulate. But it wasn't only goats that ate the grass. People had tried it too. One man had eaten it while going to the loo in the forest, with miraculous results.

'After he shit, he fly,' chuckled Dorje.

Another man who'd attempted to find it had accidentally eaten a fatal dose of aconite instead. Dorje had sampled it once himself. 'But I didn't fly,' he said seriously.

We went to sleep in lumpy piles on the floor, the light of the last embers catching on the glossy backs of cockroaches scuttling above the fire. But the night was cruelly cut short at 3 a.m. by a cockerel's premature morning reveille. There was always *something* to wake you in India, I thought, imagining the very non-vegetarian scenario of wringing the offending cock's neck. If it wasn't cockerels, it was dogs barking, children yelling, cows mooing, pigs oinking, men hoicking, or a sudden, unwelcome blast of Hindi pop. By six, everyone was up, the children sitting obediently on the floor slurping mugs of chai, Kabsang busy making *trakzen*, flat discs of unleavened bread.

I watched as he kneaded the barley flour and water into flat discs of dough, cooked them on a dry pan over the fire, then buried them in the hot ashes. After a few minutes he removed the scalding-hot loaves, beating off the ash by slapping them vigorously between his palms. We ate them warm with rancid mithun butter (there were no fridges here), rice, boiled greens and salty tea. Ah, salty tea, the gift of the Tibetan lands. The writer Charles Allen once described it as tasting like a beggar's armpit, and I have to say I agree. The Tibetans drink it in copious quantities, plunging it in long bamboo tubes with salt and butter then guzzling it down with glee, but I always had to hold my breath and gulp it down politely, hoping it wouldn't reappear. The explorer Benedict Allen (a cousin of Charles) once advised me to pretend it was soup, but it didn't seem to help.

Afterwards we continued walking along the same boggy embryo of the new road, through fog so low it was as if the earth had been swallowed by a pale ghost. It cut around the shoulders of the hills, raw and recently blasted, ripped-up trees lying like slain soldiers on the slopes below. Beside us the survivors loomed spectrally out of the murk. For a while, I couldn't help feeling disappointed. In the utopia of my imaginings this *wasn't* how it was supposed to be. I was *supposed* to be walking through a sylvan wilderness, stumbling over ancient stupas and mysteriously inscribed rocks, not walking to the heart of Pemako through the sludge of a freshly blasted road. But sadly I was a few months too late.

At a tea shack, where I fed milk and a packet of biscuits to a starving puppy, the elderly Khampa owner bemoaned the road that now ran like a scar through her mountain village. Pemako wasn't the same, she said, everything felt different now. Dorje agreed.

'Before this it so silent – just birds and insects. Now machines.'

Later, we found a section of the old footpath and followed it through a few miles of damp, slippery jungle. This was more like it – sweating up hillsides on ladders of gnarled roots through the green womb of the forest. Dorje, who wasn't prone to speed at the best of times, lagged behind, pausing frequently to catch his breath. After one worryingly long delay, he emerged with a handful of foliage that resembled red cow parsley.

'This very delicious to eat,' he announced, nibbling a red bud.

'Is it the one that makes you fly?' I asked hopefully, trying a bit myself. Sadly it wasn't.

Meanwhile the two Adi porters had downed their loads and vanished into the trees, catapults in hand.

'The Adi kill everything,' said Dorje disapprovingly. 'Birds, frogs, insects – everything. They don't understand Pemako. It mean nothing to them.'

When they caught us up, empty-handed, Dorje chastised them in Hindi and forced them to hand over their catapults. There'd be no killing on this walk, he said sternly, pocketing the weapons.

At four, having covered a leisurely ten miles, the triple-tiered golden roof of Yoldong's gompa materialized from the fog. Meaning 'curtain mountain', from Yoldong's ridge you could (on a clear day) see to the edge of Pemako at Tuting, and to its heart at Devakotta. From here on we'd be walking into the beyul's inner realms.

13

THE HEART OF THE LOTUS

The lama at Yoldong was a silver-haired colossus with a rasping voice and eyes tinged blue with cataracts. He was by far the tallest man I'd met here, even taller than the king. He towered over us all, a kindly obelisk swaddled in red. His wife, Anguk, was tiny, limping and exceptionally jolly, with a face like a happy walnut that radiated compassion and cheer. They lived near the gompa in one of Yoldong's nine houses, and had a garden fecund with mustard plants, cabbages, orange trees and radishes as big as my hand.

'This is normal for Pemako,' chuckled Kabsang, when I picked one up with astonishment.

Dorje, the lama and his wife were old friends and relatives of some sort. They sat in a row beside the fire gossiping like old biddies at a WI coffee morning, Anguk clasping Dorje's hand affectionately as they talked. They'd all had the same guru, a *tulku*, or reincarnated lama, from this village who'd died in 1970.

'He got rainbow body after he dead,' said Dorje. 'He very tall man. But three days after he dead his body become tiny, only one-foot tall. And when he cremated he produce five different type of ringsel.'

This phenomenon of 'rainbow body', the bodies of high lamas shrinking and even disappearing after their deaths, has been well documented throughout Tibetan history. Sometimes only hair and fingernails are left, or just emanations of light. Guru Rinpoche was said to have dissolved into rainbows at the time of his death and, when the Chinese imprisoned and tortured thousands of lamas after the invasion of 1950, there were reports of lamas self-realizing their own deaths and the Chinese guards finding nothing but empty robes in their locked cells. I'd heard it was common in Pemako too.

While the others caught up, Kabsang and I talked over mugs of hot chang, greasy with melted mithun butter.

'It's a blessing from Pemako,' Anguk told us, as she ladled out the steaming liquid.

The lama and Anguk had married in unusual circumstances, Kabsang told me. Anguk had been married before, to the tulku I'd just heard about, the guru whose body had shrunk so dramatically after his death. On his deathbed he'd instructed her to marry the tall lama who now sat before me, and she'd agreed, asking him to be reincarnated in any sons they had.

'Only if you have faith,' the dying tulku said.

When the couple had a son three years later it was soon apparent that her request had been granted. The infant sat, looked and behaved like the dead lama, and as a young child he could remember details of his past life and recognize his old disciples. As soon as he could talk he asked to be taken to the tulku's retreat house, where he picked out his belongings. Now that little boy, Tulku Orgyen P'huntsok, is in his forties and lives in California, where he teaches Buddhism at Santa Barbara University. I spoke to him a few months after my visit to Yoldong, his kindly, jovial voice crackling over Skype. When I asked him if he could remember anything of his past life nowadays he laughed. 'No! I'm old now and I don't remember anything – only when I was a child.'

My disappointment about the road, and the day's dismal walk, quickly dissipated among these people. They were so gentle and cheerful and, huddling around their fire, listening to stories about rainbow bodies and reincarnation, such tonic for the soul. From my fleeting, outsider's impression theirs seemed a contented existence, enfolded as they were in Pemako, nature and their faith. Almost entirely self-sufficient, they only went to Tuting two or three times a year to buy salt, sugar, tea and oil. Everything else they produced themselves.

'When I was a child,' said Dorje, 'we only went to Tuting once a year, to buy salt.' He nodded towards the smoke-blackened stack of salt packets piled above the fire.

I asked the lama about the road and he said they didn't want it, that it would disturb the peace of Pemako. After this he disappeared into his shrine room for several hours to make his evening puja, the deep, insistent pounding of his drum mixing with the din of a sudden rainstorm.

It poured all night and, in the morning, just as I finished my yoga, there was a flash of lightning and a blistering crack of thunder. Was it a portent, I wondered? Did Pemako not want me to reach its heart?

'The goddess doesn't want to see a Britisher,' teased Dorje, sitting beside the fire and chopping the plant he'd picked yesterday. 'Actually, rain a good sign. It means the protector deities are happy. They are welcoming you.'

It was good to hear, although I suspected it to be from the same strain of optimism as beliefs about birds crapping on your head and rain on your wedding day signifying good luck.

'Not everyone can reach Devakotta,' Dorje continued, looking at me with scrutinous eyes. 'You must have pure mind.'

He'd once known a Bhutanese woman who, despite several efforts, had never been able to reach the holy mountain. She'd had recurrent dreams of two naked children (Devakotta's protector deities, Dorje said) with bows and arrows, threatening to kill her if she went, and every time she tried to go an illness or accident befell her. I'd had an odd dream the previous night about my father building a replica of our old family home in the smoking ruins of Ground Zero, but there'd definitely been no angry children.

After warm goodbyes we set off in the rain, me looking faintly ridiculous with my poncho, a frilly purple umbrella and a pair of camouflage wellington boots bought at the shop in Tuting for the equivalent of two pounds. F. M. Bailey would not have been impressed. Soon afterwards we came to a road workers' hut, where we found six men sheltering from the rain. They lounged on filthy blankets, smoking and playing cards. Outside, a clot of yellow diggers idled in the mud. Dorje, it emerged, wanted to have a word with the headman: locals were worried the road was due to pass too close to Devakotta monastery, and had asked the king to intervene. The two men chatted convivially over cups of sugary tea, Dorje sitting in his usual lotus position, his hand on the smiley Monpa headman's knee. No problem, said the Monpa, tracing an imaginary extra loop on the floor; he'd happily add an extra kilometre or two. It couldn't have been more different from the suits and surveyors of a road-planning meeting in England.

At this point another road worker appeared, a Khampa, and sat down on the other side of Dorje. The king put a brotherly hand on the man's knee.

'This my . . .'

I finished the sentence for him. 'Cousin brother?'

Everyone laughed.

The discussion moved on to Tashigong, Dorje's own village. A powerful deity dwelt inside a pilgrimage rock behind the gompa there, and Dorje was adamant that the road shouldn't disturb it.

'There are so many people who have been healed by doing kora [repeated clockwise circuits] around this rock,' said Kabsang. 'One man, an Adi, had a disfigured jawbone and made one hundred kora of it. That night there was a cracking noise in his sleep and, when he woke up, his jawbone was healed.'

Again the headman nodded sympathetically and agreed to add an extra 'zig'. Being a Buddhist himself, he knew the importance of not angering such beings.

While the two men talked, Kabsang explained to me some of the vagaries of Indian road construction. The total length of the planned new road had been agreed as 90km, and was supposed to take six years to complete. But all along the route the actual kilometres constructed were inflated by the various contractors so that they could make more money. Not to mention the numerous locals who popped a few rupees in the contractors' pockets to add a little loop here, avoid that patch of forest there. Already we'd seen evidence of numerous unnecessary 'zigs' – an insane waste of land and resources in the name of making more coin. It used to be a 30km walk from Tuting to here, but by the new road it was 60km.

'This is India!' chuckled Kabsang, noticing my shocked expression.

In response to renewed Chinese claims on Arunachal Pradesh, in October 2014 Modi announced a plan to build a 1,800km trans-state highway hugging the Chinese border. The Indo-China Frontier Highway, as the paper project is known, will supposedly cut from Tawang to Vijaynagar, across the currently impenetrable, unexplored northern rim of the state. Quite apart from the obvious environmental concerns of such a project, if the Pemako road was anything to go by, there'll be bowling alleys on Pluto before it's completed.

The rain was still sieving down in great curtains when we left, swelling the oceanic puddles and veiling the mountains in grey. It dripped down our noses and pasted our waterproofs against us as we sloshed on through the mire. But I was in high spirits nonetheless. An hour later the village of Mahacotta emerged from the mist, a sprinkling of homesteads on the smooth side of a hill. Beyond it, through wandering fragments of cloud, I could just make out the golden finials of Devakotta's roof peeping from its hilly abode. The road ended here, so we bowled down a grassy hill past a mossy stupa and a parade of tall bamboo poles tied with faded white prayer flags. Under these, what looked like a stone cowshed was stacked to the roof with *tshatsha*, small devotional images moulded out of dried mud. When we stopped for tea at a house in the village, an old lady was making them in the yard, her wrinkled face steeped in concentration as she pushed balls of mud into copper moulds with stout peasant's hands. Behind her dried rows of miniature stupas and icons of a scowling Guru Rinpoche astride a tigress. She'd made 10,000 over the past few years, she told Kabsang; as she didn't know how to read or write this was her means of obtaining karma and purifying sin. When we knelt in the dirt beside her to make a stupa each, a man shouted out from the house: 'Maybe you will get enlightenment now!'

Inside we found Dorje holding court beside the fire.

'These all my relations,' he announced, as I walked in. 'This—' he pointed to a small, wizened man, 'my cousin brother. This—' gesturing towards a rosy-cheeked young woman, 'my father's cousin's sister's daughter . . .' And so on, through a muddling maze of familial connections. Already the spotted rucksack was open and he was busy distributing his blessed salt.

After cups of sweet tea, Kabsang suddenly announced: 'Come and meet my friend the tulku – he will give you a long-life blessing.'

Never one to miss out on the opportunity for eternal life,

I duly followed him to a nearby house, assuming we were just popping by for a casual cuppa and a priestly pat on the head. But as we pulled off our boots on the veranda I could hear a chorus of chanting voices, and inside we found a shrine room crammed with people. There were about thirty of them in total: older men with Confucian faces and wispy beards; fat-cheeked infants dandled on plump young women's laps; a teenage boy with red-tinted hair and diamante earrings; old women with leathery faces. They sat on the floor facing a portly young tulku, a shaven-headed Khampa with a spidery moustache, whose youth and fleshiness gave him the look of a happy cherub. He sat cross-legged, swathed in an orange blanket, the low table in front of him stacked with the tools of his trade: sutras, bells, beads and images of the Buddha. Beside him sat another lama, a slender ascetic with a sleek black plait hanging to his waist. And on the far wall was an elaborately decorated altar flickering with butter candles and thick with offerings: silver bowls full of water, *khatas* (ceremonial silk scarves), packets of biscuits, sweets, money, sutras, golden Buddhas, psychedelic images of a wide-eyed Guru Rinpoche and several extremely phallic statuettes made from rice dough and butter. In the centre of the altar was a butter carving that was oddly reminiscent of a cross.

The chanting stopped and, for a while, the villagers sat rapt, nodding in silent agreement as the tulku read passages from his sutras. When he'd finished, everyone shuffled to their feet and again took up the chant, a sonorous, hymn-like mantra that asked for wisdom from Guru Rinpoche. Their voices swelled to fill the room and they bowed their heads and pressed their hands together in prayer, their faces etched with expressions of humble devotion. As they sang, we all took turns to bow before the tulku, cupping our hands together as he bestowed on us the blessings of a long life. He cleansed us with drops of holy water, nourished us with tsampa 'long-life balls', fired our bellies with palmfuls of chang and tapped us on the head with sticks and doughy pink phalluses. Last of all, he gave us tiny handfuls of rice, which we threw all over the room and each other to signify non-attachment.

With its holy water, dough balls and sacred alcohol, the ceremony – known as *tshe-bang*, or 'life consecration' – struck me as curiously reminiscent of Christian communion. But it wasn't until a few months afterwards, when I was reading Charles Allen's *The Search for Shangri-La*, that I thought about this again. In the midst of Allen's thrilling pan-Asian quest are the Nestorian Christians, a breakaway Eastern sect of the faith whose isolated medieval communities became entwined with later Western fantasies about Shambhala. The question of whether any lost pockets of Nestorianism remained hidden in deepest Asia sent numerous Jesuit missionaries tramping across the icy wastes of Tibet in the seventeenth and eighteenth centuries, including the fictional Father Perrault in Hilton's *Lost Horizon*.

'What is intriguing,' writes Allen, 'is the survival within the two oldest religious sects of Tibet – in Bon and among the Nyingpa school of Buddhism – of a ritual known as Tshe-bang, or life consecration ... the rite is represented as a strengthening of the bla or life-force of the participants. How or when it became part of Bon ritual we will never know – but there can be little doubt that it had its origins in Nestorian Christianity.'

Reading this, I felt a thrill of discovery, a sense that I'd been exceptionally lucky to partake in such an ancient ritual. How fortunate that we'd chanced upon it that day.

Now we were so close, I didn't want to wait another day to reach Devakotta so, leaving a tired Dorje at his cousin's house, Kabsang and I set off to the holy mountain. I say mountain but, now we were so close, I could see that it was really a bouffant cone, one of the many hills, spurs, ridges and undulations that frothed up from the river in densely forested humps. Almost an island, it was cradled in an oxbow of the Yangsang Chu, surrounded on all sides by wooded slopes and the icy, purling waters of the river. But while it may have looked like just another fold in the subcontinental plate, Devakotta was the heart of Lower Pemako, one of the Rinpoche's greatest treasures, the home of the dakinis and the place where the worthy could achieve instant Buddhahood. Even if you weren't saintly, it was good luck just to walk around it. Dorje had advised that I do three koras in order to gain good fortune. As Guru Rinpoche himself had written: 'Whoever makes one complete circumambulation of Devakotta Mountain, the door to all lower rebirths will be closed.'

Perhaps after three I'd be reborn as a queen.

To reach the mountain we had to cross two rickety hanging bridges, their rusted cables almost invisible under quantities of prayer flags. As I edged over the first one I felt a strange stirring of emotion when a shaft of sunlight, the first we'd seen all week, burst theatrically through a chink in the grey. For the next half an hour we slid and scrambled clockwise around the steep shoulder of the mountain on a treacherous pilgrims' path. We grasped at slippery rocks and woven roots, slithered down muddy slopes and pulled each other over rocky ledges through damp tunnels of prayer flags, the river rushing a hundred metres below. At times there was nothing to stop us falling down the vertiginous sides of the mountain: it was not a feat for the old or infirm. At one point we slid and half-crawled into a small cave almost hidden behind soggy streams of flags.

'This the dakinis' cave,' announced Kabsang, sitting on a rock in the gloom. He rubbed his fingers on the wall and pasted a streak of red mud down both our foreheads. 'It's good luck from the goddess.'

Afterwards we climbed up to the monastery itself, a squat building perched like a stone crown on the bald pate of the mountain. Built after terton Nang Gay's original structure was destroyed by the 1950 earthquake, it was a simple affair with three golden finials on its red metal roof and large arched windows on either side of a grand red door. Prayer flags streamed from the corners of its roof and red, hand-painted prayer wheels lined the side walls. Outside it was a stone throne said to have belonged to Guru Rinpoche, the earth around it littered with offerings – rings, coins, bracelets. An oval rock beside it allegedly aided fertility, its black surface polished smooth by the hands of numberless hopeful women.

'If you carry it around the monastery maybe Guru Rinpoche will make you pregnant,' joked Kabsang.

Stranger things have happened in Pemako, I thought, keeping well clear of the stone.

Beyond the red doors of the monastery its twilight interior glittered in a haze of psychedelia. Apart from the plain wooden floorboards, not an inch had been left undecorated:

pearly white deities floated across the walls on lotus leaves, shooting rainbows into the cosmos; clouds swarmed with multi-coloured gods and goddesses; blue horses snorted beside charging white elephants wreathed in flames; meditating Buddhas emanated golden light; gods flew through space astride rainbow-powered lotus leaves. Above an altar lined with water bowls, conches and butter lamps, the carved golden figures of Guru Rinpoche, his consort, Yeshe Tsogyal, and the terton Nang Gay sat on thrones of lotus leaves, glaring into space with fearsomely bulging eyes. I later learnt that these delicately carved figures were not only modelled from mud, but that they'd been made by Dorje. There seemed no end to the king's talents. Dressed in beautifully painted robes, they wore gilt crowns and held bells and double-headed thunderbolts, their scarlet lips pursed into expressions of mild disdain. They didn't look like the sort of gods you'd want to annoy, even if the Rinpoche's rosebud mouth was framed by a curling, dandyish blue moustache. On either side of them brightly painted cupboards were stuffed with dusty, silk-bound sutras and bronze Buddhist icons.

The ceiling – carved and painted into a series of geometric patterns and hung with silk banners – was no less extravagant. It was like walking into a tiny parallel universe and being injected with LSD on the way in. If years of meditation could induce the phantasmagorical visions that sprawled across these walls, I vowed to do more of it from now on.

I sat at the front, alone, below the fat golden toes of the Rinpoche, the late-afternoon light falling in weak pools through the windows. I felt charged with emotion and elated to be there, of that there was no doubt. It had been a long journey to reach Devakotta, physically and emotionally, and one that nearly hadn't happened at all. But there was something else too. An odd light-headedness. A sense that the thickened air vibrated with an unknowable energy. Maybe I was just imagining it, transposing the emotions of my own journey onto the place. Or maybe not. I'd felt it at Kamakhya too, but it was even stronger here, the energy almost tangible, as if I could somehow scoop it from the air and hold it in the palm of my hand, a golden, pulsing orb. To my disappointment, I've never been one of those cosmic types who can 'feel the energy' in stone circles or the like. But here, well, there was *something*. Lamas and pilgrims had been meditating here for decades; who knows what invisible energies the space had absorbed.

We left as darkness fell, stumbling around the rest of the mountain in the rapidly fading light. Kabsang paused to slurp from a natural spring in the rock.

'This is holy water – it will give you long life.'

'I hope it's not holy shit water,' I added, risking a palmful. At this rate (if the water didn't kill me) I'd still be alive in 2150.

Further on, Kabsang dived behind a crumbling white stupa and pulled out a pile of musty dreadlocks from the offerings around its base, holding them up like a dead rat. 'I cut these off six months ago and left them as an offering to Guru Rinpoche.'

I wondered if the Guru appreciated such an offering, or if he'd have preferred something less noisome. I suppose it's the thought that counts.

By the time we'd squelched back up the hill to the village,

it was dark and we were soaked and dirty, but extremely happy.

'There tiger prints outside the monastery last year,' said a worried Dorje, putting an avuncular hand on my knee. 'It not good to be there at night.'

When I asked him for more tiger stories he told me that six Idu Mishmi had been killed near here ten years previously.

'It was karma,' said Kabsang. 'The Idu had gone into a monastery and made fun of our rituals – beating the drums and breaking things. Those same people were collecting medicinal plants in the forest soon after when a tiger killed them all. The strange thing was, it didn't eat them – it just killed them and went.'

We spent the night huddled around the family's fire drinking quantities of chang, a beverage I was developing quite a taste for (and hadn't yet been poisoned by). Next to me, alone among the Khampa, was an exceptionally sozzled Assamese, a labourer from the village. He sat in a crumpled heap, a dirty woollen hat on his head, mumbling to himself and letting out the occasional fulsome burp. Lulled by the chang and the chatter of the Khampa, I stared into the orange embers, lost in happy thought. I reflected how completely at ease I felt among these people, as I had on every evening around the fire with strangers in this land. At home, in our own society, we spend so much time pretending, covering up, trying to be the most interesting, wittiest versions of ourselves, striving to live up to some imagined ideal. But here, with these alien strangers, I felt unmoored from the expectations of society, of myself, of my peers, and liberated from the pressures of *being* something, or someone. There was no pretence. It was entirely uncomplicated. It was as if we met on an equal level, just as humans, curious to learn of each other's very different worlds. The longer I was away, the more I noticed a bubbling lightness of spirit, as if the journey was freeing me from a corset of expectations, allowing happiness to rise like a sap. It's why solo travel can be like a drug.

I was jolted out of my reverie when a cloud of smoke billowed from the fire and filled the room, stinging our eyes. 'That means the weather will change tomorrow,' said Dorje. I hoped he was right.

But the weather hadn't changed when we woke up, despite the king's prophecy, and it was the wettest, most dismal day of all. When Kabsang, Dorje and I made a second kora of the mountain I felt cold, wet and irritated, whereas yesterday I'd felt so joyous. Dorje, the only one sensible enough to have his umbrella, was in no hurry though, stopping frequently to explain the nuances of Buddhist belief while I stood there bedraggled, rain dripping down my nose, sleeves and neck. I felt like Lord Cawdor had in November 1924, when he'd written in his diary: 'I'd sell my soul to see some honest weather again.' A few days previously he'd referred to Pemako as 'this infernal country' and sworn he never wished to lay his eyes on another damned rhododendron. The young laird clearly wasn't cut out for a life of Himalayan plant-hunting.

Since it was too wet to go anywhere, we spent the day huddled around the fire in an absent lama's house near the monastery, drinking chang and listening to the infernal clatter of rain on the roof. It hissed down in cataracts so loud we had to raise our voices to make ourselves heard. During the afternoon Dorje and Kabsang spoke about the difficulties of being a Khampa in India, and how they often felt like out-siders in their own country. Mainland Indians treated them badly, calling them 'Chinky', asking if they were Chinese and charging them more at the market.

'It makes me so angry,' said Dorje, 'but what can we do?'

The pejorative way they were treated by their own coun-trymen sounded depressingly similar to the patronizing attitudes of British colonials. The Khampa even refer to non-tribal India, the India that begins at the foot of the hills, as *Jagar*, meaning 'white land', a reference to the fact Indians there eat white food (curds) and wear white clothes (dhotis). It reminded me of something I'd often thought here, that, although the political boundary between China and India is drawn along the ridge of the Himalayas, the cultural divide runs along the base of Arunachal's hills. For while none of the tribal people I met expressed any desire to belong to China, culturally they leant far more towards the Tibetan peoples of the north. In so many ways this mountainous, tribal land was another country entirely.

14

THE CHEERFUL MOUNTAIN

Pemako had proved itself full of magical happenings, but none were more so than the clear, sunlit sky we awoke to the following morning. After a week of rain the heavens must have finally exhausted themselves, and now the land sparkled under a perfect dome of blue. For the first time I could see the lustrous hills we'd walked through and the snow peaks that framed the valley, their freshly dusted ridges shining like mercury in the morning light. And there was Yoldong's gompa, winking in the sunshine on its distant ridge. After days of turbid weather, it was like waking up to a new world, as if the old, grey one had been soaked in colour overnight.

The dam dum flies were equally delighted and had come out in their thousands, swarming around our heads in nefarious black clouds.

Dorje caught me swatting one away. 'You mustn't kill any living thing here – even dam dum fly.'

Later, when I absent-mindedly squashed one that landed on my hand, I guiltily looked around to see if my sin had been witnessed. It hadn't.

Buoyed by the change in the weather, Kabsang and I trotted our third kora around the hill then joined Dorje at the monastery for a fire puja, an offering to Devakotta's protector deities that was enmeshed in the old ways of Bon. He was preparing the fire outside when we arrived, chanting mantras as he piled a clay platform with juniper branches and nine different types of edible, flowering plants. He was a lama now, intense, aloof, chanting, his eyes staring into space as he called on the protectors. Once the fire was lit he sat inside, behind a large suspended drum whose edges seethed with golden dragons, beating out a galloping rhythm that thundered through the monastery like an emperor's call to arms. I sat watching him, the primal pounding of the drum pulsating through the floor and my whole body, mesmerized by the noise, his voice, the place. Butter candles burnt on the altar and incense wafted through the air like dragon's breath. At the end, Dorje fixed Kabsang and me with a schoolmasterly look and asked us to internally apologize for any wrong we'd done in Pemako. I racked my mind for any significant misdemeanours but, apart from the death of the odd dam dum fly, couldn't think of any.

Since Dorje's health was holding up (thank goodness), and the weather had made such a spectacular reversal, we decided to go on to Tashigong, half a day's walk from here. Dorje still had a house in his old village, and family, and hadn't been there since before he fell ill. It was a steep uphill climb from Devakotta, on a narrow, winding footpath that would soon be superseded by the new road. It was exhilarating to be away from that blasted mud, walking through the forest under a blissfully unblemished sky. Stopping to catch my breath, I looked back at the vanishing roof of the monastery and wondered what changes the road would bring to this fantastically remote and beautiful place. Only last night a group of Adi teenagers had stayed at the simple pilgrims' guesthouse near the monastery, leaving behind all their rubbish and dirty pots and pans.

'Everyone used to cook with stone pots and use just leaves and bamboo. Rubbish only come here fifteen years ago – it like a sickness,' sighed Dorje, looking at their mess.

How many more like this would the road bring? How much longer would the monastery, with all its treasures, be able to remain unlocked? What's sacrosanct to one people means nothing to the next.

For now, though, the only major blight on the landscape was a line of sagging electricity wires marching up the hill beside us. An Assamese contractor had been paid to run power to Tashigong, but had put up the wires and pylons without installing the electricity, bribing a local politician to sign the job off as done. So now the village had the eyesore of the wires, but no power to go with it.

'It's one hundred per cent corruption,' said Kabsang.

Maybe it was the transformative effects of sunshine, or my own elevated state of mind, but to me Tashigong was a place of heart-bursting beauty. Dorje's great-grandfather had been among the village's founders, instructed to build a settlement here by the terton Nang Gay. They'd hacked their way through the forests and hewn a life out of the wild, their mithun killed by tigers and their crops eaten by bears. But in spite of the hardships they'd named the new settlement Tashigong, meaning 'auspicious mountain', and I could well see why. From its lofty hillside perch above the Yangsang Chu, its few houses looked out across hills that creased and soared and rippled beneath forest as thick as an emerald fleece. Beyond them was an encircling shield of mountains, their jagged white crowns carved by the bright sunlight into sharp fields of light and shadow. They looked crisp and pre-ternaturally perfect, as if painted onto the sky by the hand of a god. I could see the line of the river, the gleaming ridges of Padma Shri and Riwo Tula – sacred peaks only reachable in the summer months – and, to the north, Tibet, the homeland. Although we were still at only 1,600 metres above sea level, it felt like we were much higher. Guru Rinpoche had chosen his beyul well. In the village, clumps of tall white flags whipped in the breeze, bovines grazed contentedly and peach trees blossomed pink. The only sounds were birdsong, the tinkle of mountain streams, the breeze whispering through the trees and the melodic chirping of crickets. It was tranquillity itself, and I fell in love with it at once.

There was nothing grand about Dorje's house; it was a typi-cal village dwelling – stilted, wooden, slightly ramshackle, the earth around it churned to mud by the hooves of two skittish black cows. A mallard and his doting wife quacked and dab-bled in the mud outside, waddling away in stately alarm as we arrived. Below it, a fenced vegetable patch burst with yellow mustard flowers, radishes, cabbages, carrots, ginger, garlic, chillies, potatoes, onions, cabbages. But the house's position was spectacular. It sat, a fittingly regal eyrie, on top of a hill overlooking the jewel of a gompa the king had recently built. Below it, on a slope so steep it almost necessitated crawling, orange trees were hung with fruit and the grass was thick with wild mint and tiny strawberries. And all around it was *that* view, rippling away to the snows.

Dorje had grown up here, and the shrine room was still full of his father's belongings.

'My father very powerful lama. When I was child here people never get ill. If they did, they just make a few kora of the gompa and they better, or they went to my father and he did puja for them.' He picked up a smooth brown bowl from the altar. 'He use this in puja – it made from human skull, to show non-attachment to our human body. And this—' he pointed to a yellowed bone beside it, 'is drumstick made from human thighbone.' He stared silently at the altar for a minute, remembering. 'You know, when Chinese invade in 1962 everyone very afraid. Whole village want to run away. But my father tell everyone to stay, that Chinese not come here; Pemako too powerful for them. He was right. They not come here.'

His brother-in-law, Tita Guru, lived in the house now. He was a quiet man of sixty whose toned body, mop of black hair and line-free face gave him the appearance of someone twenty years younger. His wife, Dorje's sister, suffered from a serious illness and now lived near a hospital in the south of India. Their children had long moved away. So now it was just him, the cows, the ducks and a semi-resident cat – a matted, bony, madly affectionate old girl who wound around us, purring like a tractor and kneading our legs with pin-like claws.

We couldn't have timed our arrival better. The next day, 18 March, was Guru Rinpoche Day, an all-day puja that took place on the tenth day of each month in the Tibetan calendar. It was a day of feasting and worship, and no one was allowed to work in the fields or commit any sin. Each month a different family from the village would 'sponsor' the puja by providing food and chang, and tomorrow, by pure chance, was Tita Guru's turn. Given Dorje's return to his ancestral village after serious illness and a three-year absence, the luck of our timing felt strangely preordained.

Supper was a warming meal of barley flour noodles and green vegetable broth tangy with Szechuan pepper, and chang, lots of it, sucked through bamboo straws from a red jug. Afterwards I unrolled my sleeping bag on the veranda and fell asleep listening to the guttural calls of some forest bird and the roar of the Yangsang Chu, the sky twinkling cold and clear above. I briefly entertained the thought of a tiger gobbling me up from the veranda as I slept, then reprimanded myself for being such a wimp. At five, when I woke up, there'd been no feline intrusions and dawn was soaking the snowy heights a delicate wash of pink.

Tashigong was the last Buddhist village in the valley. Beyond were three Idu Mishmi settlements and then the Abroka Pass, where the Yangsang Chu rose and the Dibang Valley began. Curious to see the first Idu village before we headed back to Tuting tomorrow, Kabsang and I set off at 6 a.m., marching briskly through the dew-drenched forest in the bright morning light. Two hours later, after a lung-heaving five-mile walk, we reached Silipo, an Idu hamlet of no more than seven houses. Finding no one around, we sat on the nearest porch and devoured a packet of biscuits, sharing them with a family of chickens who dashed over hopefully. The cockerel, a gouty old duke with a fountain of glossy black tail feathers and a joggling comb, hobbled around on gnarled feet, clucking and pecking the biscuits into edible crumbs for his wives and children without touching a morsel himself.

As we admired the cockerel's chivalry, the front door behind us creaked open and a boy's face appeared from the darkness within. He dragged himself into the doorway on his bottom, his legs thin and crippled, and stared at us with a dim, uncomprehending look. He could have been twelve or eighteen, it was hard to tell, and was obviously severely physically and mentally disabled, left here alone in the dark house while his parents worked in the fields. When we gave him our remaining packet of biscuits he clutched them to his chest and stared into space, not uttering a word. I tried to talk to him in the few words of Idu I knew, but he just stared through us, as if we weren't there. What a life out here, so far from medical help, or even something as simple as a wheelchair. Amidst all this beauty, seeing him was a pertinent reminder of how difficult and unfair life could be.

The puja was in full swing by the time we returned, exhausted, at eleven o'clock. A trickle of villagers was ambling around the gompa, twirling their beads and muttering mantras, waving at us as we appeared; among them was a teenage girl with a bounding black puppy on a chain, the first pet dog I'd seen here. Above them, coloured prayer flags streamed from the golden pagoda-like roof like bunting at a village fête. Many of the villagers would walk a lucky 108 koras today, but we joined them for just three, pausing on each circuit to touch the pilgrimage rock Dorje had discussed with the road builders.

'This is only a small bit of the rock,' said Kabsang, placing his palms on the side of the lumpy black protrusion. 'Most of it is underground – that's where the deity has his palace.'

Afterwards we slipped off our muddy boots and went inside the gompa, past two buxom, tipsy old women who were sitting on the floor with mugs of chang, rocking back and forth as they turned an enormous red prayer wheel. They creased with laughter and covered their few teeth with gnarled hands when I asked to take their photographs, but happily agreed.

Inside, Dorje and three other lamas sat wrapped in maroon robes, faces intense and staring, chanting a rapid, insistent mantra while pounding on a hide drum and crashing pairs of cymbals together, the long, low table in front of them laden with sutras, bells, conches and mugs of chang. At intervals they added to this hullabaloo with shrill squalls of *gyaling*, intricately worked, oboe-like horns whose sound was strongly reminiscent of the instruments used by Indian snake charmers. At the same time, one small gathering of villagers would hold a giant conch shell to their mouths and, with cheeks inflated like puffer fish, emit a long, ear-splitting blast. The whole affair was generously lubricated by chang, served by smiling ladies who appeared every half an hour or so and wouldn't take no for an answer. If you'd been blindfolded and led in with no idea where you were you'd be forgiven for thinking Dave Grohl, a bunch of Indian snake charmers and the *Queen Mary*'s horn had somehow ended up in the same room.

Dorje, elevated to the position of head lama for the day following his auspicious arrival in the village, looked every inch the king. He sat with a fixed, faraway look in his eyes, lost in deep meditation. Beside him was his father's vacant throne upon which his reincarnation would sit once he was born.

Those who weren't in the gompa or doing koras were in the nearby kitchen hut, stirring vats of rice over the fire, plunging salty tea in a tall bamboo tube and drinking the ubiquitous chang, the air thick with smoke and chatter. One of them was a gnome-like old man with a puckered, weatherworn face and grey hair sticking out from under a red woollen hat. He laughed incessantly, an infectious, Mr Bean-like chortle, which swallowed his eyes in a canyon of laughter lines and revealed his two remaining front teeth. Kabsang sat beside him, linking his arm through his.

'He's been deaf since he was a child but he can lip-read very well, and he's always laughing.'

At this, one of the other men complained that he had a bad stomach.

'Do you want me to stick some chillies up your bum?' joked the gnome, erupting into another round of that wickedly contagious chuckle. He was cheerfulness personified.

At lunch everyone sat on tables in the sunshine outside the gompa and ate rice, dhal, potatoes and grisly lumps of mithun skin. I sat with Dorje, looking at the happy scene, struck by how this monthly knees-up was as much about worship as it was about community, mutual help and cementing familial bonds. It was like a village fête and the best aspects of Christmas Day rolled into one.

The weather had been perfect all day – cloudless and sunny with only the lightest breeze. But in the middle of the afternoon, just after the lamas had chanted a mantra for the local protector deities, a storm appeared out of nowhere. It howled around the mountain in angry gusts of wind and a fit of sideways rain, clattering on the roof and dripping through the open windows.

'It means the protectors are happy,' assured Kabsang, raising his voice over the din. 'It's normal. We've seen rainbows appear from the top of the monastery during puja here.'

It vanished half an hour later, as quickly as it had appeared, the sky as clear and blue again as if it had been a dream. As the sun sank behind the mountains and the gompa fell into darkness, the puja reached a horn-blowing, drum-beating, conch-blasting crescendo. We threw rice offerings all over the floor, took (more) swigs of holy chang and were given silver trays piled with *prasad*, blessed food: popcorn, strips of mithun skin, biscuits, sweets and doughy rice phalluses. By the time we'd finished, the place looked like the aftermath of a children's party.

The greying, day-old rice phalluses looked singularly unappetizing when Dorje pulled them out of a plastic bag and fried them in oil for the next morning's breakfast.

'This prasad blessed by the Guru Rinpoche in Pemako – it *very* lucky,' he said, handing me a plate. I looked at them suspiciously; thoughts of food poisoning nudging at my mind, then I remembered that even if I did die in Pemako I'd be fast-tracked to enlightenment. But in spite of my misgivings they were surprisingly tasty, like hot buttered toast. I even had seconds.

I'd learnt by now that the king didn't do anything fast, and this morning was no exception. He'd said we'd leave Tashigong at 7.30 but, by the time we'd had breakfast, cooked omelettes for our lunch and packed, it was already 8.30. Then, just as we were shouldering our bags to leave, Dorje announced that he hadn't washed his face. There followed a very thorough, unhurried face-washing ceremony (with pink soap) under the freezing-cold outside tap, then a leisurely application of Nivea face cream. (Aha, so that was the secret of his wrinkle-free skin!) Twenty minutes later we'd said goodbye to Tita Guru and were off, Dorje – Nivea'd and puja-powered – springing down the slope in his trusty gold wellies, humming the Rinpoche's mantra. After a last look back at the sunlit gompa, we were into the forest again, the last glimpses of Tashigong swallowed by the trees.

It's easy for an outsider to romanticize life in a place like Tashigong, to be swept away by the beauty of the mountains, the space, the quiet, the rarity of its near-pristine wilderness; to turn it into some rose-tinted paradise where the happy natives skip merrily about their daily tasks. But life wasn't easy here, and it would be naive to assume so. There was no medical care, or electricity, or schools. Many of the villagers were illiterate. They lived hard, physical lives in an often extreme climate: planting, harvesting, cutting, collecting firewood, milking, cooking. It was an existence that left little room for the luxury of idleness. Most of the young people had either gone to boarding schools in Dharamsala or colleges in Delhi and Assam. The younger generation didn't want to be subsistence farmers anymore – they wanted mobile phones, labels, the internet, cars. When Dorje was a child here there had been sixty houses but now that number had shrunk to fifteen. Like so many of the rural villages in Arunachal Pradesh (and so much of the world) it was a village in decay, a place that people were draining away from. Perhaps in one sense the road, ironically, might save it, by stopping the younger generation deserting it entirely when their parents and grand-parents are no longer.

But in spite of all this, the one thing that struck me most about the people of Tashigong was how *happy* they seemed. No one was hurrying around, shoulders tensed, faces frown-ing with worry. Instead their eyes were creased with laughter lines and bright with mirth. They laughed easily and often. There was a lightness of spirit, a deep-seated cheerfulness. People had time for each other, stopped and said hello and shot the breeze. And Tita Guru wasn't alone in looking astonish-ingly young for his age. It wasn't just in Tashigong, either; it was my abiding impression of all the remote tribal villages I visited in Arunachal Pradesh. I'd felt it among the Idu too – their cheerfulness, the affection between people, the sense of community and mutual help. There was a very different feel here to the tribal communities I'd travelled through in southeastern Laos. As one anthropologist put it, life there was 'brutish, Hobbesian and short', and many of the villages reeked of poverty and malnutrition. People were so poor they risked their lives to search for scraps of unexploded ordnance left over from the Vietnam War, selling the metal for a pit-tance in order to feed their families. But I saw no evidence of hunger here, quite the opposite. People were round-cheeked and well-fed, their gardens overflowing with fruit and vege-tables. They might not have owned cars and televisions, those modern barometers of wealth, but it would be wrong to say they lived in poverty.

Despite the hardships, I felt life here to be the antithesis of our fast-paced, mechanized, materialistic, Western existences – a life that's become so driven by artificial wants. Life in Tashigong was *real*. It was about food, shelter, family, community, togetherness. It was about need, not greed. It was about living with nature, the seasons and the cycle of night and day. People produced their own naturally organic food, breathed pure mountain air, spent the majority of their time outside and were free from the tyranny of the sedentary, screen-addicted lifestyles so many of us now lead. British children aged between five and sixteen spend an average of six and a half hours a day in front of a screen, a figure that's doubled in twenty years. The average American adult spends ninety-three per cent of their lives in cars or buildings, while the average American child plays outdoors for only half an hour each week. But here no one spent their days sitting in cars and air-conditioned offices, working in pointless jobs to pay the mortgage and buy more stuff they didn't need. They weren't subjected to the same drip-feed of distressing news that filters through our media channels every day. They lived in multi-generational households, looked after their elders, brought up their children together. Theirs was an existence of genuine togetherness, not one lived through the distorting, distancing filters of emails and social media.

Being there for those few precious days swelled in me a sense of loss, of want, of nostalgia. Maybe I'm guilty of putting the villagers' lives on a pedestal of lost pastoralism, but I saw Tashigong as a paradigm of a disappearing way of life. It made me feel as if we've gone wrong somehow, that progress and modernization are taking us away from the essence of what makes us human. We evolved in nature. We're animals. We need the wild, community, a sense of purpose, emotional connection. Yet we've bound ourselves to this speeding missile of progress, and are hurtling away from the things that really matter. As His Holiness the Dalai Lama wrote in 'The Paradox of our Age':

> We have bigger houses but smaller families;
> More conveniences but less time . . .
> We've been all the way to the moon and back,
> But have trouble crossing the street to meet
>   a new neighbour.

And look at the effect it's having on us. We have more money, more choice, more medicines and more conveniences than ever before, but every year the human race gets fatter and more miserable. Rates of depression among British teenagers alone have increased by seventy per cent in the last twenty-five years. Obesity in Britain has more than doubled in twenty years. The same patterns are true for the United States, Canada, Australia and South Africa, with research showing that people who live in cities experience far higher incidences of anxiety and depression. And it's only going to become worse. If urbanization continues at its current rate, seventy per cent of humans will be living in cities by 2050. How ironic it is that the richer and more 'civilized' we become, the harder we find it to experience happiness, the one thing we strive for above everything else.

I'm not an anthropologist, and my ponderings and impressions of Tashigong are based on a few, precious days spent on that auspicious mountain. I would love to return, to spend months there, to try to understand – as much as an outsider can – whether the villagers really are much happier than us, and why. But to me it felt like a Shangri-La – as much as such a thing can exist in human society, with its grief and passions and transience. Now that the road was coming, my short time there felt even more poignant.

15

GOODBYE TO PEMAKO

Not only was Dorje a restaurateur, lama, politician and artist, he was also an accomplished jungle apothecary. Striding through the forest that morning, down the steep footpath we'd sweated up two days previously, he waved his staff around like a wizard's wand, pointing out various edible and medicinal plants. There were sprays of wild cardamom, unripe bunches of wild kiwi fruit, vines of wild pepper, a type of green tea, and a magenta flower whose petals Khampa women used to crush up to use as dye for their cheeks. Occasionally he'd pause to rummage around in the shrubbery, coming out with the sweet, fleshy hearts of palm fronds or red, rhubarb-like stems that we sucked on as we walked. At one point he stopped and waved at a clump of ordinary-looking greenery beside the track.

'All this edible. This good vegetable, and this, and this, but *don't* eat this one.' He tapped an unmemorable-looking plant with broad green leaves. 'If you do, you dead in an hour. *Very* painful.' He grimaced, then waved his wand at a nettle-like plant next to it. 'That one *very* poisonous too.'

I decided it was probably best I leave my foraging ambitions to the less fatal fields of Somerset.

Kabsang knew a thing or two as well. 'My brother once wiped his bottom with one of those leaves after going to the loo,' he grinned, pointing to another harmless-looking shrub. 'Afterwards he couldn't sit down for a week.'

The king was also an amateur birder.

'That one green bird, long tail. Bad people like to eat it,' he said, pointing to a flash of green in the treetops. 'That one red bird. Bad people eat it too.' He waved his stick towards a trilling coming from somewhere above us.

Later he stopped, cocking his head towards a shrill '*Pap, Mapap. Pap, Mapap. Pap* . . .' noise piping through the canopy. 'This one mean rain come.' But since the first drops were already tip-tapping on my newly put-up umbrella, I pointed out this was cheating. He laughed and patted my shoulder.

By lunchtime we'd reached Yoldong, stopping to eat our omelettes with the tall lama and his jolly wife, Anguk. She clasped my hands affectionately and asked Kabsang if I'd found it difficult, walking in all that rain, then gave me a tshatsha of Guru Rinpoche astride a tiger. We wrapped it in a white khata and cardboard in the hope it would reach England safely. Afterwards she hobbled beside me to their gate, holding my hand all the way, asking me to come back and visit again soon. I dearly hoped I would, I told her truthfully, although

I didn't know when. There are some people you meet in life who, even though the meeting is brief and you don't share a word of mutual language, make a lasting impression on you. Anguk was one of those – a beacon of warmth and compassion and a shining, wise old soul.

We stayed in the village of Paynigem that night, reaching it on a little-used footpath that wound steeply upwards through thick, dark jungle.

'This real Pemako track. Maybe bears here,' said Dorje, sniffing the air. I hoped he was just saying it for effect. For now, though, the only wildlife we could see were leeches waving around on their posterior suckers, sensing fresh blood. When we paused, Kabsang found ten of them shimmying hopefully up his gumboots.

'They want to get drunk,' he joked, referring to the several glasses of chang he'd had with lunch.

Dorje picked another one off my cheek, patting me comfortingly on the shoulder when he saw me recoil. 'Don't worry, leeches our friends, they take away sin.'

It was 5 p.m. when we were delivered from the trees onto a high grassy plain grazed by fat-bellied Tibetan ponies – descendants of a pair brought here by a lama decades ago. Soon afterwards we were sitting in heaps around the fire of one of Dorje's relatives, reviving ourselves with rice and chang. It had been a tough fifteen-mile walk up and down a concertina of ridges, and even Kabsang, a stripling of twenty-eight, was exhausted. The Adi porters had taken up their usual position in the corner, silently playing games on their mobile phones.

A few hours later two smiling young Tibetan men burst

in from the dark and joined us by the fire. They were polling agents for the Tibetan government in exile and had walked from Tuting that day with a ballot box, stopping in every village for beer and chang. Tomorrow the Dharamsala-based government's new prime minister was to be elected, and all Tibetan refugees who lived in India were allowed to vote. This didn't include ethnic Tibetans like Dorje and Kabsang, who'd been born here in India, but those who'd fled their homeland following the Chinese occupation. Dorje's wife, whose family had escaped in 1962, was one of these, as were around fifty others from the Yangsang Chu Valley. The men would carry the ballot box to a nearby village in the morning and wait all day for voters to appear. It was a long walk for some of them, and the agents thought only about thirty would show up. I asked them how they made sure there was no cheating.

'Cheating!' exclaimed Dorje. 'No problem. Everyone in India cheats. In some states they just swap in fake ballot boxes.'

'Is that what you did?' I asked him, jokingly.

He looked at me with an expression of mock offence. 'No need.'

It was simple, one of the men explained: all the voters' names were listed in a green book they carried and each person was ticked off when they arrived. Anyway, they were sure the current candidate, a Harvard-educated Tibetan called Lobsang Sangay, would be re-elected anyway. As it turned out, they were right.

Sitting on a motorbike for six weeks isn't the ideal training for a walk in Pemako, and the next morning my tired, clumsy legs felt like they'd been filled with concrete. But we had a long way to walk that day, to Tuting, almost twenty miles to the west. From Paynigem's ridge we could just make out the town's distant roofs glinting beneath the white wall of the Tibetan frontier. It looked a *very* long way to walk by sunset, I thought, lacing up my boots. But if Dorje, a sexagenarian survivor of heart surgery, could make it, then so jolly well could I.

We set off at a lick and, by 10 a.m., we'd wound down a knee-jarring 800 metres and crossed the roaring river on a hanging bridge that was more air than anything else. Most of the slats had rotted away and I inched across, stepping carefully on the metal cables, my stiff legs pummelled to jelly by the punishing descent. On the far side we met an Idu family trotting the other way, their heads bowed under loaded bamboo baskets. A boy of about eight jogged at their heels, letting out a startled yelp when he saw me. If I thought we had a long way to walk today, it was nothing compared to them: as they dashed past they said they were going to the last village in the valley, a sixty-mile journey.

'It nothing for us mountain people,' said Dorje. 'I went on my first two-week pilgrimage to Padma Shri when I eight. My parents say no, so I run away with a lama. I had no shoes and we sleep in jungle.'

It was midday when we sat under the branches of a mountain ash to eat trakzen and omelette for lunch. Beside us the river thundered around a boulder-strewn bend between forest that pressed against the water's edge like crowds jostling for a riverside seat. It was a beautiful spot. But black swarms of dam dum flies put paid to any ideas of a restorative snooze under the whispering boughs. We tucked our trousers into our socks and wrapped our jackets around our heads, but there was no stopping the determined little blighters. After twenty minutes they'd doubled the mass of red, itching, oozing bites on my hands, neck and ankles. It was astonishing that something so miniscule could produce such a maddening bite.

Afterwards we swung along a flat footpath beside the river, through rice paddies dotted with stilted grain stores. It was hot now, and we strode along on tired legs with our umbrellas up for shade. Suspecting I already knew the answer, I gently asked Dorje why we hadn't taken this route on the way. He'd been worried about his heart, he admitted, and when the tractor appeared he'd jumped at the chance of a lift. I wasn't cross; things happen for a reason. If we hadn't taken the tractor I wouldn't have experienced the impact of the new road to the same extent. Looking at the Dorje that walked through the sunlit paddy now, he seemed years younger than the man who'd climbed aboard that tractor only a week ago. Perhaps the Rinpoche was right – maybe Pemako really could make old men young again.

In a forest clearing a few miles outside Tuting we came to Garuda Rock, a grey, car-sized monolith with an uncanny resemblance to an eagle with outstretched wings. Garuda, if you remember, was the name of the sacred eagle ridden to Mount Kailash by Vishnu in the story of the goddess Sati. Believed to cure pain and illness, it was draped in white khatas and surrounded by offerings of biscuits, alcohol and oranges. Around it the clearing was thick with prayer flags.

'It used to have beak,' said Dorje, muttering a mantra as he walked around it. 'But long time ago some Adi hear it make a noise like eagle and they very afraid. They come here and break beak off. When they do this, big white bird appear from rock and fly into jungle. Soon after, most of Adi village die from dysentery.'

When we reached the bridge at Tuting we found that the same sudden storm that had struck Tashigong after the puja had wreaked havoc here, destroying much of the hanging bridge and ripping off a number of roofs. Now the bridge swarmed with Adi, cutting and fitting new slats and lashing them on with strips of cane. We stepped over men and gaps, our feet on the steel cables, the peacock-green waters of the Siang whorling below. Soon afterwards we flopped down on the veranda of Dorje's house, jubilant, panting, soaked in sweat. Dorje removed his boots to reveal shredded socks and blackened, blistered toes. Kabsang did the same, then pulled a bottle of chang out of his rucksack and took several large gulps.

'Painkiller,' he gasped, grinning as he handed me the bottle.

Excellent idea, I thought, downing some myself. I couldn't have walked a step further.

Kabsang was staying in Tuting so, the next day, Dorje and I travelled south without him, roaring down the mountains in another juddering disco bus. I'd felt a lump in my throat hugging Kabsang goodbye, but it was time to leave Pemako, time for the next chapter. Numbed by the usual cocktail of jolting and ear-perforating Hindi pop, I looked pensively out of the window on what I'd come to know as a typical Arunachal day. Clouds drifted through the valleys like smoke and clung to the dark shoulders of the mountains, casting their gossamer veils around the slopes with a wraithlike possessiveness. I imagined them as shape-shifting dakinis, masking the secrets of those unknown forests from prying mortal eyes. Never the same for more than a second, it was a view you could gaze at forever and not become bored.

Time plays tricks when you travel. It slows and thickens, like a river turning to treacle. Rich with new experiences, vistas, people and insights, my time in Pemako had felt like a month. It was almost impossible to imagine that we'd roared up this road only nine days before. So much had happened since then. There'd been no witches, or poisoning cults, or fanged beasts, or vipers, or demons, or cannibals armed with poison darts. Nor had I found the key to eternal life, a portal to another dimension or plants that magically propelled me into the stratosphere. But then again, I'm not a naked, dreadlocked Tibetan mystic who's spent decades meditating alone in a Himalayan cave, guided by visions of a tiger-riding Tantric sorcerer. I might know my *utkatasana* from my *trikonasana*, and do the occasional twenty-minute meditation with Andy on Headspace but, well, it's not *quite* the same.

What I did find, though, was a breathtakingly beautiful, remote valley inhabited by people of exceptional jollity and occasionally astonishing youthfulness. I'd met reincarnated lamas, heard wondrous stories and spent numerous happy nights around glowing fires. And I'd been fortunate to travel in the company of two marvellous people. Dorje, the king, had in many ways remained an enigma, as hard to fathom as the mysteries of Pemako itself. A man of contradictory nature, he was at once childlike and wise; a lama and a politician; intense yet light-hearted; of this world yet drifting in and out of it; affectionate and aloof.

Just before we said goodbye the following morning he told me he'd move to Tashigong soon, to go on near-permanent retreat in his father's old hut in the forest.

'I'm tired of samsara,' he'd sighed. 'Inside, outside, middle side. I need to relax.'

How lucky I'd been to find him and Kabsang, to reach Pemako, to experience the place before the road was completed. My time there had been everything I'd hoped for, and more.

*

I'm sitting on a *chair*, at a *desk*, in a hotel with *sheets*, *towels* (white, medium fluffy), hot water and REAL GIN. So excited was I by all this when I arrived last night that I'm having a day off to rest, wash my fetid belongings and wallow in gin.

So read my diary entry from Daporijo, the headquarters of the Upper Subansiri district, three days later.

Reunited with my Hero, it had been a long two-day ride down from Yingkiong, via Along, following the spiralling descent of the Siang through a landscape that eased from a sharp undulance of hills to gently rolling hummocks. By the time I dragged my luggage into the pristine reception of the Singik Hotel in Daporijo, I was dog-tired and in dire need of a wash. Catching sight of myself in a mirror, I hardly recognized the thing that stared back at me. Half-human, half-hobbit, it had wild, strawlike hair forming dreadlocks at the back, a face smeared with dust and oil, black creases of grime encircling its neck, and stinking, mud-caked clothes.

The shower water (my first hot shower since Kaziranga) went an unmentionable shade of brown, the white towels would never be the same again, and I gingerly handed a reeking bag of laundry to the set of teeth on reception. There was of course a man attached to these teeth – a young Assamese with a permanently startled expression. But his teeth were so prominent it was hard to see beyond them. They stuck out like bowled wickets, exactly like a set one might buy in a joke shop. How the poor boy was ever going to kiss anyone was a mystery.

The only disappointment was the gin. Sitting down for supper, my gaze wandered lovingly across the alluring shelves of bottles behind the bar. They promised a wildly decadent night of gin and tonics sipped from long, cool glasses fizzing with ice and fresh lemon. How I'd looked forward to this moment.

The barman walked over to take my order. 'A gin and tonic please.'

He looked at me blankly. 'Tonic?' he repeated uncertainly.

Thinking this to be a simple matter of a barman who'd never made a gin and tonic before, I offered (perhaps a little eagerly) to come and make it myself. But a search behind the bar revealed a far more critical situation. There was no tonic. Not a whiff of it. Instead I had to make do with gin and soda water; a poor, but drinkable, substitute.

My impromptu rest couldn't have fallen on a better day. It was Holi, the Hindu festival of colours – a riotous celebration that marks the arrival of spring and the triumph of good over evil. For two days India turns into a joyous orgy of colour, its cities, towns and villages thronged with merry revellers armed with bags of multi-coloured powder. It's perfectly acceptable to smother a stranger's face in yellow powder, pump them with a water pistol and smear their cheeks pink. Men, women, children, rich, poor – everyone is fair game. Lubricated by copious amounts of *bhang*, an edible cannabis preparation, and booze, it's like playschool with intoxicants. Holi was my idea of a good day out.

Holi isn't celebrated by the tribal people of Arunachal Pradesh, but there were enough Hindus living among the Galo, Tagin and Nyishi population of Daporijo to make it an event. Most of the shops were shuttered and the streets were staggering with drunks, their faces and clothes splodged in a messy kaleidoscope of powder. I spotted a colour-smeared rabble of about thirty men sitting around a table inside the Border Roads Organisation compound, their fat bottoms overflowing the edges of white plastic chairs. Empty bottles of whisky lay like fallen skittles between them.

Excitable shouts of 'Madam! Madam! Please come! Please come!' erupted from them as I walked past.

I looked at the green moustaches, powder-splatted turbans, ruined shirts, blue foreheads, and thought, *Why not?*

'Happy Holi!' they yelled in a fug of boozy breath, eager hands rubbing my face with green, yellow and pink powder. It flurried around me, trickling off the end of my nose and settling on my clothes and camera. A chair was pulled up, a glass of whisky thrust into my hand and the usual round of questions flung at me in rapid succession.

'What is your good name?'

'What is your country?'

'Where is your group?'

'Where is your husband?'

At the hotel, I lied.

A wall of wobbling heads and smartphones popped up around me. 'One click, Madam?'

More hands smeared green powder on my cheeks. Sweaty, moustachioed faces loomed close. Arms slid around my shoulders. Men from Bihar, Assam, Uttar Pradesh and Punjab took it in turns to grin triumphantly at my side. A toast was made in my honour.

Sensing the alcohol might loosen the odd wandering hand, I left a while later, happily returning to the hotel smeared in a messy array of colours.

'Happy Holi!' shouted passers-by, bounding over to proffer a hand and ask my good country. When I stopped to take a selfie, a drunk, shrivelled old Tagin appeared behind me and pressed his nose against the lens, as if he'd never before seen such a contraption.

While I enjoyed a Holi-day it seemed only fair that my Hero have some attention too. It had been spluttering on the ride down from Yingkiong and the waterlogged horn had now given up the ghost completely. I wasn't in the mood for mechanics, so readily handed the keys to a lanky, enthusiastic teenage porter at the hotel when he offered to help, watching as he sprang onto the Hero and careered off to the local mechanic, my 'Be nice to my bike!' falling on absent ears. Feeling like a duchess, I retired to my room to sit on my *chair*, at my *desk*, and write. But I was disturbed five minutes later by a knock on the door. It was the porter, wide-eyed with urgency and panting slightly.

'Madam. I need one hundred and fifty rupees for oil change.' I handed over the notes and, with a brisk head-wobble, he was off, dashing down the corridor like a terrier after a ball.

Five minutes later there was another rapid knock at the door.

'Madam, bike need new horn. Need extra four hundred and fifty rupees.' I dug around in my pockets for a 500-rupee note, passing it to him without question.

He returned fifteen minutes later, breathing heavily and flushed with success. As evidence of his good-doings he held up the ruins of the old horn and handed me the bill, then off he galloped, happily pocketing his tip. Who's to say I wasn't ever so slightly had by him, that I was too trusting. But if he had diddled me, it was to the tune of no more than two English pounds, and I admired his cunning and entrepreneurial spirit.

When I checked the bike afterwards I found that the new horn had the pitch and tone of a startled guinea pig. My poor Hero. But in India any horn was better than nothing.

I hadn't come across any tourists since Kaziranga, but that evening, as I ate rice and vegetable curry in the empty white dining room, a minibus disgorged a noisy Italian tour group into reception. Grey-haired, mottle-skinned and chattering, they swarmed around poor Teeth in a sea of functional clothing, pressing him with passports and questions. One of them, I noticed, had lips like Lola Ferrari, grossly swollen from collagen injections. Compared to the people with whom I'd spent the last few months, they appeared another species entirely, and their presence gave me a sinking feeling that I'd left Arunachal's Wild East behind me.

A few minutes later, a harassed-looking Teeth hurried through the dining-room door and stopped beside my table, addressing me with all the whispering urgency of a presidential aide in a nuclear crisis.

'Madam, we must make adjustment to your room. We must remove one bag.'

'Which bag?' I replied quizzically, wondering which of my bags had so offended the staff, or if I'd exceeded some small-print bag quota.

He shook his head and corrected himself. 'Sorry, Madam. One bed.'

A troupe of six staff followed me up the stairs, and I watched as they disassembled one of the twin beds and dragged it down the corridor to an Italian's room. Escaping to the quiet of my single-bedded room after dinner, I slipped between the sheets with a tumbler of Jura. At the cost of five pounds from the hotel bar, it was worth every sip.

A crowd gathered around the bike to watch me pack after breakfast, hands behind their backs, necks craning for a closer look.

'How does your husband allow you to roam around like this?' asked a middle-aged Assamese man as I battled with a bungee.

'It's very dangerous to travel alone here, you know,' he added, sucking his teeth. 'Arunachal is full of outsiders.'

Being an outsider himself, I wasn't sure what he meant by this, but by now I'd learnt to largely ignore people's warnings and negativity, seeing them as more a reflection of their own fears than anything else. It was clear, though, that a lot of men in India were unsettled by the idea of a woman travelling alone, as if the natural order of things had been unlawfully rearranged. Women were for cooking, cleaning and having sons, not for gallivanting around the jungle alone on a motorbike.

Ignoring his naysayings, I rode out of Daporijo, its patch-work of corrugated roofs and the idle, inky waters of the Subansiri falling away as I climbed back into the hills. It was a perfect day for riding, and I buzzed west under a flawless sky on a narrow tarmac road that snaked around the shoulders of shining, forested hills. They pressed against the road in a tangle of greenery – ferns, palms, bamboo, wild cardamom, thorny lianas and feathery tufts of pampas grass – and the warm air hitting my face carried with it the intoxicating scent of herbs, pines and flowering frangipani. Small scarlet-bottomed birds skipped through the air ahead of me. Pairs of kites wheeled overhead. Fantastic, saucer-sized emerald green and turquoise butterflies danced around a waterfall where I stopped to fill my water bottle. A snake as black and shiny as polished onyx slithered across the hot tarmac. The first rho-dodendrons dotted the forests red. And as far as I could see the hills bubbled away to the distant horizon, a roiling ocean of wilderness, fading from green to blue to grey as they merged with the adamantine sky. It was as if nature, like a strutting male peacock, was showing off its spring wares. In the villages chickens clucked across the road trailed by a fluffy wake of chicks, reminding me that today was Easter Friday. Hymns and Easter eggs couldn't have felt further away. I swung happily around numberless corners, beeping my guinea pig horn, a rising sense of anticipation as to what lay ahead. For somewhere, hidden among those hills ahead of me, was the fabled Apatani Valley.

PART THREE

UP AND OVER

16

Easter in the Hidden Land

In the chaos of the Great War and the intervening decades, China's 1914 rebuttal of the McMahon Line had all but been forgotten. As far as the British were concerned the matter was settled and the mountainous, tribal lands that lay between Tibet and the Brahmaputra were unquestionably pink. But the issue resurfaced in 1943 when the Chinese produced maps that claimed the territory as theirs; awkward timing, given the Allies were currently spending billions propping up Chiang Kai-shek against the encircling Japanese. Afraid of risking this valuable East Asian alliance, the British quietly dispatched an army of surveyors, anthropologists and Political Officers into 'The Excluded Areas of the Province of Assam', north of the Brahmaputra. Their aim was to map the frontier zones and 'make India's right to the ... boundary very clear indeed'. If we couldn't fight the Chinese with gun and sword, we'd fight them with compass, pen and quadrant instead.

Accompanying one of this erudite force was a remarkable young woman called Ursula Graham Bower. More at home holding a Bren gun than a Bacardi, the 31-year-old anthropologist was fresh from a wartime stint in the Naga Hills, where her original mission 'to potter about with a few cameras and ... maybe write a book', had turned into captaining a 150-man-strong Naga guerrilla force against the advancing Japanese. One of the very few women to fight in the Second World War, and the only female guerrilla commander in the history of the British Army, her 'Bower Force' proved so effective that the Japanese put a price on her head, and many a downed Allied pilot owed her their life. Indeed, she was lucky to escape with her own life. Allied losses in this forgotten theatre of the war were heavy and the Japanese showed no mercy to captured enemies: one British guerrilla commander had his eyes gouged out before being executed. So as to avoid such a fate, Ursula had arranged to shoot herself if ever threatened with capture. Her loyal Naga servant would then chop off her head and take it to the Japanese in order to prevent a manhunt. Fortunately, such a situation never arose.

Adored by the Naga – who believed her the reincarnation of a goddess – and her Allied commanders alike, her gutsy jungle endeavours caused quite a stir. Dubbed the 'Naga Queen' by British troops, she even graced the cover of the January 1945 edition of *Time* magazine. Inside, an article titled 'Ursula and the Naked Nagas' wrote breathlessly of the bravery of 'pert, pretty Ursula Graham Bower ... Roedean-educated debutante, rally driver, traveller and anthropologist', the soldier who looked 'like a cinema actress'. And well they might be breathless. Our Ursula was one hell of a girl, a gun-toting glamazon who broke every mould in the book.

One of the many people who fell for her charms was tea planter turned soldier, Tim Betts, a cool, no-nonsense sort of chap who'd also led a guerrilla unit against the Japanese in Burma. Upon hearing of this famous Naga Queen, he resolved to seek her out and marry her – which is exactly what he did. 'As we both seemed to be mad along the same lines, it appeared a very suitable match,' Ursula later wrote. When Tim was appointed Political Officer of the recently established Subansiri Area soon afterwards, the newly married couple were dispatched to build a new British outpost in the wilderness. At first the government didn't want Tim to take his young wife, believing the job unsuitable for a lady, but thankfully they were persuaded otherwise. As Ursula wrote in *The Hidden Land*, her thrilling and often hilarious account of their tenure:

'The Subansiri Area was a weird, unexplored, strange and unchartered [sic] world. Its tribes came from no one knew where, its hinterland held no one knew what ... The map showed it as a blank, a vast virginal space ... a mountain labyrinth of unbelievable difficulty ... and nobody knew what lay further in at the foot of the snow ranges ... from one end of the Area to the other there was nothing but cliff and torrent, harshness and savagery. It was wild, sinister and unbelievably beautiful.'

The heroically unflappable pair spent eighteen months among Subansiri's 'fantastically Martian' Apatani and Dafla (since renamed as the Nyishi) tribes, attempting to establish a modicum of government control in this forgotten corner of India. Fresh from a war in which the Allies and Imperial Japanese armies had been pulverizing each other with tanks and bombs, they now found themselves in a society frozen in a medieval time warp. Their new subjects were a Rabelaisian bunch who inhabited a torrid world of constant tribal warfare, 'horrid butchery', slavery, kidnapping, mithun theft, polygamy and animal sacrifice. The men were scantily clad in loincloths, cane hats and primitive (yet highly effective) cane armour, their long black hair tied at their foreheads in topknots secured by brass skewers. Daos, Tibetan swords and tiger jawbones hung permanently at their sides, ready for any sudden skirmish. The Apatani women – allegedly as a deterrent to slave-raiding neighbours – had their 'noses turned into hippopotamus-snouts by large black resin discs' and their faces heavily tattooed. It was a galaxy away from the genteel society of postwar England.

It wasn't your typical honeymoon. But by the time the rushed Indian Independence forced Tim and Ursula to return to England, the couple's initial uncertainties had given way to love and ardent loyalty. They were heartbroken at having to leave.

'We'd come to care passionately, vehemently, fanatically for the area and its people,' our heroine writes. 'Home was in the Assam Hills and ... there would never be any other ... for the rest of our lives we should be exiles.'

Their Apatani and Dafla subjects had come to equally love the couple, affectionately nicknaming the tall, lanky Tim *soping*, meaning lizard, and the curvaceous Ursula *yaping*, meaning rice bowl.

Coincidentally, while writing this book, I discovered that Tim's cousin was the surveyor Henry Morshead, F. M. Bailey's fearless companion in *No Passport to Tibet*. Hardiness obviously runs in the family.

Seventy years later here I was, sputtering up to the crest of a 2,000-metre pass, keen for my first glimpse of Tim and Ursula's beloved valley. How much would life here have changed in the intervening decades? Would I still find men garbed in loincloths and cane armour, their bare, brown bottoms winking in the sun as they jogged barefoot across the fields? Would I experience the same weak-kneed awe as Ursula upon first seeing the valley? When they'd arrived in 1946, panting up from the plains with their butterfly nets, linen, lamps and Union Jacks, they'd been amazed at what they saw – for the Apatani may have been primitive by Western standards, but they lived in a wide, flat-bottomed valley 'as rich, cultivated and serene as an Italian garden'. Excellent farmers, they practised a settled form of wet rice cultivation that was far superior to the shifting cultivation practised by almost all the other tribes in the Northeast. Amidst the untended wilderness of the surrounding hills this neat complex of rice paddies was an unexpected oasis, the sight of which caused Ursula to fall to her knees in wonder.

But Tim and Ursula had walked north from Assam and I was approaching from the east. Before I knew it the road had carried me down into a tunnel of tall, fragrant pines and debouched me onto the hem of the valley itself. It fanned ahead of me, a wide, flat plain covered in a seamlessly inter-locking maze of rice paddies; not the phosphorescent green I'd expected but brown, waterlogged and humming with frogs. Pines marched around the edge, walling in the amphibian din, and here and there villages bulged up from the paddies like islands. It was a landscape like nowhere else I'd seen in Arunachal Pradesh.

By now the sun had lowered and the air was too cold to linger. Riding slowly on, I found myself in Ziro, the main hub of the valley, a dusty, dishevelled place where cows munched on piles of rubbish and curs sniffed at the gutter. Grimy buildings jostled for space. Wires sagged. Cars beeped. Signs advertised the numerous Baptist and Revivalist churches that were springing up in the area. Satellite dishes budded from walls and roofs. Shops spilled with car parts, plastic toys, cheap clothes, medicines; proof that commercialism had long taken over from the bartering economy of Ursula's time, when the Apatani traded with neighbouring, and occasionally distant, tribes, swapping smoke-dried rats for safety pins, handfuls of rice for matches, pine resin for Tibetan turquoise. Not everything in Ziro had changed, though. Among the people I rode past were old Apatani women with black resin nose-plugs and tattooed faces, the last to undergo the tradition before the newly formed Apatani Youth Association banned these old-fashioned, non-progressive practices in the mid-1970s. When I stopped to ask one of these leathery old ladies for directions she just looked at me in silent astonishment and shyly scurried away.

The hotel, when I found it, was a Swiss-style chalet surrounded by pines and croaking paddies whose manager, a pudgy, eager Apatani, bobbed around me as I unloaded the bike.

'My name is Haj Lodhe,' he chirped, dragging my dusty panniers across reception, 'but you can call me Abraham.'

Abraham, like so many of his people, was a recent convert to Christianity, baptized six years ago at the behest of neighbours who told him God would cure his father's alcoholism. But, alas, God hadn't cured the man and he'd died not long afterwards. As it was Good Friday, I asked Abraham if he celebrated Easter by gorging on chocolate, as we do.

He giggled, a little guiltily, I thought. 'No, we sacrifice mithun.'

Easter, ironically, coincided with the Apatani festival of Myoko, a ten-day bacchanal in honour of the arrival of spring and the strengthening of clan ties. For centuries every Apatani had revelled in Myoko's sacrificial rituals, but missionaries from the evangelist-dominated states of Mizoram and Nagaland were sweeping away the old ways in a proselytizing tide of Christianity. Now, while half the valley spent Myoko divining omens from the livers of sacrificed animals, the other half sang 'Praise the Lord!' in crude bamboo churches. I was curious to find out more.

Myoko is hosted by a different village each year, and this time it was Hong's turn to lead the festivities. Allegedly the second largest village in Asia, Hong was a stilted metropolis of 10,000 people, its numbers swelled to double that by the Myoko celebrations. Traditional bamboo huts stood eave to eave with modern concrete houses in tight, ordered rows and cars clogged the narrow streets. Locating Takhe Kani – a local historian I'd been told about by Tim and Ursula's daughter, Catriona – here could prove harder than finding a grain of rice in a paddy. But pointed hands and pattering feet soon led me to Kani's house and, before long, I was seated beside an Idu-style fire with his round-faced wife pouring me a mug of *o a la*, or rice beer, and handing me a lump of Apatani salt. A briny, solidified ash made from burnt plant matter, the idea was to take a glug of beer followed by a lick of the salt. A few minutes later a small man of about fifty, with gold-rimmed spectacles, a flop of hennaed hair and flecks of chewing tobacco on his lips, tumbled into the flame-lit hut. It was Kani, swaying slightly, fresh from a nearby party. Apart from the faded 'T' – signifying the Tani people – tattooed on his chin there was nothing to mark him out as Apatani. No cane hat, dao or palm-leaf cloak, just a very ordinary T-shirt and jeans.

Takhe Kani and I had communicated briefly by email a few weeks ago, but I hadn't been able to reach him since, and he certainly wasn't expecting me tonight. Entirely unperturbed, though, he shook my hand warmly and we sat by the fire to chat, his wife handing us a plate of small, green berries to nibble on.

'Don't eat too many,' said Kani (in Apatani the first name comes second) in good English, biting into one of the hard, peppery berries himself. 'They make you fall asleep.'

Whether it was the berries, or the slight altitude – 1,500 metres – or today's eight-hour ride, or the rice beer, I can't recall much of the few hours I spent at Kani's house. I can see the dark hut flickering in the firelight, and Kani rolling tobacco in his palm as he talks. I can remember him telling me the Apatani came from somewhere near Mongolia, but no one knows why, or how or exactly when. And I can picture myself walking out of the hut into the bitterly cold, starlit night and being told to come back the next morning. The family were holding a private Myoko ritual, he said, and I might find it interesting.

I arrived to find Kani and five other middle-aged men standing in a cluster outside the house examining a small, slimy piece of reddish flesh. One of them held it delicately between his rough fingers while they all took turns to peer at it, muttering and adjusting spectacles as they did so.

Kani grinned when he saw me. 'It the liver of sacrificed chicken. We look for omens,' he explained. 'You see here—' he pointed to a piece of the liver with his little finger, 'those red lines mean there will be a death in the clan.'

'How many people are in the clan?' I asked.

'About a thousand.'

Another liver, a tiny yellow one, delivered another dubious prophecy. 'This one says there will be a fight in the family,' said Kani, pursing his paan-flecked lips.

Next, a handful of boiled eggs were sliced in half and examined for signs. Kani held one up to his glasses to make sure he didn't miss anything. 'Sometimes the eggs are very precise and tell you to sacrifice a dog, and then we find an omen in the dog liver. Shaman also use eggs to check if two people should marry. If egg says so, the marriage not happen.'

But today the bright-yellow yolks were silent.

Inside the dark hut a *nyibu*, or shaman, was sitting beside the fire, showered in ash, chanting as he dangled a tiny, chirping chick in the smoke. You didn't need a degree to work out things weren't looking good for the chick. The shaman, a sinewy old imp with dark, impudent eyes and a face like crumpled leather, wore a black embroidered waistcoat and

267

near-indecently short shorts, out of which stuck a pair of twig-like legs.

'What are they for?' I asked Kani, pointing to tight white bands of cotton around each of the imp's upper calves.

'They vital. If the nyibu isn't dressed properly the spirits won't listen to him.'

I wondered if the spirits had noticed that the nyibu's long black hair, knotted at the forehead in the old Apatani style, was actually a wig. Or perhaps the spirits weren't bothered by toupées.

Scattered around the fire was a handful of other men, bottles of Royal Stag at their feet, laughing and talking noisily. Like Kani, the only thing that marked them out as Apatani were the faded blue tattoos on the older men's chins.

In a grim parody of Easter today's ritual involved the sacrifice of a number of tiny chicks. They cheeped in a basket beside the shaman, balls of yellow fluff no more than a few days old, soon to be offerings to the many Apatani gods. To appease Luto, the spirit of domestic animals, the imp went outside and squatted in front of an egg on a leaf, muttering as he doused a dangling chick in flour and beer. Seconds later he'd slit its throat and blood was dripping onto the egg from its limp body. Other chicks were hung upside down on a bamboo and leaf altar by the door while the shaman plucked bleeding wing feathers out of a squawking black hen.

'This altar to keep spirits out of house – like security guard,' explained Kani over the cheeps and squawks.

Minutes later their charred bodies were being turned on a spit over the fire and the hut smelt of blood and burning feathers. When the bloodshed was over everyone sat around the fire and ripped at bits of cooked chicken and egg.

'We're "all-a-tarian",' quipped Kani's son, a policeman, when he discovered I didn't eat meat. 'We eat everything. Dogs, cats, frogs, rats, tadpoles . . .'

At one point the conversation turned to my apparent bravery. The men, most of whom spoke some English, were astonished that I was travelling alone on a motorbike.

'We tribals are afraid to even go to Guwahati,' said one of them. 'We get called "Chinky" and treated like outsiders when we leave Arunachal Pradesh.'

His work done, the nyibu sat coquettishly on a stool, one scrawny leg crossed over the other, holding forth about the need for more people to become shamans. Like the Idu, none of the younger Apatani wanted to be shamans anymore, and the nyibu were dying out. When I asked to take his photograph he puffed out his chest, stuck out his chin and held up a surviving chicken in mock-ceremony, vainly rearranging his wig when I showed him the image. Maybe I'm being unfair, but from my outsider's perspective I felt him to be more a strutting showman than a genuine conduit to the gods.

Dawn broke with a record-breaking round of epiglottal exorcism; a concerto of throat-clearing, spitting and gurgling of phlegm that lasted at least ten minutes. Of course I was accustomed to the unsavoury noise of the Indian male's morning ablutions by now. I'd got over the urge to dash into the communal bathroom and perform the Heimlich manoeuvre on its occupant. I'd trained my mind to recognize that no, that violent choking coming from the next room wasn't the sound of someone being strangled. But I was still dumbfounded by the range and volume of hoicks, gargles and chokes that rico-cheted through the musty corridors of Indian hotels at dawn. I mean, *what exactly were they doing in there?* This morning I loitered outside my room, curious to see what Goliath could produce such a racket. But when the bathroom door opened one of the kitchen boys walked out, a reedy Assamese of no more than twenty. I'd hate to hear a heavyweight Indian wrestler at their morning toilet.

Later I asked Abraham, the enthusiastic manager, the pur-pose of such forceful ablutions. He looked shocked.

'You mean you don't do this in England?'

I shook my head.

'But it's very necessary to do this, to clean your throat and tongue. Otherwise—' he scrunched up his chubby face and fanned his hand in front of his nose in distaste, 'little smelly.'

It was Easter Sunday, and by ten o'clock a deserted, foggy Ziro rang with the sound of electric keyboards, tuneless sing-ing and shouts of 'Pays da La!' (Praise the Lord). Kani had told me only four per cent of the Apatani were Christians, but I'm sure the figure is far higher. Intrigued as to what went on in these services, I followed the sound of singing into a barn-like Baptist church. Inside, about a hundred people, nearly all women, clapped and swayed and sang along with a smiling, clean-cut youth who, with his gelled hair and denim jacket, reminded me of an eighties *Blue Peter* presenter. Beside him ten teenage girls in shirts and sarongs, pretty and sinless-looking, led the congregation in a choreographed dance. They shimmied and clapped and wiggled their hips, and the worshippers shufflingly followed. I noticed, among the smooth-skinned youths and young mothers, a number of old women, their tattoos and nose-plugs seeming oddly out of place in a church. It was easy to see why young people, influenced by travel and the media, might be cynical of the old animist ways. But it was harder to understand why the old would turn their backs on the Apatani gods in the twilight of their lives.

There was nothing *Blue Peter* about the Revivalist church I visited next. Here, in a large bamboo hall near the village of Hong, a packed congregation sat listening to the hellfire of a screeching young virago. She strode back and forth across the stage, Bible in one hand, microphone in the other, belting out the word of God with deafening machine-gun rapidity. Every few minutes her indecipherable rantings would be punctuated with sudden shouts of: 'He died to set us free: Praise the Lord! Hallelujah!' To which the audience would respond with fervent cries of 'Pays da La!' It was exhausting just watching her.

When she'd finished her sermon, if that's what it was, she whipped the audience into an evangelical frenzy, conducting them with stabbing fingers and goading shrieks. They wailed and shook and waved their arms above their heads. They moaned and stamped and flapped their hands. Old women rocked back and forth in their chairs like confined lunatics. Young women convulsed as if having fits. The few men just sat there, inscrutable, observing the hysteria. When I left I found a gaggle of children peering in through the open door, as wide-eyed and disturbed as I was. While I might expect to see such scenes in New Orleans or Nigeria, I hadn't expected to see it here.

I met two recent converts to Christianity that evening, crouched beside the fire in Abraham's family hut. Chigin

Yami didn't know how old she was. Probably more than a hundred, she guessed. But she looked nearer seventy. A plain, thick-set woman with an orange headscarf and a crucifix around her neck, a single faded blue line ran from the top of her wrinkled forehead to the tip of her distended nose. Another four lines were tattooed between her mouth and bottom of her chin. She'd been ten when she was tattooed, Abraham translated for me, held down by her parents and two others while an old woman inked her face with sharpened bamboo. I asked her why it used to be done.

She shrugged and shuffled her bare, blackened feet. 'I've no idea. I just followed the tradition of the elders.'

Three giggling girls were sitting beside us, listening to our conversation. They must have been about ten years old. 'Would you like to be tattooed like this?' I asked them.

'No!' they cried, bunching together in shy titters.

Ten years ago Yami's husband had fallen ill with cancer. Doctors hadn't been able to help. Nor had the village nyibu, despite Yami spending a fortune sacrificing mithun, dogs, goats, pigs and chickens. After her husband died Yami started suffering from severe headaches, but again the doctors and nyibu were unable to help. When friends suggested trying Christianity she'd resisted at first, but after seven visits to a Catholic church had converted. It had worked, she said; her health was much better now and she only had headaches when she sinned. Another woman, a sad-looking, hunched old shell with nose-plugs the size of fifty-pence pieces, told a similar story of illness and spiritual bargaining. Her back pain was much better since she'd been baptized in the local river, she said: her only worry was that in the afterlife she wouldn't be able to find her husband, who'd died a follower of the Donyi-Polo faith.

I could see now why some old people were turning to Christianity. Good health is everything when medical facilities are poor and your livelihood depends on being able to work in the paddies. And Christianity was a far simpler, less threatening belief system than Donyi-Polo, whose spirits were both numerous and prone to malevolence. They lurked at crossroads, hid in the wind, whispered through doorways and attacked unwary people in the forest. Be it a nosebleed, headaches or a poor harvest, any illness or misfortune was interpreted as the work of malicious spirits, and sacrificing chickens, dogs, pigs and mithun to keep them happy was expensive. At least with God there was only one of Him, and it didn't cost valuable livestock to assuage his thirst for vengeance. But these two old women were unquestionably the most miserable people I met in all my travels here – sad, downtrodden individuals whose very souls seemed to have been extinguished. God may have proved a good anaesthetic but He certainly hadn't brought them happiness.

Another reason for the rise of Christianity was, I later heard, the old Apatani social system of the patrician *mite* and the plebeian *mura* classes. In Ursula's time the mite married only within themselves, creating 'a network of alliances ... comparable to that of European royalty in the years before 1914'. The mura, meanwhile, were often kept as slaves. Although slavery had stopped in the 1950s, the class system still persisted and Christianity was seen as a way for the mura to liberate themselves from these age-old bonds. It was a sort of religious communism.

The Ziro I rode away from in the morning was smothered in mist and impending rain, the dusty streets turned to mud by an overnight downpour. There were no longing backward glances as I climbed through dreich pines to the Jorum Top Pass. The Apatani Valley had left me cold. It was my fault really. I'd fallen in love with the cane-armoured warriors of Ursula's *Hidden Land*, and it was stupid of me to think I'd still find such a place. The 1940s were a world ago. Look how much England has changed since then; if an Indian read a memoir of a wartime Wiltshire village and went there expecting to find farmhands in hobnail boots leading carthorses up the street, they'd be sorely disappointed. Ursula and Tim felt like they'd landed in one of 'Edgar Rice Burroughs' interplanetary romances', but I felt like I'd glimpsed a fractured society riven by God and Progress. Throughout my travels I'd been asking tribal people if they identified more with their tribe, or with being Indian. The Apatani were the first to answer that they felt Indian first. In another seventy years' time it's possible their culture will have vanished altogether.

17

A RISKY BUSINESS

Every journey has its doldrums, and Itanagar was mine. I found Arunachal's state capital to be a smutty, congested town whose streets were choked with frustrated drivers and foul with exhaust fumes. Rickshaws wove in and out of crawling lines of traffic. Jeeps nearly took off my legs as they barrelled impatiently past. Slums teetered on rooftops above billboards advertising the 'Ecstasy and Serenity' of new apartment complexes that spread gaudily across the green hills. Seen through different eyes, on a different day, the blue, pink and yellow buildings might have looked attractive. But not today. I was tired, that particular type of cumulative tiredness that breeds on these long journeys, and I wanted Marley, proper chocolate and a hot bath.

None of which I was going to find in the dive of a hotel I checked into, a mephitic place on the main drag whose rooms overlooked a rubbish tip, a slum and a half–built tower block. Its walls were stained with damp and squashed mosquitoes. Cockroaches as big as golf balls scuttled across the concrete floor. The tiles around the squat loo looked like Jackson Pollock had been experimenting with a palette of excrement, paan and mosquito blood. My sleep there was equally bad. Buried in my sleeping bag, fully clothed, I was woken in the middle of the night by the sound of a young man sobbing and screaming hysterically in a nearby room. Other voices were trying to console him, but the poor man's despair lasted at least an hour. At six, when the ceiling started to clank and thud with the sound of metal weights being dropped, I realized there was a gym above my room. Blearily emerging from my orange cocoon just afterwards, I saw that something had burrowed its way through my layers of cotton and fleece and left a trail of red, itchy bites across my stomach and back.

My mood wasn't improved by a morning in Itanagar. I couldn't find an ATM that worked. The Research Publication Department, where I'd been told I might pick up some interesting books on the area, was closed, and the electricity at the Jawaharlal Nehru State Museum had gone out. Instead I peered around its glass cases in the dark, the stuttering beam of my dying head torch falling on badly labelled textiles and terrifying–looking mannequins.

The best thing about Itanagar was receiving a text from Tapir, the Adi guide I'd briefly met in Roing who'd identi-fied Ata as Dorje Tenzing. It read: 'Mem, i meet u tomorrow Sagalee.' It was all set. Tapir and I were heading into the jungle on a thrilling wartime mission.

*

On 7 December 1941, when the Japanese attacked Pearl Harbor, Jay Vineyard was an ordinary American eighteen-year-old. He was a freshman at college in Arkansas, loved going to picture shows and played French horn in the college band. Two and a half years later the recently qualified pilot was flying his Curtiss C-46 Commando across the high mountains and deep gorges of Japanese-occupied northern Burma, resupplying China over the notoriously lethal 'Hump'. Stationed at a crude base on a tea estate in Upper Assam, Jay spent eight months flying supplies into western China, risking his life almost daily navigating a series of 5,000-metre ranges in an unheated, unpressurized plane with a nasty reputation for mechanical failure. The twin-engined C-46 wasn't dubbed the 'flying coffin' for nothing. As one Hump pilot said: 'Let there be no question about it! Flying the Hump was risky business.' Pilots had to wrestle their planes through 200-mile-per-hour winds, icing, violent storms and severe turbulence, all with a dearth of reliable charts, little weather data and no radio navigation aids. At times the visibility was so poor they may as well have been flying blindfold – but the pressure to deliver enough fuel, weapons, ammunition, rations (and occasionally mules) to China meant taking off in all weathers. As if this wasn't enough, Japanese fighters prowled the skies over Burma, waiting to pick off the lumbering, unarmed planes whose pilots could do no more to defend themselves than fire a Browning automatic rifle desperately out of the cockpit window.

Crashes were so frequent that the monthly losses sometimes equalled fifty per cent of all the planes flying the route; on the night of 6 January 1945, fourteen planes and forty-two crewmen were lost in a single twelve-hour period. Jay Vineyard was flying the last plane to cross that night.

'The wind was over 200 miles per hour and there was thunder and extreme turbulence,' said the disarmingly young voice of the 92-year-old at the other end of the telephone from his home in Texas. 'We were flying blind – lots of pilots got lost. I didn't know how lucky I was until afterwards.'

There was never any mention of casualties, though. The only way you knew if a crewman had been killed was if you shared a room with them.

'It always shook us up a bit,' Jay told me. 'You knew any of us could go out and never come back.' Jay's own roommate was a brilliant pilot called Danny Edwards. 'He was the best pilot we ever had – but he died one night trying to land with one engine on fire. The next day the quartermaster came in and took his clothes away.'

Even if you did manage to parachute to 'safety', your chances of survival were slim. The downed Allied pilots rescued by Ursula's Naga 'Bower Force' were a lucky minority. Some crewmen were lost for weeks in the jungle. Others suffered cruel deaths at the hands of the Japanese. RAF pilots flying in the China–Burma–India theatre were issued with a survival guide: next to the section about tigers, it simply said, 'pray'. A US general wasn't exaggerating when he wrote: 'It was safer to take a bomber deep into Germany than to fly a transport plane over the Rockpile from one friendly nation to another.'

Life wasn't much better on the ground. When they weren't in the air, crews passed the time in mind-numbing inactivity; sitting around on their makeshift bases reading and playing cards. Malaria was rife, the food was disgusting and conditions primitive. Radio operator Private Robert L. Looney summed up his frustrations in a poem.

> I am weary of bathing with Lysol
> And washing with carbolic soap.
> I am tired of itch and spin diseases
> Mosquitoes and vermin and flies ...

Another young pilot, Freddie 'Buzz Boy Pete' Raubinger, wrote to his brother back home in Michigan:

> It rains almost every night and the humidity is so high that nothing will dry unless it's put out in the sun. We live in bashas made out of bamboo, with thatched roofs and they're none too weather proof. I woke up at about 5 a.m. today with water dripping in my face and my right shoe half full of water ... Ah yes! All the comforts and facilities of home.

Neither man lived to see the end of the war: Looney's C-87 vanished on 9 April 1943; Raubinger's C-46 crashed into a mountain north of Itanagar in February 1945.

In total, 594 planes and 1,314 people were lost over the Hump. The grainy photographs of dead crewmen show the boyish, smiling faces of men too young for such an ordeal, let alone for death. Jay Vineyard was one of the lucky ones. He flew 660 hours – 174 missions – over the Hump and made it home unscathed. But despite the human tragedy, the airlift did achieve its purpose. In February 1942 Roosevelt had ordered that 'the pathway to China be kept open at all costs'. And it was. By July 1945 a plane was crossing the Hump every few minutes. With the Burma Road closed by the Japanese, and the Stilwell Road a failure, it was Jay and the other brave pilots of the Hump who kept China in the war. Without them, the outcome could have been disastrously different.

But like the soldiers who toiled in the mud of the Stilwell Road, the bravery of these men has largely been forgotten. Whereas the US military spends millions of dollars each year recovering remains from the Vietnam War, they've done almost nothing to bring home the estimated 400 airmen whose remains still lie in the jungles of Arunachal Pradesh. Written off as unrecoverable after the war, Chinese objections to the US military being in 'their' territory of Arunachal Pradesh have hamstrung recovery operations since. When the Indian government finally allowed an American MIA (Missing in Action) team to investigate a site in 2008, complaints from China forced the mission to be pulled after only a few weeks and the Indian government blocked any further recovery efforts by the US military. When this unofficial moratorium was lifted in September 2015, the same happened again: an MIA team investigating the same site in the Upper Siang Valley were booted out after a month. A year later, despite huge pressure from the families of those still missing, there is little sign of change.

There is one American, though, who has investigated the crash sites. Intrigued by the tale of these missing planes, Arizona businessman Clayton Kuhles has, since 2003, undertaken numerous privately funded expeditions to the farthest

corners of Arunachal Pradesh, Yunnan and Burma, sometimes spending weeks trekking to extremely remote locations.
So far he has found twenty-two planes and the remains of 193
men, documenting all his finds on a meticulously recorded
website. One of these planes was the C-46 that Freddie
Raubinger, the young pilot who'd written to his brother, had
been a passenger on. The circumstances of this crash were
particularly poignant. The plane had taken off from Chabua
in Upper Assam on 4 February 1945, carrying two crew and
thirty-two American airmen home to the USA. But not far
out of Chabua the plane developed mechanical problems and
caught fire, ploughing into the summit of a 2,000-metre ridge
near the Nyishi village of Karoi. Only one man, 22-year-old
Technical Sergeant Marvin H. Jacobs, survived. Asleep on a
pile of bags at the rear of the plane when it went down, he was
flung 600 yards – the length of *five* football pitches – clear of
the wreckage, and later told how he'd woken up in a thicket
of bamboo, cut, bruised and with one broken ankle. A few
days later he was rescued by amazed 'natives'.

After talking to Clayton, and reading a collection of
Freddie's letters home, I decided to try to reach the Karoi site
myself. But if I wanted to go there and talk to local villagers
I'd need a guide. And by pure chance I'd already met the perfect person. In the short time we'd spent together in Roing,
Tapir had told me he'd been one of Clayton's main guides,
trekking with him to ten of the sites. Not knowing when I
might reach Itanagar, I hadn't called him until reaching the
capital, but fortunately he had a few spare days and immediately agreed to come. Luck, once again, was on my side.

*

Tapir had caught a Sumo from Pasighat and was waiting at a roadside shack in the small, muddy town of Sagalee when I arrived. He bounded into the road waving when he saw me, his small, stocky frame clad almost head to toe in camo. With a tent and a waterproof roll-bag slung across his pack, a camo baseball cap and a karabiner dangling from his belt, he looked like he was ready for some serious adventure.

Karoi was only fifteen miles away, but somehow Tapir, me, his bag, a tent and all my luggage had to squeeze onto the Hero and wobble along what promised to be a narrow, boggy mountain track. Thank goodness I'd packed duct tape. Digging out a roll I set to work taping my rucksack and sleeping bag onto the lid of my Number One Indian Quality Top Box which, by now, had lost another bolt, rattled horribly and was cracking underneath. Loading it with a wobbling tower of nylon wasn't going to boost its chances of survival, but we didn't have much choice. Once it was done I swung my leg over the saddle and shunted forward onto the tank, holding the bike steady while Tapir squeezed himself, the tent and his bag into the gap behind me. Twenty or so Nyishi had by now gathered to watch, including a scraggy old man in a cane hat topped with a fake wooden hornbill's beak, the environmentally friendly version of the Nyishi's traditional headwear. They tittered in amusement at Tapir's efforts to mount.

'I'm short man!' Tapir giggled. 'Your bike too big!' Tapir, I was soon to learn, laughed at everything.

The track to Karoi was the worst I'd ridden on yet. It clung to the flank of a forested mountain, a slick of orange mud gouged into lakes and boggy ruts by bikes and the odd car. We splashed and slid and splattered our way slowly along,

Tapir giggling every time we skidded or veered too close to the edge. At times the only way through it was to balance on a narrow strip of grassy verge, with just inches between the mud-caked tyres and a plunge into the valley below. By the time the first huts of Karoi came into view an hour later, my shoulders and arms felt like they'd done five rounds with Mike Tyson.

We stopped outside the first house in the village, a long bamboo dwelling beside the track, overlooking a valley dense with trees. It belonged to the gambura, said Tapir, bouncing out a few minutes later – we were more than welcome to stay. Inside, the house stretched away in a flame-lit tunnel of homely activity. There were no windows, just doors at either end, and clusters of people were bent over the fires of three centralized hearths. Bosomy, rosy-cheeked women with sarongs and grubby cardigans bustled about cooking and making tea; lean men in jeans and old tracksuits pushed logs into the fires and, at the far end, two teenage boys watched a television. Clothes, daos, cane baskets and calendars hung from the woven bamboo walls. It was the biggest hut I'd seen, and must have been forty metres long.

It needed to be big, for it was home to an extended Nyishi family of forty-nine, nineteen of whom were here now. Head of the clan, and of the village of twenty houses, was the gambura, a wizened old soul with filthy bare feet, a tatty baseball cap and earlobes that hung down like a pair of socks on a washing line. He sat cross-legged by the end hearth, turning a log in the fire as he spoke, his bald, cadaverous but extremely cheerful eldest son translating for Tapir from Nyishi to Assamese. Of course he knew about the crash; it was part of village history, and you could find something from the wrecked plane in every one of Karoi's twenty houses. At this the son dashed down the hut and returned with a silver Chinese coin and a rusted, circular object that looked a bit like a wheel hub – a section of the plane's landing gear. The villagers had seen the plane burning in the sky, the gambura said, and heard the explosion as it crashed. The following morning a group of them had trekked to the still-smouldering wreckage and found one man alive. He had a broken ankle, so they gave him drops of water collected in bamboo and carried him back to the village. Two of the Nyishi then walked to the nearest tea estate in Assam in order to send a message to the Americans, and a doctor was parachuted in soon after.

'But doctor parachute stuck in tree,' laughed Tapir, 'so willagers had to rescue him too!' Tapir had an endearing way of mispronouncing certain letters.

Three weeks later, once the Nyishi had been able to clear a landing strip with axes and dynamite supplied by the Americans, Jacobs and the doctor were evacuated. Apart from an American team, who returned a few months afterwards to remove the human remains, Clayton and I were the only foreigners to have come here since then.

It could have been down to the three-way translation, but the story seemed a little muddled. Clayton had been told a hunter was the only one to witness the actual crash, but the gambura told it differently. The gambura also told us seventy people died, including women, and that the villagers carried Jacobs to the village the following day. But in his report Jacobs said he was carried down from the mountain on 11 February, days after the accident. It was like Nyishi whispers, handed down through largely illiterate generations, morphing as it travelled through time. When I asked the old man when he'd been born, several minutes of debate with his son ensued. Finally, he said, 'I was born after the earthquake, after 1950.'

By the end of the conversation it had been agreed that the gambura's younger brother would take us to the site the following morning. It was about six miles away, on the summit of a mountain south of the village; if we left soon after dawn we'd be back before nightfall.

As we finished talking I noticed a woman walk past with a protesting white hen under her arm. It wasn't difficult to guess the chicken's fate.

'No, Tapir! Please tell them I'm a vegetarian and not to kill the chicken for me!' I pleaded. The woman laughed and carried the hen off in the other direction, and I was sure it had been granted a reprieve. But when supper appeared Tapir's plate steamed with rice and boiled chicken.

'It tradition,' said Tapir. 'Respect for the guest.'

As he ate, Tapir told me about various other meats he was partial to. Being an Adi, the list didn't exclude much. Crow, snake, elephant, bear, porcupine, barking deer, his friend's dog – he'd eaten them all.

'Your friend's dog!' I exclaimed, appalled. 'What did your friend say about that?'

'He bring dog round for us to eat – he eat it too!' he laughed. 'Oh, and many cat too. But I no like cat.'

His favourite was a particular type of poisonous beetle the Adi literally go wild for. Eating these was a bit like a game of entomological Russian roulette; you popped the crunchy little morsels in your mouth whole and hoped it wasn't the one in a thousand that would kill you, put you in a coma or send you crazy.

On telling me about this, Tapir shook with laughter. 'Sometime the poison make you think you beetle and many Adi hurt their heads trying to get under rocks. Doctors very angry and not treat people.' It was a ludicrous vision.

After supper – a very normal plate of rice and sweet potatoes – Tapir showed the family photographs from other crash sites he'd reached, his finger swiping across images of femurs, skulls, rotted leather brogues and bits of fuselage jutting out of snow.

'The man who willagers rescue here lucky,' he said. 'At one crash site I see, one man live too. He walk to nearest willage but the people newer see white man before and he was so long [tall] with pale hair and pilot uniform that they afraid. They think maybe he yeti, so they kill him with bow and arrow.'

Next it was my turn to take centre stage.

'Mem, you lady – you sleep in tent,' said Tapir.

'No, no need, I'll just sleep here by the fire,' I replied, not wanting to be a spoilt memsahib. But Tapir insisted. A lady must have her privacy and, before I had time to protest, he'd whipped out the tent and was laying it out in the space between two hearths. Nineteen pairs of eyes turned to look at us. Even the teenagers dragged their gaze away from the television to watch us wielding tent poles and nylon, almost poking granny's myopic eyes out with the end of an unruly pole. Careful inspection of the tent followed, the family members walking around it, stroking, prodding and peering at it from every angle. Even more entertaining was the sight of me blowing up my inflatable sleeping mat. Eager to see what was next, they pulled up cane stools and sat with expectant faces in a semi-circle around me. Rising to my new role as stand-up comedian, I lay on my inflated mat with a panto-mime 'aaaaah'. They slapped their thighs, rocked on their stools and broke into peals of laughter. Next I pulled out my fluffy anteater and handed it to the bald son. This caused another outbreak of mirth. He stroked it, convulsed with a fit of high-pitched, infectious laughter, then passed it on around the giggling circle.

'Are you married?' the son asked, probably thinking a grown woman with a teddy bear was a highly unsuitable wife. I told him I wasn't.

'And ladies and gentlemen, the final exhibit of the evening,' I said, unpacking my bulky sleeping bag and diving into the tent. Everyone laughed and filtered back to their hearths. What a very jolly family they were.

My night's sleep was less entertaining. Someone was watching television until the early hours. I had to 'attend to potty', as Mark Shand called it, in the outside shed around two in the morning, my knotted, paining stomach having a rare revolt against something I'd fed it. Then a pair of cockerels started crowing at three, after which the Noah's Ark under the hut mooed, oinked, clucked and bleated until I crawled out of my tent at five. I felt nauseous, under-slept and about as fresh as a week-old turd.

Tapir, who'd spent the night curled up on the bamboo floor like a cat, was already up and packing away his sleeping bag. The family were stirring too.

'No problem!' he laughed, when I commented on his

sleeping arrangements. 'I sleep anywhere. When hunting I sleep in tree so safer from leffard and python.'

Given that this pocket Rambo had told me he was Arunachal Pradesh's former kick-boxing champion, I wondered if it was really the 'leffard' and python that should be hiding from him. Next he checked his anti-venom kit to make sure the syringe-like suction pump was working properly.

'If mountain pit wiper bite we suck out poison with this. Otherwise you die after five, maybe ten, minute.'

Discussing sucking fatal doses of snake venom out of my body wasn't my usual pre-breakfast conversation. 'Do you think we'll need it?' I asked.

'I hope not. But many people die here from pit wiper and we need to be careful of snake today. They wake up this time of year.'

I didn't need reminding. I'd seen two black and yellow ones slither across the road just yesterday.

Powered by tea and Maggi noodles, we set off with the headman's brother just after six. A slight man of about sixty with wire-rimmed spectacles, greying hair and a blue tracksuit, he led us into the forest on a steep footpath, his flip-flops squelching in the mud. Below us Karoi's roofs looked like flotsam in a sylvan sea, lapped at by roiling emerald waves of valley, ridge and spur. A laughingthrush whooped and trilled somewhere down in the valley and above us an unseen bird wolf-whistled cheekily as we sweated past. I asked Tapir its name.

'I don't know name in English. But this bird seasonal. When it make this noise we plant paddy. And we no get married now – wery unlucky!' As with everything he said, he followed this with a tumble of laughter. If I were a doctor, I'd prescribe Tapir as an antidepressant: I have no doubt that a few days in the jungle with him could banish all but the worst cases of the blues.

It was a hot, sultry day and we climbed steadily through a sombre forest of slender, mossy trees, ferns and clumps of bamboo. Sunlight filtered through the canopy, fracturing the crepuscular light with beams and stippled pools. There was almost no birdsong now, just the sound of our feet scrunching through the loam, my breathing and the *thwack thwack* of our guide's dao on bamboo and branches. It seemed that everything in the jungle was out to get us. Barbed stems of bamboo and vicious, thorny creepers clawed at our shoulders. Dam dum flies swarmed and bit. Leeches wriggled. The friendliest creatures in the forest were the biggest – the village mithun, docile beasts that eyed us idly as we passed. One, a massive piebald bull, ambled up to me and licked the salty sweat off my hands and arms, wrapping his long, rasping tongue around my fingers. The last time I'd seen a mithun tongue it was hanging from a piece of cane in Sadhu Mihu's house during the reh festival. I much preferred this one.

For the last half-hour we climbed steeply to the summit of the ridge where the plane had crashed, hacking a path through bamboo and shrubs. By now sweat was sluicing down my back and the effort and slight altitude (2,000 metres) making me breathe like a pair of overworked bellows. Then I saw it – the first bit of wreckage: a bent, four-foot-long propeller, its tip still painted yellow. Beyond, spread over an area about half a kilometre square, was the rest of what remained of the plane. The majority of the metal had long been salvaged by entrepreneurial locals but the parts that were either too heavy, or not worth taking, were still here. In one small clearing lay the main arm of the landing gear, a riveted, rusted column of steel at least five metres long. All around it, half-rotted into the leafy mulch, were disintegrating lengths of rubber piping, crumpled bits of aluminium tube, twisted sections of panel, shards of pottery and damp, mouldering bundles of white nylon. It was this that affected me most, the nylon – the remains of the thirty-four men's unopened parachutes. Among this heap of metal, it felt like the only direct link to the men themselves – a visceral reminder of their deaths here. Squatting down beside the landing gear, I picked up a decaying rag, suddenly acutely aware of the stillness and silence of the forest. A lot of lives had been cut short here, and for a few moments I imagined I could feel the men's ghosts among the guard of trees. How sad that they'd died here, on this lonely mountaintop, thousands of miles from their families. And what cruel, cruel irony that they'd been on their way home.

Further down the same slope lay the rusted, mossy hulk of one of the radial engines. Two of its propellers were still attached and the third lay bent among the leaves. At all the sites he'd seen, the propellers were always intact, said Tapir. The main engine had once been near here too, our guide told us, but the 1950 earthquake had dislodged much of the wreckage and now it lay at the bottom of a deep ravine.

I wandered among the remains of the C-46 for an hour, examining bits of metal, thinking about the men, their families and Jacobs' miraculous escape. I thought of the parents of the plane's pilot, Cecil Weaver, who lost their other son, Ralph, a bombardier, just two days later when his bomber crashed in England on its way home from Germany. I thought of 21-year-old Freddie Raubinger, who was on his way home to Michigan to start a job as a mechanic and delivery driver for the local newspaper. A brilliant fighter pilot and a 'prince of a fellow', he'd survived 120 combat missions flying P-51 Mustangs against the Japanese over Burma, only to die on his way home. I thought about Jacobs' rescue by the 'natives', and his crash report saying how they'd been so fascinated by the zips on his flying suit they 'nearly wore them out, zipping them back and forth'. I thought of the wake of heartbreak this single crash had left behind it, and how what was left of these men was flown back to America to be buried in a mass grave at the Jefferson Barracks National Cemetery in Missouri, five years later.

Afterwards the three of us sat on a fallen tree and Tapir produced a tiffin of rice and omelette for our lunch. Every time we'd paused that morning he'd magicked something different from his 'I could swim across a river with this' waterproof bag – toffees, biscuits, Pepsi, water. I was beginning to wonder if he had a lamp and a coatrack in there, à la Mary Poppins, and asked him this as we ate.

He chuckled and reached into the bag's apparently fathomless depths. 'When trekking you need everything.' Out came a first-aid kit, torch, power bank, waterproof poncho and Swedish FireSteel. He proudly gave me a demonstration of the latter.

'At high altitude matches not work, so this very useful. Sometimes I use gunpowder from bullets I find at crash site to make fire too.'

Tapir made Ray Mears look like Barbie.

It began to rain as we left. Not the sort of rain that pitter-patters down in delicate drops, or sploshes playfully on the end of your nose, but a thunderous, blinding wall of water. We trotted, slid, squelched and half-tobogganed down the mountain, flayed by the cataracts of rain. Tapir galloped ahead, bamboo staff in hand, his hooded green poncho slapping and billowing behind him like some fleeing wizard of the woods. In his wake jogged the gambura's brother, jaunty red umbrella held aloft, jumping over roots and fallen logs as nimbly as a goat.

What a relief it was to be back beside the middle hearth three hours later, drinking tea and eating popcorn made in a wire basket over the fire, a kitten curled in the nook of my arm. Tapir, meanwhile, was showing the family how the FireSteel worked. They crowded around him, like children around a magician, exclaiming, 'Oooooh!' and 'Aaaaah!' as the sparks made a ball of cotton wool leap into flames. Afterwards we gave the gambura a list of the Americans who died here, as well as Jacobs' full name and the correct date of the crash. It was an important part of Karoi's history, and the family were grateful for the information.

The thought of peeling ourselves away from that warm fire was almost too much to bear. But Tapir needed to return home to plant his rice and was catching an early Sumo from Sagalee the next morning, so we had to make it back there tonight. I packed up the bike, took photographs of the family outside their hut, and gave the plump, jovial matriarch 2,500 rupees, around twenty-five pounds, for having us to stay. A fortune by local standards, she smiled delightedly and enveloped me in a warm, bosomy hug. How different I'd found these laughing, kindly Nyishi to the warring, slave-raiding, 'barbarian' Dafla of Ursula's *Hidden Land*, or the 'cruel and stupid village people' the Adi hotel manager in Itanagar had warned me I'd find.

The track had been pummelled to liquid mud by the night's rain, and it was a hellish ride back to Sagalee. How we stayed upright I'm not sure. When we reached the yellow Inspection Bungalow at dusk, the swarthy, moustachioed Nepali care-taker said there was only one room left, and it had just one double bed. By that point I was so insensible with tiredness I'd have shared a bed with Donald Trump if I'd had to. Besides, unlike Trump, I felt sure Tapir wasn't the groping type. But when we unlocked the door to the musty white room we found two double beds – *quelle luxury* – plus a bathroom with someone's dirty Y-fronts hanging on the door.

I washed under the trickle of a shower, hopping and swear-ing at the cold, and then sat on the steps watching purple fingers of lightning bolt across the black sky and listening to cracks of thunder and rain hammering on the metal roof. All I wanted was to eat and fall into bed. But the gas and electricity had gone out, the cook was drunk and the firewood was wet. In the end Tapir cooked us chapatti over a smoking, sputtering fire, the cook lolling and blathering on a stool beside him. By nine o'clock I was asleep.

18

THE SELA PASS

I'd spotted it when riding out of Itanagar a few days ago: an impossibly shiny tower of gleaming glass with the words HOTEL emblazoned across the front. A beacon of order and cleanliness, it rose out of the dust and disarray of the town centre like the sword of hope, as at odds with its surroundings as an alien spaceship. I didn't care how much it was. I was going there, and that was that. As much as I adored staying with families, I had a long few days' riding ahead of me and, for one night only, wanted space and quiet. I wanted to wash in hot water, to sink into a soft bed, to eat something that wasn't rice, chapatti or Maggi noodles and to not be woken up by cockerels, pigs or people at 3 a.m.

It was only here, amidst all the polished glass and pressed uniforms, that I realized I was emitting a most unladylike stink. My panniers were damp and fetid, I reeked of sweat, and my boots, clownishly swollen with mud, smelt like a dead stoat was rotting somewhere in their depths. I suspected only a sheep dip would really clean me, but for now a hot shower would do. Soon the bathroom tiles were spattered brown, my clothes were dripping muddy puddles onto the polished white floor, and I was sprawled across the soft, king-sized bed in a white, towelling robe.

At supper, in the empty hotel restaurant, I was waited on by seven nervously obsequious staff. They stood stiffly in starched white shirts and blue waistcoats, pretending not to watch me eat, the occasional scrape of my cutlery amplified by the formal silence of the room. It all felt very sensible and serious, a world away from the cosy fireside humour of my tribal friends. As glad as I was that I'd spent an extravagant 4,000 rupees, about forty pounds, for a hot shower and the comfortable bed, the hotel was a soulless place, with little relation to the Arunachal Pradesh I'd come to love.

Before I left town the following day I took the Hero for a service.

'This wrong bike to go to Tawang,' said one of the men watching the thin Bengali mechanic tighten and oil the Hero's chain. I ignored him but he went on anyway, his words toppling out in an irritating know-it-all whine.

'The road to Tawang is very bad, and *very* high. It not possible on this bike. It too old, and too small. You should have chosen Bajaj Pulsar instead.'

I'm generally extremely polite when I travel, particularly in places where a vituperative remark or a sulky face could be someone's first experience of a Westerner. But I'd come to be extremely fond of my Hero, and the man's unsolicited negativity made my hackles rise.

'It *is* the right bike, and it *is* going to get me to Tawang,' I snapped, suppressing the urge to swear. 'I've been two thousand miles on it so far, and it's done nothing wrong. It's *much* better than a Pulsar.'

Despite my angry retaliation, the naysayer did have a point. The former Tibetan stronghold of Tawang sits, eyrie-like, in a mountainous cul-de-sac between the Tibetan and Bhutanese borders. Cut off for centuries from the outside world, now the only way to reach it is by the single winding road that connects it with the rest of India; a road which crosses, at its highest point, the 4,175-metre Sela Pass. Even riding at 2,000 metres had deprived the Hero's 150cc engine of enough oxygen to make it struggle and splutter – now I was expecting it to cope with double that altitude. A thorough service and new battery would help, but it might not be enough.

For now, though, I rode south towards Assam on an empty dual carriageway freshly carved and blasted through the receding hills. The lines hadn't been painted, the crash barrier was half-built and the odd road worker ambled along the new tarmac, spade in hand, but it was still the best road I'd ridden on here. I belted along at an unheard-of fifty miles per hour, a hot wind on my face, occasionally having to swerve violently on rounding a corner to find a lone car or truck hurtling towards me on the wrong side of the carriageway. Thinking back over my journey I realized that, in two months, I hadn't ridden on a single road that wasn't being upgraded. From east to west, the arteries of Arunachal Pradesh were being dug up, blasted and sealed with tarmac. After decades of not investing in Arunachal's infrastructure, lest the Chinese invade again, and only building roads for troop deployment, the Indian government has only recently altered its policy. Never in its history had the region undergone such rapid transformation, and I felt sure that if I returned in five years' time I would find a very different place.

A few hours later I reached the toe of the mountains and was kicked out into the pandemonium of Assam. It was a shocking transformation. One minute I was swinging along an empty road in Arunachal Pradesh, the next I was in the midst of a honking, yelling, fist-pumping, flag-waving, political frenzy. State elections were coming up and today, Saturday, tens of thousands of people had converged on the roads to show their support for Modi's Bharatiya Janata Party and Sonia Gandhi's Indian National Congress. I've been told that voters are paid between 300 and 1,000 rupees, roughly three to ten pounds, each to rally for a particular party, and they were definitely earning their keep. Convoys of white pickups thundered along the main road, bumper to bumper, crammed with shouting mobs. Men hung out of overcrowded rickshaws, yelling and waving flags. Lanes were ignored. Motorbikes swerved and beeped.

With no choice but to navigate ninety miles of this madness, before turning north again towards Tawang, I rode west, beeping and swearing liberally, one fume-filled eye on the wing mirror, the other on the verge I'd probably need to dive towards at any minute. 'Concentrate!' I berated myself, after several close shaves saw me skittering sideways, yelling with frustration. Astonishingly, amidst all this, the cows remained unfazed. They lay in the middle of the road, chewing their cud, while the maelstrom belched and listed around them. Whether they were Zen masters of the highest order or exceptionally stupid, it was hard to tell.

When I did dare take my eyes off the road I saw how different Assam looked to the drear place I'd ridden through two months ago. Now February's dull brown plains yawned south in an infinity of green, the mirror-flat panorama broken only by betel palms, the occasional adobe hut and grazing cows – the green so vast and the cows so small they looked like farmyard toys scattered across a baize cloth.

What a relief it was to turn north at Balipara and buzz along a miraculously peaceful road flanked by palms, paddies and neat bamboo huts in swept earthen yards. Here little boys sold coconuts from roadside shacks, men in white dhotis led dun cows home from the fields and the air flashed blue with dragonflies. Soon afterwards, as the sun slid beneath the tips of the palms, I stopped for the night at a basic tourist lodge on the edge of Nameri National Park. The concrete huts had definitely seen better days, but at least it was quiet. Or so I thought, until a group of people arrived after I'd gone to bed and decided to have a party until cock's crow. In between their drunken shouts, the *doof doof* of their sound system, and a burping gecko nearly giving me a seizure when it landed on my pillow, sleep was scarce. At 5.30 a.m., when a pair of young goats took to bleating plaintively outside my room, I packed up, rode noisily past the sleeping revellers' huts and set off towards the mountains. Find me a noisier country to travel through than India and I'll find you the goose that lays the golden egg.

From there the road ran like an arrow towards the blue

massif, a grey causeway carrying me across a green sea. In Bhalukpong, a scrappy frontier town at the juncture of plain and mountain, a swaggering Monpa policeman sat at the desk in a tiny hut and copied the details from my Protected Area Permit, looping my long surname across two rows of the ledger. With his black beret, fake Ray-Bans and gold watch he could have been a border guard in a hundred different countries.

'Where your guide?' he asked, in a manner which suggested he didn't really care.

Although the police had seemed more relaxed the further west I travelled, I thought it best to fib a little. 'In Tawang,' I replied.

He then pointed to John's name. 'Where John? He coming?'

I lied again. Anyway, for all I knew, I might find the mysterious John in Tawang.

Beyond Bhalukpong the road wound steeply into the mountains between sheer walls of jungle and the hurtling waters of the Kameng, the blue skies of Assam soon giving way to a wadded ceiling of grey. Before the road was built in the mid-1960s it was a nine-day walk from here to Tawang: the Monpa trekking down with woollen blankets and returning with dried fish, matches and Assamese silk. Now the Sumos did it in one long day, and slow English motorcyclists in two. A sign warned people not to travel after sunset, another: SHOOTING STONE SLIDE AREA STARTS. DRIVE CAREFULLY – which I presumed to mean landslides and not some novel form of recreation. Now Buddhist prayer flags streamed between jerry-built roadside shacks and the people were stocky mountain folk with the weather-burnt features of Tibet. Up, up, up the road climbed, clawing its way around the mountains in a series of steep, precipitous switchbacks, a ruched quilt of green falling away below. Soon the Hero was struggling – by 2,000 metres I was crawling up the inclines in first gear, slower even than the merrily painted trucks that rumbled past me in stinking clouds of diesel smoke and dust.

Respite came in the form of a sudden drop in altitude to an arid, pine-scented valley where a cold river clattered over its shallow gravel bed. In the brief Sino-Indian War of 1962 the Chinese had focused their invasion on Tawang and advanced south through this valley. Since then, the Indian Army wasn't taking any chances. For twenty miles the road was flanked by check gates, military truck parks, officers' messes, mule lines, barracks, shrines and dusty football pitches. Gung-ho motivational sayings such as: 'Winning is a habit', 'For Guns, Guts and Glory' and 'Truth Alone Triumphs' lined the roadside, and sentries with sunglasses and slick moustaches stood to attention under signs for battalions with names like *The Formidable Five*, *The Balls of Fire*, *The Thundering 13th* and *The Soaring Eagles*. I imagined soldiers with nicknames like 'Bear Killer' and the 'Madras Marauder' spending their evenings here waxing their taches and watching *Top Gun*.

Climbing again towards Bomdila, a Monpa town straddling a 2,700-metre pass of the same name, the Hero really began to falter. Above 2,000 metres it seemingly couldn't draw enough oxygen from the thinning atmosphere to function properly, and now it slowed to the speed of an asthmatic slug. I forced its strangulated engine upwards around a string

of hairpin bends, bunny-hopping past a sign warning: IF
YOU'RE MARRIED DIVORCE SPEED at the dangerous speed of
seven miles per hour.

'Come on, little bike, be my Hero. Please!' I urged, leaning
over the handlebars like a jockey.

I finally crawled into Bomdila in the early afternoon.

Ursula Graham Bower had once walked across the mountains
to Bomdila and found 'cheerful peasants who whipped their
hats off and put their tongues respectfully out at us' in the
traditional Tibetan greeting. She'd dined in 'Oriental splen-
dour', then bought some sheep and herded them back across
the mountains to the Apatani Valley, clipping them with nail
scissors when she arrived. But I found a foggy, shuttered town,
deserted on this chill Sunday afternoon. A 'fooding' sign led
down some steps to the only open restaurant, a tiny, garishly
pink room lit by a single bulb, underneath which six Monpa
men were hunched over plates of momos. In the corner, an
ample woman stood behind a counter making more, filling
the anaemic circles of dough with minced beef before deftly
pinching them into dumplings. Falling hungrily on a plate of
rice and dahl, I thought about the Hero. At least from here it
was only a few more miles to the head of the pass, then down
just twenty-five miles to Dirang Dzong. While I should easily
reach there tonight, in the Hero's present state there was no
chance of making it over the Sela Pass tomorrow. Either I'd
have to take a Sumo from Dirang Dzong, or find some way
to fix it.

I'm not mechanically minded, but I knew the Hero's altitude sickness arose from a simple case of too much fuel and too

little air. There was *some* way of rectifying this – of fiddling with the carburettor to alter the ratio of fuel and air reaching the engine – I just didn't know what. Luckily Bomdila had telephone reception, and I knew a man who would. Half an hour later Marley had searched his prolific brain and the internet and found a possible solution. All I had to do now was reach Dirang and find a mechanic.

I popped over the pass an hour later, grinding the last mile so slowly I feared we might slide backwards. On a clear day my efforts would have been rewarded with a view of Arunachal's highest peak, the 7,090-metre Mount Kangto. But, alas, the gods had drawn a thick grey curtain over the line of the Himalayas, and all I could see was cloud. From here the road slalomed down through a necklace of pretty Monpa villages, completely different to anywhere else I'd been on this journey. The houses were tall and robust, half-tawny stone and half-painted wood, their brightly coloured balconies spilling with pots of scarlet geraniums, while strings of yellow maize dried under the eaves. Earthquake resistant and weatherproof, they were typically Himalayan, the same style as houses from Ladakh to Tawang and all the mountain kingdoms in between. Prayer flags flew over white brick stupas and everywhere were neat stacks of cut firewood, essential for surviving the harsh mountain winters. Even now, in early April, my hands ached with cold.

The Monpa, Arunachal's largest Buddhist tribe, were hardy, weather-bitten people in black yak-felt skullcaps, and their animals were huge and hairy. Shaggy yaks grazed on steep hillsides and mastiff-type dogs lay on doorsteps or trotted along the road, bushy tails aloft. Thankfully, unlike their distant cousins in Mongolia and Central Asia, they didn't seem interested in chasing motorcycles. Of all the days on this journey, none had passed through such differing landscapes – it was bewildering to think I'd begun today in Assam and was now riding through 'little Tibet'.

I stopped at the first place I came to in Dirang, a simple wooden lodge on a hillside overlooking the town, and immediately set to work on how to fix the Hero. Marley had told me that by stuffing electric wire inside the main jet of the carburettor and removing the air filter, I should be able to alter the fuel-to-air ratio sufficiently for my Hero to wheeze over the Pass. While the wire would restrict the fuel flow, removing the air filter would allow more oxygen to reach the engine. It was the equivalent of putting the bike on a homemade respirator.

Two hours later the amiable Nepali manager of the lodge had called a local mechanic and the three of us were squatting around the Hero, studying its carburettor by torchlight. The mechanic, a young Manipuri, had at first ignored me when – through sign language, pointing and the Nepali's basic English – I'd explained what I wanted done. Instead he'd checked the sparkplug and battery, listened to the engine and poked around the bike for other explanations for its sickness, while I hopped around behind him in frustration saying, 'No – carburettor, carburettor!' But I was a woman, I couldn't possibly be right. Only when he failed to find anything else wrong did he reluctantly follow my instructions, screwing apart the carburettor to poke a length of thin copper wire inside the main jet. For an hour's work he charged just 150 rupees. Call me idle, but I'd prefer to spend the equivalent of one pound fifty than stay up all night trying to decipher the inner workings of a carburettor. Whether the bodge would work or not, only tomorrow would tell.

*

Swaddled in thermals and down, I began the eighty-mile, 3,000-metre climb towards the Pass, zigzagging upwards through taupe, pine-clad hills half-obscured by cloud. Convoys of army trucks clanked by. Sumos dashed past. Trucks ground up the steep inclines in noxious clouds of black smoke. Yaks shambled across the road, skittering nervously as I passed – compared to the docile mithun the *Bos grunniens*, or grumbling ox, was a far more anxious creature. Stopping at one of the many Buddhist roadside shrines, I drifted my gloved fingers along the line of red prayer wheels and asked to reach the Pass. And at 3,000 metres, when the trees had thinned to nothing and the clouds reduced my vision to a white void perforated by a strip of dusty road, the Hero was still going. Onwards I climbed, slower and slower, crawling steadily towards the summit through a wilderness of cloud. 10km ... 8km ... 6km, said the white marker stones by the road. When we crept past the 4km stone I knew we'd make it. Even if the bike conked out now I could push it to the top.

It was cold. Dregs of snow lay on the rocky verge and the freezing air bit through my two pairs of gloves. How odd to think I'd been in the tropical heat of Assam only yesterday.

'Come on, Hero! Come on! We can do it!' I yelled excitedly.

Then, rounding a bend, there it was: a large, pagoda-like gate over the road, the words 'Welcome to Tawang' written beneath its golden roof. A line of prayer flags flapped in the breeze and a wonky sign beside a café said: YOUR [sic] ARE NOW AT 13700 FEET. It was the Sela Pass.

'Yes!' I whooped. 'We've done it!'

I parked under the gate, did a celebratory jig around my Hero, then dived into the café, where a soldier wearing a woollen balaclava silently served me a cup of tea. Lightheaded from the altitude, I stood in the unlit, empty room stamping my feet and warming my hands around the cup, thinking about how the last few days had been a series of reliefs: escaping Assam's pre-election fervour in one piece; making it to Bomdila; finding a solution to the Hero's problem, and now, the relief to be standing here. Each one was a small but significant triumph, a journey within the journey. Now it was just fifty miles to Tawang.

The road descended through a stark, rocky defile streaked with snow and scattered with miserable-looking army camps patrolled by soldiers in woollen hats and balaclavas. As if these weren't reminder enough of the 1962 war, below them was a grand roadside memorial to a Sikh rifleman whose death here has become the stuff of legend. According to local lore, 21-year-old Jaswant Singh ignored the orders for his division to retreat from the Chinese in November 1962, instead remaining at his post with two Monpa girls. Only after the heroic trio had killed 300 enemy troops was their position overrun, Singh killing himself with his final bullet. The official story, though no less heroic, goes a little differently. According to a plaque at the memorial, he and two other soldiers volunteered to attack a Chinese machine-gun post, crawling to the enemy lines under heavy fire and killing the three gunners. Retreating with the captured gun, they were shot dead just as they were climbing back into their own trenches.

The memorial is a paean to one man's bravery. A bronze bust of Singh stands on a marble plinth in the middle of the temple-like complex and, beside it, in a glass box, is his immaculately made-up bed. The army treat him as if he's still alive, stationing six soldiers here at all times to attend to his every need. They serve him bed tea at 4.30 a.m., breakfast at nine and dinner at 7 p.m. His boots are polished every day, his bed made, his uniform ironed. He's even still awarded promotions. Every passing soldier stops here to pay their respects and legend has it that Singh can be seen guiding military convoys over the mountains in dangerous weather. The Monpa worship him too, believing him to be a local protector spirit. Whatever the truth, Singh's bravery provides the army with a useful diversion from the embarrassing reality of that thirty-day war. And for passers-by, it's a welcome chance for a free cup of tea and a samosa, lovingly baked by Singh's attendant soldiers.

The clouds thinned. The air warmed. Colour leached back into the barren landscape. Rocks gave way to sparse pines and, later, the town of Jang and a brief, magnificently forested gorge. After this I snaked skywards to Tawang around a foggy, potholed procession of hairpin bends. On another day I might have been able to see Tawang's monastery – a mighty fortress resplendent atop its narrow spur, the snow-dusted ridge of the Bhutanese border just beyond. But now all of that was hidden somewhere in the clouds. Instead I admired the gangs of female Monpa road workers who hammered at heaps of grey stones, babies peeping from their backs. They raised their masked faces as I passed, returning my greetings with girlish voices and dusty, bandaged hands. Others shifted rocks and shovelled mud, but they always paused to wave. Around five o'clock, sapped from the ride and the changes in altitude, I was riding through the dusty, half-shuttered streets of Tawang's old market. How happy I was to be here.

Compared to the rest of Arunachal Pradesh, Tawang is a tourist mecca. They come here by the minibus-load in late autumn, when the weather is clear, trundling over the Sela Pass to be wowed by the views and the world's second largest monastery (only Lhasa's Potala is bigger). But now the giftshop owners dozed behind their glass counters, the few restaurants were a sea of empty tables and my Monpa guesthouse – a new concrete building off the old market – hadn't had another visitor for weeks. Instead the town was overrun with dogs. They were everywhere. Mangy old mongrels lay on the steps outside shuttered shops. Shaggy, swaggering hounds trotted between parked cars. Half-starved bitches lay on piles of rubbish, bundles of puppies tugging at swollen teets. At night the feral packs roamed the empty streets, barking, howling and fighting, and the cold mountain air echoed with the canine hullabaloo. It was dangerous to walk alone after dark, someone told me, and I well believed them.

It wasn't difficult to find the monastery the next morning. It dominates Tawang and the surrounding mountains, a vast white and gold citadel raised high on its rocky plinth. Gold roofs gleamed wanly through the cloud and, below its formidable walls, the town straggled in obeisance. Built around 1680, under the orders of the 5th Dalai Lama, it was designed as both a fortress and a monastery – a two fingers up at the marauding Bhutanese. This is Tibetan territory, it said, and we've got twenty-foot walls, defensive ditches and an army of monks to prove it. The story goes that the Dalai Lama gave a local lama a ball of wool and instructed him to build a new monastery whose boundary walls were the same length as the wool. For months the lama searched fruitlessly for the right place to build this great edifice. Then one day, while meditating in a cave, he emerged to find that his faithful horse had vanished. Following its hoofmarks, he found it at the end of a rocky spur, pawing at the ground. Seeing it as a divine sign, the lama renamed the place Tawang, meaning 'chosen by horse', and began work on the Tawang Galdan Namgey Lhatse Monastery, meaning 'Celestial Paradise of the Divine Site Chosen by Horse'. To further seal Tibet's claim on the area, the 5th Dalai Lama chose to be reincarnated here and his successor was born in a nearby village.

Despite British efforts to prise it away from Lhasa – including a 1938 expedition led by the fabulously named Captain Lightfoot – Tawang remained under Tibetan rule until February 1951. Only then, when an Indian Army delegation walked over the mountains from Assam, was it officially handed over to India. Fed up with the heavy taxes levied by Tibet, the Monpa agreed to India's claim without the spilling of a single drop of blood.

Inside, the monastery was like a town – not quite a medieval one, but close. Worn stone steps led me through a labyrinth of narrow alleys between high walls of rough, whitewashed stone. Stray dogs scavenged. Cocks crowed. Neat stacks of firewood were piled outside the painted wooden doors of the monks' quarters. In the richly ornamented gompa a twenty-foot golden Buddha sat on a lotus leaf, looking sternly down over rows of empty platforms. There were no cars, or advertisements, or shops, or crowds; just an air of stillness and order. Of the almost 500 monks who lived behind those doors, I saw curiously little. They must have been studying, praying or sensibly sheltering from the cold. Occasionally the low, monotone chanting of a single ascetic would drift down from one of the brightly coloured windows, or I'd hear footsteps and a maroon figure would hurry past. Mostly boys of fifteen or less, they smiled shyly and hurried on, clutching their robes about them. Although it was no longer compulsory for the Monpa to send their middle child to the monastery (or nunnery), many poorer, rural families still did – some of these boys would have come here as young as five. Others, like Dorje's son in Tuting, would have chosen to come themselves.

For some time I sat on a step in the central courtyard, writing my diary and watching monastic life trickle by. A monk carrying a stack of tiles walked past and asked me where I was from, frowning in surprise when I told him.

'Oh! Out of country,' he said, as if he'd thought me Indian.

After him came two young monks – no more than ten years old – who leapt about giggling as they tried to catch wind-blown flurries of dead leaves. They ran over when they noticed me, said 'Hello!', then rushed off again, boys in monks' robes. It struck me, sitting there, how fortunate it was that India had claimed Tawang in 1951. Had it not, this great monastery would very likely have fallen foul of the ravages of China's occupation of Tibet: by the end of the 1970s fewer than ten of Tibet's 6,000 monasteries remained intact and unknown thousands of monks and nuns had been killed, imprisoned and tortured. The cultural genocide continues to this day.

Tawang would be the centre of more controversy in October 2016, when the Indian government announced that His Holiness the Dalai Lama would visit the town in March 2017. The announcement sparked a diplomatic furore with China, who threatened a breakdown of border peace and bilateral ties if the visit goes ahead. The visit of a US envoy to Tawang in autumn 2016 similarly incensed the Chinese, but thankfully the Indians seem to have taken little notice of either tantrum.

The benefit of coming to Tawang now, when it was grey and drizzly, was the absence of tourists. The only other lay-person I saw was a tiny Monpa woman shuffling across the main courtyard, her yak-felt hat framing features that age had whittled to a husk of crinkled skin and angular bone. She wore the traditional maroon and white striped woollen dress with a red felt cape fastened over her shoulders and, around her neck, hung weighty necklaces of coral and turquoise beads. Drawn by her appearance, I followed her into a dark shrine room, watching as she slowly filled twenty silver bowls with water and lit some incense under a bronze Buddha. Noticing my presence, she gave me a handful of puffed rice, putting one hand to her mouth to tell me to eat it. Afterwards she hobbled, muttering, around the four ten-foot prayer wheels that occupied the back of the small room, while I sat on a bench and turned one by pulling on a worn leather strap attached to a well-oiled cog beneath it. Rocking backwards and forwards as I turned the wheel, the chimes clanging melodiously off the old stone walls, I could see the appeal of monastic life.

*

Shaven-headed and dressed in a maroon robe, Lobsang Gyatso looked like an ordinary monk. Kindly eyes twinkled from behind thick spectacles and his soft, round face exuded cheerfulness.

'Come in! Come in!' He greeted me enthusiastically, ushering me into the small house on a hillside below Tawang.

But as we drank tea on a bench beside his wood-burning stove, I learnt that Lobsang was in fact no longer a monk at all. A Monpa from Tawang, his parents had sent him to a monastery in Mysore aged eleven. But in 2011, after twenty-three happy years, he decided there was something more important for him to do than to remain a monk. With the permission of his abbot he left his monastery, sold his house and land and – with the 25 lakh, around £25,000, he'd raised – set up the Save Mon Federation, an organization dedicated to preserving the fragile ecology of the Tawang region. A rash of hydroelectric projects was threatening Tawang's rare wildlife and sacred pilgrimage sites, and Lobsang felt that something had to be done about it. And besides, it was madness to build so many dams in an area prone to earthquakes and landslides.

Indeed, just after I finished my journey, the Northeast was hit by a magnitude 6.9 earthquake. Amazingly no one was killed or injured, but the combination of heavy rain and earthquake-loosened soil triggered massive landslides in Tawang a week later. Sixteen people were killed by a single landslide in a village just south of the town that I'd ridden through on my way.

'There are already twenty-eight micro and mini hydroelectric projects in Tawang district – none of them working well due to bad work and corruption.' He shook his head in weary disbelief. 'Most of them haven't lit a single bulb.'

It was true the electricity situation in Tawang was dire. I'd spent the previous evening shivering under the blankets with no lights or hot water in my room. It was the same every day apparently.

He nudged his spectacles up his nose and carried on. 'The latest mini hydroelectric project was six megawatts and cost nearly one hundred crore [around £11 million], but after three and a half months the spillway collapsed and the local villagers had to flee for their lives. One local politician involved with the construction pocketed *a lot* of money.'

In between fielding calls on his mobile, Lobsang told me that several far bigger projects were being planned: dams which would threaten the habitats of rare species such as black-necked cranes, snow leopards, Tawang macaques and red pandas. Not only that, in the same way as the Idu Mishmi feared for their culture, Lobsang felt that thousands of migrant workers brought here to build the dams would swamp the region's 40,000 Monpa. But Lobsang had already succeeded in halting the forest clearance for one dam, and was determined to stop them all.

'One hundred per cent we will succeed in stopping these projects. The government can't do the forest clearance without the agreement of the local villagers.' He opened a folder and showed me a piece of paper covered in thumbprints – the signatures of illiterate villagers. 'See, all the villagers have signed this resolution against the clearance.'

Until Lobsang stepped in, villagers were routinely bullied and tricked into signing agreements with dam companies.

For these largely older, illiterate people who'd lived in the mountains herding yaks all their lives, understanding issues such as environmental impact assessments, dam heights and compensation was beyond them.

In Laos and Cambodia, where I'd last travelled, outspoken environmental campaigners like Lobsang were harassed, abducted and even killed by their governments. I asked Lobsang if his efforts had placed him in any danger.

He laughed, a quiet, rueful chuckle that lit up his whole face. 'Oh yes, we face so many difficulties. I've been beaten up and received more death threats than I can remember. But I have to face the consequences of my actions – whether they are positive or negative.'

'Have you ever been in prison?'

More laughter. 'Yes, I've been put in prison twice. But both times there was so much protest they had to let me out the next day.'

On another occasion, when he was organizing a peaceful rally in Tawang about the poor state of their roads and rampant corruption within the Border Roads Organisation – 'They're the worst!' – a man turned up at his house the night before with a suitcase full of money.

He shook with mirth as he recounted the story. 'They tried to bribe me to stop the rally, but I told them I didn't want the money and we went ahead anyway. Four thousand people attended.'

As he showed me out, I asked him if it had been hard leaving his monastery after all those years. For a moment he looked wistfully across the foggy valley.

'Oh yes, it was very emotional for me. I loved my life there.

But my monk's training has helped me so much. I'm always happy, whatever difficulties I face.'

At that we shook hands and he climbed into the battered blue van he used as a taxi. 'I have to earn money somehow!' he said, smiling.

Just two weeks after we met, Lobsang was arrested again, this time charged with some dubious allegations about insulting the abbot of Tawang Monastery. When several hundred local people gathered outside the police station to protest peacefully against his arrest, the police opened fire on the crowd. Two people were killed and several others seriously injured, among them a young monk and a woman. Lobsang was released soon afterwards and continues his campaigning. What an incredible human being he is.

19

SISTER ACT

The weather wasn't kind to me in Tawang. At 3,000 metres the air was thin and cold, and most of the time the surrounding mountains were shrouded in a hoary quilt of gun-metal grey. Venturing for a ride along the Tawang Chu Valley one morning, I ended up racing back to town in a storm of bouncing hailstones, watching curtains of rain and hail sweep down the valley and forks of lightning streak across the angry sky. In the villages sodden dogs trotted along the road with their tails between their legs and cows sheltered against the houses, their heads lowered in sullen patience. What I would have done to have been in a hot bath at that moment, with Marley feeding me gin and tonic and slabs of salted caramel chocolate.

With no heating, and infrequent electricity, it was too

cold to linger in my room, so much of my time in Tawang was spent with my Monpa hosts, huddled around a gas fire in their large modern house. We sat on blankets in the small white room, warming our hands around cups of tea and talking, the various family members wandering in and out. The elderly parents – doughty villagers with farmers' hands, their faces broad and kindly under knitted woollen hats – had been born when Tawang belonged to Tibet. People were happy when Indian soldiers arrived in 1951, they told me; the Monpa were fed up with Tibetan tax collectors arriving each spring to levy a share of the harvest. Apart from access to the Tibetan salt trade, they gained nothing in return. Life under India was better. They had never gone to school and grew up helping their parents farm and look after the family's yaks. But how things had changed since then: their two daughters were sassily dressed women with iPhones and painted nails who were planning a shopping trip to Bangkok; one ran a prosperous travel agency, the other taught English at a local school. Their son, Chopa, owned a Sumo business and had a house in Itanagar, where he spent most of his time.

One evening, as we drank hot *arag* – a clear, potent rice wine poured from a silver teapot – I asked the father, Thutan Lama, if he remembered the events of 1959. On 17 March that year the Dalai Lama, along with twenty of his closest aides and family, had slipped out of the summer palace in Chinese-occupied Lhasa and begun a perilous journey to India. Nine years after China's 'Peaceful Liberation of Tibet', scattered revolts had turned into a full-scale uprising and it had become too dangerous for the 23-year-old spiritual leader to remain. Travelling at night, so as to avoid detection, he walked for fifteen days across the blizzard-driven Himalayas, reaching the safety of the Indian border on 31 March. The next day, when Jawaharlal Nehru announced to parliament that he would be granted asylum in India, his speech was met with cheers and applause. Two days after this the Dalai Lama arrived in Tawang.

'We must have been a pitiful sight,' His Holiness later wrote, 'physically exhausted and mentally wretched from our ordeal.'

I was lucky. The old man didn't just remember the Dalai Lama's stay; he'd played a part in his journey. Thutan was eighteen then, he told me, and working as an errand boy for the Deputy Commissioner of Tawang. As he spoke, his youngest daughter – the glamorous English teacher – translated what he said.

'The Dalai Lama stayed at the Deputy Commissioner's office for a night and I was the only one allowed into his room to take him his food and make his fire.'

'What was the Dalai Lama like?' I asked eagerly, wondering if he'd seemed tired or afraid.

Thutan laughed at the memory of his younger self. 'I was only a teenager and too shy to talk to him – he was so important! But I don't remember him seeming scared or upset.'

The Dalai Lama and his entourage had left for Assam the next day and Thutan was instructed to follow with his mother, brother, two sisters and their Tibetan porters, plus nine ponies for their luggage. For five days they walked south to Bomdila, greeted in every village by crowds of Monpa bearing khatas, tea and food.

His eyes lit up at the thought of it. 'They were so happy

to have their *Kundun* and his family among them. It was like one big party!'

At this he poured me another fiery cup of arag and ushered me to drink. After taking a swig, I asked him how the Dalai Lama's family had felt, knowing they'd almost certainly never return to Tibet.

'They seemed happy, to be enjoying the journey,' Thutan told me. 'I remember his mother fussing over me because I was the youngest. I didn't appreciate the importance of what I was involved in at the time, but now I look back at it as one of the key experiences of my life.'

Until then, despite the simmering border disagreement, relations between China and post-colonial India had been cordial. But Mao Zedong was incensed at Nehru granting asylum to the Tibetan leader and bilateral relations rapidly deteriorated. Three years later, China invaded Arunachal Pradesh – a war that cost an estimated 2,000 Indian lives, many of them from the cold.

By the time the war broke out Thutan was working as a porter for the Indian Army, carrying air-dropped rations up to the border post north of Tawang.

'We knew something was wrong when we saw injured Indian soldiers being carried down from the border and, a few days later, the main Chinese force invaded on foot. The Indian soldiers were poorly trained and badly equipped, and the Chinese quickly drove them back. Our group of porters hid in a forest, but two of them became afraid and ran away – they were later shot by the Chinese. And a female porter had a lucky escape when a bullet hit her thick silver bracelet.'

Thutan was leaning towards me now, talking animatedly.

'When it got dark the rest of us left the forest and ran through the night, reaching our village by the morning. The next day everyone in the village, except a few old people who refused to leave, loaded our belongings onto ponies and fled to Assam.' He swept one arm through the air to indicate their flight. 'Our village was just below Tawang and, as we left, we could hear gunshots and see people running away from the approaching Chinese. Everyone was panicking. The Chinese were already attacking the Sela Pass, so we trekked over the mountains into Bhutan, and then on to Assam, where we stayed in a refugee camp for three months. When we returned home we crossed the Sela Pass and saw dead Indian soldiers everywhere. They were rotting and dogs were eating the bodies. But there were too many of them to bury.'

A few hours later I asked Thutan if the Monpa believed in the yeti. His daughter didn't understand what I meant at first, then said: 'Oh! You mean the *gret*!'

'Of course,' the old man replied. 'It lives in the mountains; it walks like a human and looks like a big monkey. The *brokpa* [nomadic yak herders] often see it, but only at night, and it always hides its face.'

Once, in the 1960s, he and four friends had stopped for a night at an abandoned hut in the mountains while on their way to Assam. 'We lit a fire to keep warm and all at once a gret came and shook the hut from the outside. It felt like an earthquake! The gret is afraid of fire and we knew it wouldn't come inside, but we were still very scared.'

There was another thing I'd heard about the Monpa, which particularly intrigued me, and that was their traditional way of disposing of the dead. Unlike other Buddhist tribes they don't burn bodies or leave them on mountaintops for vultures to eat. Instead they chop the corpses into 108 pieces and throw them into rivers. Through this, they believe, the deceased is guaranteed a good rebirth. Surprisingly it isn't a priest or lama who undertakes the gruesome task of dismemberment; any male in the community can volunteer. In a macabre version of community karma service, the more dead you chop up, the more karma you accrue: if you hit the magic 108 corpses you'll have climbed several notches up the ladder towards enlightenment.

Fascinated by this, I asked the family about the practice. It still happened, they said, but not everyone did it now and the government was trying to discourage it. But a few hours later, one of the English teacher's friends popped in: a suave-looking, middle-aged man in jeans, he sat down next to the teacher and began absentmindedly scrolling through his phone.

'He's cut up the bodies for river burials – ask him,' said the teacher, giggling. The man looked embarrassed and buried his head in his phone. But after some gentle persuasion he opened up, telling me in good English about his experiences. The first body he'd ever done was a three-year-old female relative, and he'd chopped at least twenty bodies since. Young people's bones were much harder, but old people's were soft and broke easily. It had been difficult at first, he said, especially since it was a young child but, like anything, you soon become used to it. Fascinated by the gory details, I asked him what it was like to do it.

'You have to cut the body in a special way. First you cut the head off and hide it so it can't see; then you cut up the rest of the body, counting the pieces and throwing them in the river as you do it. The head goes in last. You have to cover your face when you chop the body—' he lifted his hand in front of his face to show me, 'because the blood spray everywhere.' I grimaced at the mental image.

'Why do you do it?' I asked. Notching up karma points was one thing, but actually chopping up the corpses quite another.

'People don't want to do it anymore, and no one in my village was volunteering, so I thought I should.'

'You're not a vegetarian are you?' I quipped.

'Yes. Pure veg. For twenty years.' Everyone in the room laughed.

Maybe if you weren't a vegetarian, it would be enough to make you one.

There was a third daughter – a quiet, gentle woman of about forty who often sat in the corner of the room knitting socks for her father. With her shaven head covered by a pink woolly hat and a coat over her robes, I hadn't noticed at first that she was a nun. Of the four children, she was the only one who didn't speak any English, but her sisters told me she'd made the choice to enter a nunnery when she was nine years old. Now, having studied away for several years, she was about to return to her old nunnery in Tawang. Wanting to experience what life was like for the nuns in these cold mountains, I asked if I could go and stay there. Several phone calls later it was all arranged – I'd walk to the nunnery tomorrow afternoon and take Chopa, her younger brother, to translate. Although he was a man, as a relation of one of the *ani*, nuns, he was allowed to stay there too.

*

No one is sure how old the Bramdung Chung Ani Gompa is: some say it was built by an eighth-century Tibetan king as a place for his wife to meditate; others that it was founded by the same lama who constructed Tawang. A cluster of white buildings muscling out of the face of a mountain, it sits amidst slopes thick with juniper, pine and scarlet rhododendrons. Below it, in bald, grassy clearings, yaks graze around the small stone huts of brokpa, the alpine tinkle of their bells drifting up to the nunnery's whitewashed walls. Inside these walls, worn stone alleys run between rough whitewashed buildings with painted windows and gold corrugated iron roofs. Firewood is piled up to the eaves. Baskets of chillies dry on the balconies of the nuns' wooden houses. Androgynous, bald-headed figures in maroon robes walk past windowsills bright with old paint pots planted with primroses and geraniums. In the middle of it all is the main gompa, its ornate windows and soaring main doors looking down across a deep gorge to the main monastery and Bhutan beyond. Compared to the sprawling monastery, though, it's much smaller: just forty-seven ani live here; a tenth of Tawang's monks.

Phurpa was eight when her parents sent her to the nunnery. She'd been too young to fully understand what was happening, she said, but remembers all the other nuns looking after her. Now the woman sitting on the floor beside me was twenty-seven, a striking-looking Monpa with wide-set eyes and full lips. I asked her if she was happy here.

She replied in faltering English, her voice soft and lilting. 'Yes, I like very much.'

Chopa and I had arrived at the spartan, two-roomed house Phurpa shared with two other nuns just as a storm broke, and now the three of us were huddled around the wood-burner, our voices competing with the clatter of hailstones on the metal roof. A bright young woman fizzing with energy and intelligence, Phurpa bobbed up and down – pushing logs into the wood-burner, pouring tea, chopping vegetables. In between this we warmed ourselves around the fire and spoke in broken English, with Chopa filling in the linguistic gaps. Although Phurpa had only started learning English at the nunnery's school a month ago, she could already hold a basic conversation.

'I want to be an educated nun.' She said it like a mantra, her brow knotting in determination.

'Why English?' I asked.

'I speak Monpa, Hindi and Tibetan too. But English is most important language. With English can communicate all over world.'

We hadn't been there long when a frail-looking, toothy nun and an adorable little girl in a pink, sparkly woollen hat walked in – Phurpha's two housemates returning from a visit to some healing springs near Jang. Sitting with us by the wood-burner, Legpe, the older nun, immediately unscrewed a flask of hot arag and poured me a bowl.

She nudged the bowl of steaming liquid across the wooden floor, smiling and talking in Monpa. 'She's telling you it's cold – that you need to drink,' translated Chopa, accepting a bowl himself.

This is not what I'd expected in a nunnery, I thought, trying not to gag as the taste of greasy, rancid melted yak butter hit my tongue. (Just as in Pemako, the Monpa melt butter in tea and alcohol to help with the calorie-burning effects of the cold.) But as soon as I'd taken a few sips, Legpe was topping me up, encouraging me to drink in the same way a kindly nurse might administer medicine to a sickly child. If I paused for too long she'd tip the bowl towards me, saying: 'It's a cold place here – you need to drink. You need it to sleep better!'

Between sips, I jokingly admonished her. 'Legpe, you're so naughty! You're a bad influence. A nun shouldn't be getting me drunk.' But she just smiled her gap-toothed grin and poured me more. When she wasn't administering arag, she fetched pillows from the bedroom they shared, plumped them behind my back and worried that I wasn't comfortable enough, ignoring my assurances that I was.

'You're a guest, you've come so far, it's my duty to look after you.'

At this rate, the 3 a.m. alarm call for morning prayers was unlikely to be pretty. Drinking forty per cent proof alcohol is likely to affect you on most occasions, but on an empty stomach, at the oxygen-starved altitude of 3,200 metres, it was even more potent. I was drunk in no time. Not head-spinningly, throwing-up drunk, but the sort of inebriation where details fade, conversations converge and your brain retreats into a warm, fuzzy, booze-filled cocoon. I know that Phurpa bustled about and cooked us dinner on the gas stove in the corner of the room, but for the life of me I can't recall what. Rice perhaps, and some sort of vegetables. And I can picture little Tenzin, an angelic-looking girl of eleven, falling asleep across Legpe's lap as the old nun lovingly stroked her head. I would have liked to talk to her more, to ask her how she'd felt when her parents sent her a year ago. But she spoke only a few words of English and the older nuns always answered for her. She was still adjusting to the rigorous discipline of her new life, they told me.

'She's naughty – she has a lot to learn, but she's only young,' said Legpe, looking down at her adoringly.

The three of them were related, I found out, and came from the same village near Jang. Phurpa and Tenzin were first cousins, and Legpe – who'd been here for forty of her fifty years – their aunt. In the absence of their own parents or children, they were like a close family.

With such an early start, the nuns normally went to sleep at eight, but it was after ten by the time Legpe refilled my bowl for the last time. Chopa slept by the fire and us girls in the bedroom: Legpe and Tenzin snuggled up together in one bed, Phurpa and I were in the other two. Phurpa coddled me like a child before she turned out the light, pulling the blankets around me and tucking them under the thin mattress. Afterwards I fell asleep in a drunken, happy stupor, tears of contentment and gratitude wetting my cheeks.

'Sister! Sister! Wake up!' It was the middle of the night and Phurpa was gently shaking me. A bulb flooded the room with harsh yellow light. 'Sister, time for prayers.'

I groaned. Odd dreams, a midnight stumble to the outside loo, and a nun snoring thunderously in a neighbouring house had made for a fitful sleep. All I wanted to do was burrow into the blankets and stay in bed for another five hours. But instead I blearily pulled my jeans over my thermal leggings and followed the nuns into the black, starless night, our breath ballooning in freezing clouds as we trotted down an alleyway to the main gompa. From across the inky darkness of the gorge came the solemn blasts of conches calling the monks to prayers.

The gompa flickered in semi-darkness, the light of yak butter candles falling on silk banners, golden icons and rows of shaven heads. Sitting cross-legged between Tenzin and Phurpa, on one of the low platforms that ran at right angles from the altar, I watched the nuns rub sleep from their eyes, yawn and pull their woollen shawls about them, their breath rising in the gloom. It was just above freezing now, but even when it was minus twenty they were forbidden to wear warm coats over their robes during morning prayers. It was a form of mental training, Legpe had told me: the older nuns used a type of meditation called *nen jurma* that generated internal heat.

'But you have to control your mind first. It's very hard.'

It sounded just like *tumo*, meaning warmth, an advanced form of meditation used by Tibetan monks and ascetics to raise their core temperature. The great traveller and Tibetologist Alexandra David-Néel witnessed new initiates of tumo proving their abilities by drying freezing wet towels on their naked bodies in the middle of the Tibetan winter, and Tibetan hermits surviving winters in freezing caves with nothing but tumo to keep them warm.

At 3.30 a.m. the head nun, a bullish woman of about fifty, took her seat nearest the altar, drilbu and *vajra* in hand, and led the nuns in a low chant. At times the chanting was drab and dirge-like, at others more urgent, but always it surged on in the same flat tone, the voices of the younger nuns shrill above the rest. Some of the women looked bored and half-asleep; others, like Phurpa, belted out the prayers with evident gusto. Tenzin soon nodded off, her chin dropping into the folds of her robes, and the nun next to her, a child of about the same age, giggled when she saw. Every ten minutes or so a shy nun of about fifteen came round and poured a steaming flask of salty butter tea into our wooden bowls but, in spite of the cold and my need for caffeine, it still made me gag.

Warming my hands around the bowl instead, I closed my eyes and let the sound of the chanting wash over me, my mind floating across an hypnotic, changing landscape of voices and tinkling bells. Several times the chanting paused and, in its place, the silence fidgeted with the slurping of tea and the shuffle of robes being pulled tighter around cold bodies. By 5 a.m. tiredness overtook me, and my head lolled into a doze, but soon a revived Tenzin was prodding my knee, smiling conspiratorially as I groggily caught her eye. At six the prayers ended and we emerged into a grey dawn. Below us, blue smoke curled from the yak herders' huts and Tawang slumbered in a pallid light. To the southeast, a thick blanket of dark grey clouds smothered the peaks of Bhutan.

'Has she had her breakfast?' bellowed the monk, half-jokingly.

It was morning assembly and twenty nuns were standing in sheepish rows outside their two-roomed concrete school-house above the gompa. Their teacher – a wiry, elfin-faced 26-year-old monk whose pointed features made me think of Mr Spock – had asked one of his pupils to stand at the front and recite a Tibetan verse. Now she blushed and mumbled shyly at the ground, her thin voice barely audible.

The monk paced up and down beside the nuns, a sergeant major drilling his troops. 'Has she had her breakfast?' he repeated. But the nuns just tittered coyly in response. It was obvious that the young monk took his job extremely seriously, chivvying and goading his pupils with a zealot's intensity.

'It is my duty to educate these nuns. I want to do the best for my disciples,' he told me earnestly.

All morning the nuns sat obediently behind low wooden desks – Phurpa and six older girls in one room, Tenzin and the youngest nuns next door – the monk pacing between the rooms, teaching two classes at once. In the first class, Buddhism, the rooms rang with the pupils' enthusiastic, if not always tuneful, singing. The monk danced around the front of the class, bursting into snippets of Hindi song. He was a funny character, half-stern, half-comic, but the nuns clearly liked him and I wondered if any of them harboured secret, un-nunly crushes. Sitting quietly against the side wall in the older nuns' classroom, I watched the nuns whisper and chew the ends of their pens, their fingers following the lines of text, while in the front row Phurpa hunched studiously over her books, furrowing her brow in concentration. She was a whirlwind of energy, that girl, determined to learn and make the most of her opportunities.

At one point the monk leant over to correct her work, the top of his robe flapping open to show a pale-blue Real Madrid shirt underneath. 'She's my best student,' he said, unabashedly.

By mid-morning the nuns' efforts not to be distracted by me had largely failed: every time the monk went next door their curiosity fizzed out in a torrent of excitable questions.

'Sister, you like nun?' Seven expectant faces looked at me.

'Yes, of course!'

'Sister, why you not become nun?'

I could see the appeal of life here – not having to worry about money or finding a job or a husband, sheltered from the tumult of the outside world. One nun I spoke to was thirty-seven, the same age as me, and had only just arrived. Painfully shy, she could hardly look me in the eye, but through Phurpa she said she'd come to escape life's difficulties. But I knew I wasn't cut out for life in a nunnery, especially the 3 a.m. starts.

'Erm, I don't think so. I've got too many sins,' I replied.

'Sister, are you married?'

'Sister, what class did you reach?'

'Sister, what are your responsibilities?' I had to think hard about this one. 'My dog?' I ventured.

'Sister, what is your hobby?'

This needed less thought. 'Travel.'

'Sister, how many countries have you visit?' They gasped when I said fifty-two.

'Sister . . .'

When the monk walked in the nuns looked down at their books and fell guiltily silent. But at least they were practising English.

Chopa had returned home that morning, so I walked back to Tawang alone just before dusk.

'I miss you,' said Phurpa as I left. 'Please come back.'

Then, in a rush of affection, she presented me with a string of prayer beads she'd been given during the Dalai Lama's visit in 2009. 'Please have this, so you no forget us.'

I was extremely touched, and have written this book with

those prayer beads beside me, and thought of my friends at the nunnery often. After giving Tenzin, Phurpa and Legpe big hugs, I shouldered my rucksack and walked out of the gates, brimming with happiness.

20

YAK TO THE PLAINS

I left Tawang under a brilliant blue sky and understood, for
the first time, the true beauty of this place. For five days the
town had drowsed under fog and cloud, the surrounding
mountaintops severed by cantankerous banks of grey. But
now I rode away squinting into dazzling sunshine, the mountains transformed to a glittering wall of white. In the middle
of this magnificent arena rose the monastery, shining like a
knob of fresh yak's butter on its mount. A few times over the
previous week I'd stopped to look at a view and felt oddly
unmoved by the scene, as if I was trying to save photographs
to a memory card that was already full. But now, despite the
freezing wind that flayed my cheeks, I gloried in the astound-
ing vista, and couldn't have been happier. Around my neck
was a white khata, given to me by Thutan's family as I left.

I'd tucked it under my down coat and waved goodbye until the bulky, coated figures in my wing mirror had vanished around a corner.

From Tawang I span down towards Jang through slopes dotted with crimson rhododendrons and puffs of white blossom, the silver thread of a river becoming a foaming torrent beneath a clanking Bailey bridge. In the villages women were laying out wide, flat baskets of onions, garlic and red chillies to dry in the sunshine, waving as I passed. Climbing beyond Jang, the view was even more fantastic, and I stopped beside a friendly yak to imprint the moment on my memory. A hidden river meandered north between steep, pine-furred escarpments and mountains that heaved and tumbled in a mosaic of every imaginable green. Stone villages dripped down slopes felted emerald with fields of young barley and rice. I could hear dogs barking, children shouting, yaks' bells. There were frothy copses, grassy knolls and black dots grazing around brokpas' huts. The occasional house stood alone at the end of a ridge, around which prayer flags flapped in the breeze. To my far left, the golden roofs of Tawang glinted on the crest of a green wave and, behind, that perfect line of white. How thankful I was that the weather had given me this chance to witness the magic of the place. The yak stood beside me as I took it all in. Perhaps he was enjoying it too.

But by the time I reached the Jaswant Singh memorial a rumbling tide of cloud was rolling in from the north, suffocating the tops of the mountains. So sharp was the contrast between blue sky and the advancing line of grey, it was as if an invisible hand was pulling a sheet of iron across the sky.

Fresh snow covered the barren slopes around the Sela Pass and I rode the last few miles to the summit shivering in the freezing air. But my Hero was uncomplaining.

Apart from being woken by some drunk hammering on my door at 2 a.m., it was an uneventful night in Dirang. In Bomdila the next morning plump, Monpa women sat at market stalls behind bags of walnuts, kidney beans, maize, peanuts and cubes of hard yak cheese. Rough tin ladles, saucepans, yak-tail dusters and red woollen shawls hung behind them. I stopped to buy a shawl, handing the woman the equivalent of eight pounds without bothering to bargain. Not once had I tried to quibble over prices here, and not once had I felt ripped off. When I asked to take her photo she shrieked with laughter and pointed to her paan-stuffed cheek, as if to say, 'What about this?' But she laughed and posed anyway. Never had I travelled among people so quick to laugh. I'd miss that ready cheerfulness.

I'd packed badly that morning, shoving too much into my dry bag (now ripped and definitely *not* dry) and securing the disintegrating top box with worn-out bungees and the last of my trusty duct tape. By now the box was cracked halfway across the bottom, held on by just one and a half bolts, and rattled so loudly you could probably hear me coming from two valleys away. I'd be lucky if it lasted until Guwahati. But after the addition of the bulky woollen shawl, my luggage situation deteriorated. Now the dry bag didn't close properly, the bungees wouldn't quite stretch, and its bulging form kept slipping sideways as I rode. Stopping near an army camp to rectify the situation, I moodily wrestled with the bungees, vaguely aware of a white pickup pulling up beside me. Two men got out, stood beside the car and stared wordlessly. After a minute or so one of them, a fleshy, charmless fellow, said: 'Where you from?'

I was in the middle of trying to secure the dry bag with a bungee that didn't stretch.

'England,' I replied, without looking up.

'Where your husband?'

The damn bungee still wouldn't stretch. I was sweating now. 'England.'

They looked at me with blank, witless stares and tried again. 'Where your husband?'

They were annoying me now. 'England.'

'No!' The man shook his head uncomprehendingly and pointed to a group of Indian men who were splashing around in a river just below the road. 'Where your husband? Bathing?'

'No! England!' I snapped, wondering how long this would go on for.

At this, clearly thinking me idiotic, he gave up and fell back into gawking silence.

A minute later came the inevitable: 'One click?'

I wasn't in the mood for smiling sweetly as the men slipped their arms around my shoulders for a grinning selfie and, for the first time on my journey, I replied, 'No, not today.'

Feeling mildly repentant I rode away, the two still staring sullenly after me. But guilt soon turned to regret that I hadn't thought of a better response to the numberless selfie requests of the past few months. Damn, I thought, if only I'd replied: *Yes, but only if you pull a* Saturday Night Fever *pose*, or *Yes, but only if we all stick our tongues out*. But one always thinks of these things afterwards.

It had been sunny when I left Dirang at seven, but the weather changed again beyond Bomdila and the blue sky flooded grey. So near the end of my journey, my mood fluctuated as frequently as the weather. At lunchtime I pulled over at a roadside shack for rice and dahl and found three young Dutch motorcyclists inside, two women and one man – the first independent travellers I'd met. Bonded by two-wheeled camaraderie, we crowded around a small table piled with helmets, gloves and maps, stories bubbling out of us excitedly, my belligerence over the men forgotten. They were riding around the world on 250cc trail bikes (which I somehow hadn't noticed outside), visiting Tawang before crossing India to Pakistan and riding home through China, Central Asia and Iran. It was a brief but high-spirited meeting, and we parted ways with warm hugs and photographs.

Finishing a journey is always like this – a tidal bore of emotions raw with elation, exhaustion, wonder, relief, sadness, nostalgia and gratitude. I didn't want it to end, to leave behind the wild mountains and all the exceptional people I'd met here. And this journey had meant more to me than any other. It had healed me. I was a different person to the one who'd nervously boarded the plane almost three months ago. I felt alive, happy (apart from the odd moment of irritation), restored to the essence of myself, as if the real me had emerged from the diminished shell I'd become. I'd been reminded that the only way to beat fear is to face it head-on, to look it in the eye and see it for the gutless bully it is. Fear itself can't hurt us. Only our reactions to it can. But on the other hand I desperately wanted to see Marley, my family, our dog Seamus; to sleep in my own bed, wash in something that wasn't a cold bucket and not be woken up by bugling cockerels, volleys of phlegm, or drunks.

Coasting down to the plains around the same switchbacks I'd trundled up a week ago, dropping so fast my ears popped, I kept telling myself to smell, savour and *really look* at the lush hills around me. All too soon, they'd be gone. Then, distracted by the view, I turned a tight hairpin bend to find a lorry hurtling towards me on the wrong side of the road, trailing a pall of black smoke. Swerving to miss it, I looked down and shuddered to see my wheels just inches from a vertical drop.

'Concentrate!' I berated myself. 'This is India! For goodness sake, don't get run over now.'

When an army convoy of forty trucks rumbled past soon after, I pulled over, wincing as the three-foot wheels rolled by, uncomfortably close. My final images of Arunachal Pradesh were three monks squatting beside a white Sumo, changing its front tyre, and a soldier having a crap beside his roadside sentry post. Then I was beside the boiling brown waters of the Kameng, dense, humid jungle rising on either side, and before I knew it the road had spat me out at Bhalukpong. In place of the mountains was a grimy town: dingy 'fooding and lodging' joints, tangles of wires, half-built houses encased in rickety bamboo scaffolding, cows lying in the road, wine shops, *people*. I parked my Hero beside the red and white barrier gate into Assam, scribbled my name beside the details the policeman had taken from me a week ago, and BAM! I'd left Arunachal Pradesh. It was 13 April, the date my permit expired.

A vermilion sun was sinking between the palms as I

drove down the sandy track to Nameri eco-camp. A veritable oasis, its thatched huts and safari tents sat among tall palms and silk-cotton trees, beneath which colourful gardens flitted with birds and saucer-sized butterflies. The only other guests were a group of elderly American birdwatchers, some of whom had travelled to over a hundred countries in search of the avian grail. They'd come to the right place: in the morning I was awoken not by howling dogs or violent hoicking, but by the mellifluous trilling, cooing, whistling and piping of an orchestra of koels, barbets and a hundred other exotic birds I didn't know the name of. The twitchers were long gone, striding through the park with spreadsheets and binoculars, fervently ticking off their morning's feathered conquests.

That final morning's riding comes to me in a sequence of mental images: a troop of red-bottomed monkeys under a row of palms, glaring at me with nasty yellow eyes as I buzzed past; a black goat dashing across the road dangerously close to my front wheel; a policeman in miraculously white uniform standing beside the 'Welcome to Tezpur: Town of Eternal Beauty' sign, behind him a brackish, rubbish-filled pond; crowds of people waiting to cast their electoral votes at roadside polling booths, the women in saris with parasols up; the bike gusting sideways in the wind as I crossed a bridge over the immense brown waters of the Brahmaputra; a woman walking over the same bridge, red sari slapping at her legs and silk scarf streaming out behind her. On the wind-blasted plains betel palms arched sideways and paddies rippled like sheets of emerald silk. It was surreal to think that only yesterday my wheels had crunched over the snowbound

4,175-metre Sela Pass, yet now I was skimming along the Brahmaputra Valley, sweltering in thirty-seven degrees.

Ten miles from Guwahati, by the side of the same road I had left in February, Manash was waiting on his Enfield, looking the epitome of cool in a black T-shirt and jeans. It felt like a year since we'd drunk Tango-flavoured gin at the Paradise Hotel in Jorhat, and I rode the last stretch in the sputtering slipstream of his bike, on roads strangely emptied by the election, smiling from ear to ear.

At some traffic lights on the edge of the city, Manash turned to me, jubilant, and said: 'Welcome to Guwahati!'

I felt oddly numb at first – neither happy nor sad. Just aware that the grand adventure was over and I'd ridden my Hero for the last time. Reaching Guwahati felt almost inconsequential: it was the journey that had been important, not my arrival into the traffic, concrete and heat of the city. I suppose it was a culture shock, too – going from the stark cold of Tawang to the breathless pre-monsoon heat of Guwahati; from hard beds and cold bucket washes to a marble-floored apartment with a maid and a bed big enough for ten. My hosts, journalist friends of Manash, took me out for dinner and presented me with a beautiful red and blue *mekhela chadar*, the traditional Assamese dress, the last in a long line of people who had shown me extraordinary kindness over the past few months. The two nights I was there I lay awake, sweating in spite of the air-conditioning, my mind flicking through an album of images from the journey: elfish Idu faces lit up in the firelight, the view from Tashigong, the heaving flanks of dying mithun at the reh festival, frayed parachutes amidst the wreckage of the C-46, nuns, monks, mahouts . . .

I'd travelled through Arunachal at a critical time in its history, when the homogenizing juggernaut of globalization was colliding with tribal cultures that had flourished in near-isolation for hundreds of years. How long, I wondered, would Idu shamans chant to Inni Maselo Jinu or the Monpa throw their dead into rivers? Would Lobsang Gyatso succeed in stopping the dams that threatened his native Tawang? How would the tribes manage to retain their cultural identities in the face of rising pressures from both Hindus and Christians to reform?

Abhra arrived the next afternoon, fresh from six weeks filming snow leopards in Himachal Pradesh for *Planet Earth II*. His hair was a little greyer than when we'd last met in Delhi two and a half years ago, but he was still the same laughing, laid-back Bengali. Juggling ten different television projects at once, he spent half the evening with his phone and power bank hanging off his ear, fielding Skype calls from demanding producers at the BBC and elsewhere. It was funny being at the other end of the line, seeing him answer his constantly ringing mobile and say, 'Yes, now's a good time to talk,' and meaning it, whether he was in a car, walking along the street or sitting down to dinner. Answering phone calls at all hours of the day would drive me potty, but Abhra is a man of fath-omless energy and good cheer. And he still had the stamina to stay up with Manash and me until 3 a.m., drinking the bottle of Bombay Sapphire he'd brought. This time the gin was at last accompanied by tonic. Real Schweppes tonic water, hunted down by Manash from some obscure shop in the city.

We didn't have ice or lemon, but just the fizzing, bitter taste of a bona fide gin and tonic was enough. Abhra flew back to Calcutta the next morning to celebrate Bengali New Year, before flying up to Uttar Pradesh the day after for a BBC recce. That man never stops.

My journey had been sewn with such good fortune that it seemed only right I end it at Kamakhya, the temple I'd been blessed at before I left. But a clammy, head-drilling hangover and lengthy farewell lunch with my hosts meant it was late by the time we were ready to leave. Manash and Abhra would be looking after my loyal Hero from now on, while the top box would be immortalized as an *objet d'art* in their office. After patting both bike and box goodbye I slung my bags into Manash's car and we set off through the city's traffic.

With the temple's usual crowds swelled by both *Navratri* – a Hindu festival associated with the goddess – and the start of *Bihu*, the Assamese New Year, we'd be lucky to even make it into the compound. Tens of thousands would be descending on the temple today, some who would have queued for a puja since dawn. With my flight just three hours from now, the best we could hope for was a quick blessing at the gates from Manash's family priest.

We ran past the gaudy stalls and the dreadlocked sadhus, pushing our way through the throng. Then suddenly the panda, the same bony, bespectacled old priest I'd met in February, was at our side and whisking us through the main gates, past the coven of cunning priests and milling crowds. We ducked and jostled past hubbubs of people, billy goats and paving stones spattered with the sticky blood of recently sacrificed animals. Then we were in a small room behind the temple and the panda was hurrying us towards a desk, where a woman was stamping two red tickets printed SPECIAL ENTRY COUPON and saying something about it being a gift from the District Commissioner's office. Bewildered, slammed by heat and my hangover, I was hurried by the priest into the black maw of the temple, past a crush of people shuffling forward behind a grid of metal fencing.

'They'll have been queuing all day,' said Manash's voice behind me.

Glancing briefly back at the line I saw it snaking back and forth inside the metal cages, a heaving press of thousands. It must have been fifty degrees inside. Sweat sprang instantly, copiously, from my forehead and back. My head swam. Sweaty bodies crushed against me on all sides. A minute later the panda was thrusting me down the steps into the inner sanctum and one of the temple priests was pulling me to my knees beside the yoni, telling me to touch the water, throw marigolds, give money – all the while unseen bodies pushing me from behind and our panda chanting urgently in my ear. It was fuggy with sweat and incense, charged with fervour. Somewhere behind me was Manash, kneeling and muttering too. Then we were stumbling into the sunlight again, blinking, smeared red, poorer, bewildered, buzzing with adrenaline.

I looked at Manash, wide-eyed and ecstatic. 'That was insane! What on earth just happened? How did we get in like that? What did you do?'

But Manash, his forehead daubed in three lines of red tikka, looked equally confused. 'I've no idea. That just doesn't happen. The panda must have arranged it but I've honestly no idea how. You are quite unbelievably lucky.'

He was right. I *was* lucky. It was an extraordinary end to a quite magnificent journey.

ACKNOWLEDGEMENTS

I never understand how some authors' acknowledgements contain just a brief thanks to their other half, editor and cat. So many people have been involved in this journey, and have shown so much kindness and generosity, that I'm afraid mine are going to be more like a Kate Winslet Oscar acceptance speech.

Without a doubt the person who has played the biggest part in this journey is Marley, my amazing boyfriend, who has encouraged and supported me every step of the way – from those dark months of panic attacks to the writerly angst of completing this book. He told me I could do it when I didn't believe I could, put up with my long absence, talked through chapter plans, proofread my manuscript and generally showed boundless love and patience: I couldn't have done it without him.

Huge thanks go to the stellar team behind this book – my brilliant agent Imogen Pelham, my excellent editor Kerri Sharp and Simon & Schuster UK's Editorial Director, the lovely Claudia Connal. Thanks also to Jack Smyth from Simon & Schuster's design department for designing such an excellent cover, to Jo Whitford for her production wizardry and Sue Stephens for her stellar work on press and PR. All of them have been an utter delight to work with and I feel extremely lucky to be working with such a superb and talented team. I must also thank the late, great Gillon Aitken for the role he played in accepting me into the illustrious bosom of Aitken Alexander Associates, and to Ted Simon, for the introduction. I must also thank Ted for his useful comments on the manuscript and for having me to stay while I wrote some of the book.

The idea for this book began with meeting Abhra Bhattacharya in Delhi in late 2013. And what a fateful meeting that was. Abhra played an absolutely pivotal role in my journey, and somehow – in between the dozens of television projects he was handling – found time to handle my permits, help me with contacts and give me endless advice. By the time this book is published, Abhra and I will have worked together again – this time on an ITV series about India. In Abhra's absence, Manash Das, his business partner in the Northeast, was unfailingly brilliant and resourceful. Between the two of them they were my Indian fairy godfathers. I can't thank them enough.

Thank you to my family, Fiona, Noel and Zara Bolingbroke-Kent, and my stepfather Mark Wrigley, for putting up with my lengthy travels. Sorry for any sleepless nights . . .

More than any other journey, this was about people. Countless people gave me their kindness, their time, their knowledge, their stories, their laughter, their firesides, their spare beds: Mishmi, Khampa, Monpa, Adi, Nyishi, Apatani, Assamese and Bengali. I can't name them all, but a few

Acknowledgements

who really stand out are: Jibi Pulu, Phupla Singpho, Maini Mahanta and Bani Das, Apedo Rondo, Sipa Melo, Dorje Tenzing, Kabsang Jurmey, Phurpa Lamu and Tapir Darang. Others who were enormously helpful with fact-checking and information were: Sahil Nijhawan, Mirza Zulfiqur Rahman, Aparajita Datta, Catriona Child, Jay Vineyard, Gary Zaetz, Clayton Kuhles, Amy Johnson.

The kindness didn't end when my journey did. I wrote much of this book in a shepherd's hut on a farm in Somerset's Chew Valley. The owners, Simon and Barbara Banks, didn't know me at all when a mutual friend asked if they might consider allowing me to use their hut to write in, but they gave me the key and said I could use it when I wanted. They, the hut and their dogs became an integral part of writing this book, and I have been bowled over by their saintly kindness towards me. Looking over the farm and the hills, with cows, dogs, buzzards, wrens, badgers and a green woodpecker for company, I couldn't have wished for a more peaceful and idyllic place to write. Thank you.

A big thank you to Liz Rigby – you always told me I could do it, even when things were at their worst.

Thank you to my sponsors and supporters: Native Route, the Transglobe Expedition Trust, Sir David Tang, Sir Charles Blois Bt, Snugpak, Chris and Michele Kohler, Edge Expeditions, the Visa Machine, Stanfords, Water to Go. Without them I'd be poorer, colder and probably still at home.

Thanks to Anna Bywater for her insightful comments on parts of my manuscript, to Ed and Lil for picking up the pieces in Thailand, to Olivia Donnelly for the support and wisdom, to fellow lady travellers Dervla Murphy, Lois Pryce and Joanna Lumley for the support and inspiration.

And finally, a word for Seamus, the Buddhdog, who very sadly died a few weeks after I returned from India. He was the wisest, kindest old Labrador in the world and we miss his thumping tail and cheerfulness every day.

GLOSSARY

Adi: Tibeto-Burman tribe who live in the East Siang, Upper Siang, West Siang and Lower Dibang Valley districts of Arunachal Pradesh and also in Tibet. A sub-group of the Tani people, along with the Tagin, Galo, Nyishi, Hill Miri, Mising and Apatani. Formerly known as the Abor, which is now seen as an outdated, pejorative term.

Ahom: A Shan people who ruled the Brahmaputra Valley for six centuries, from 1228 to the British annexation of the region in 1826.

Amrahla: A bandolier of tigers' teeth used by Idu Mishmi shamans, or igu. Believed to ward off evil spirits. Only about a dozen remain in existence.

Ani: A Buddhist nun.

Animist: Someone who believes in the existence of individual spirits that inhabit natural objects and phenomena.

Apatani: Sino-Burman tribe who live in the Ziro Valley, in the Lower Subansiri district of Arunachal Pradesh. A sub-group of the Tani people, along with the Adi, Tagin, Galo, Nyishi, Hill Miri and Mising.

Apong: Adi rice beer. Delicious.

Arag: A clear (and fairly lethal) Tibetan or Bhutanese rice wine. Often served hot with yak butter or yak fat. Not always delicious!

Beyul: According to the Nyingma tradition of Buddhism these are hidden valleys in the Himalayas, created by the eighth-century mystic, Padmasambhava – otherwise known as Guru Rinpoche. They will provide refuge to believers in future times of war or trouble. Pemako is one of these beyuls.

Brokpa: Nomadic Monpa yak herder.

Carrom: A sort of finger billiards played on a square board, whereby players stand around the board and flick small, round wooden discs. Thought to originate in India, the game is hugely popular in Asia.

Chang: Tibetan (and Nepalese) rice, barley or millet beer that can be drunk cold or hot. Delicious.

Chulikata: Meaning 'crop-haired' – this was the name given to the Idu Mishmi by the British, on account of their unique fringed coiffures.

Coolie: A nineteenth-century colonial term meaning an indentured labourer or servant.

Curtis C-46 Commando: Transport plane widely used by the Allies to fly over 'the Hump' in the Second World War.

Dafla: The old name for the Nyishi tribe of Lower Subansiri. Now seen as extremely insulting.

Dakini: A female Buddhist deity.

Dao: A single-bladed, square-ended, machete-type knife, probably originating in China. Used for slashing and chopping. Ubiquitous among the tribes of Northeast India. Usually about a foot long.

Dhaba: Simple roadside eateries found all over India.

Dhoti: A garment worn by male Hindus, consisting of a piece of material tied around the waist and extending to cover most of the legs.

Donyi–Polo: Animistic, shamanic religion followed by certain Tibeto-Burman tribes in Arunachal Pradesh, such as the Apatani. Centred around the worship of *donyi*, the sun, and *polo*, the moon.

Dorje: In Tibetan Buddhism this is a representation of a thunderbolt in the form of a short double trident or sceptre, symbolizing the male aspect of the spirit and held during invocations and prayers.

Dorje Phagmo: Buddhist Tantric Goddess whose supine form is said to mirror Pemako. Also known as Vajira Yogini.

Drilbu: Ritual Tibetan bell.

Engoko: Idu Mishmi fireplace central to every Idu house. These are square hearths set into the floor, above which hang racks for storing firewood and drying meat.

Etokojo: Traditional sleeveless jacket worn by Idu Mishmi men. Black with beautiful red, orange, yellow and gold horizontal strips of embroidery around the lower half. A similar garment, the *etoma*, has fewer strips of embroidery.

Gambura: Village headman.

Gamosa: Traditional Assamese white rectangular piece of cloth woven with red embroidery. Translated as 'something to wipe the body with', it is used variously around the neck, for worship, around the waist, around the head, on altars or as a welcome for guests.

Ganesh: Hindu elephant god.

Gompa: A Tibetan monastery or temple.

Gret: Monpa word for the yeti, a large mythical creature that walks like a human but looks like a monkey.

Gyaling: An oboe-like reed horn used in Tibetan ritual music.

Hindutva: 'Hinduness' – the predominant form of Hindu nationalism in India. Hindutva is the official ideology of the ruling BJP.

Idu Mishmi: Tibeto-Burman tribe who live in the Dibang Valley region of Arunachal Pradesh.

Igu: Pronounced 'eegoo'. Idu Mishmi shaman or priests. Central to Idu society, these men and women are powerful inter-mediaries between the worlds of the seen and the unseen.

Jathaap: Khampa fireplace and oven made of dried and packed mud.

Kachin: Northernmost state of Burma that borders eastern Arunachal Pradesh and China's Yunnan. A multi-ethnic state riven by border disputes, smuggling, independence movements and civil war.

Kalita: Non-hallucinogenic root used by Idu Mishmi shamans in their rituals. Looks very like ginger.

Kani: Northeast Indian word for opium.

Khampa: Buddhist tribe from the Kham region of southeastern Tibet and, more recently, the Upper Siang region of Arunachal Pradesh.

Khata: Tibetan ceremonial silk scarf to represent purity and compassion. Usually white. Called a *khadag* in Mongolian Buddhism.

Khepa: The Idu Mishmi name for the yeti, a ten- or twelve-foot-high gorilla-like creature which lives in the forests.

Khinyu: Idu Mishmi word for spirits.

Khundu: Idu Mishmi word for the area where the mithun are sacrificed at reh festival.

Koonki: Domesticated elephant used in mela shikar, the capture of wild elephants.

Kora: Tibetan Buddhist word for a clockwise circumambulation of a temple, religious structure or sacred site.

Kundun: Tibetan term for His Holiness the Dalai Lama, meaning 'the presence'.

Lakh: Unit of Indian currency: 1 lakh rupees is 100,000 rupees, which (at the early 2016 exchange rate of £1 to 100 rupees) is around £1,000.

Lama: A lama is a Buddhist teacher (translation of the Sanskrit word 'guru') and a monk is a man who has renounced worldly life to (usually) live in a monastery and follow the monastic rules that were decided by the Buddha. Many lamas are monks, but there are many monks who are not lamas and there are lamas who are not monks.

Mahout: Man (or occasionally a woman) who works with and rides elephants.

Mekhela chadar: Traditional Assamese women's dress.

Mela shikar: Wild elephant hunt.

Merum: Centrally located, square hearth and fireplace of Adi houses. Almost identical to the engoko of the Idu Mishmi.

Mite and mura: The old Apatani social classes.

Mithun: Or *Bos frontalis*, a large, semi-wild bovine indigenous to Northeast India, Yunnan, Burma and the Chittagong Hill Tracts of Bangladesh. Often sacrificed or used as dowry payments.

Momo: Meat- or vegetable-filled dumpling popular among Tibetan peoples.

Monpa: Buddhist tribe who live in the Tawang region of northwest Arunachal Pradesh. Largest Buddhist tribe in the state.

Musth: The frenzied state of certain male animals, especially elephants or camels, that is associated with the rutting season. Not a good time for a cuddle.

Navratri: Nine-day Hindu festival dedicated to the deity Durga, celebrated in the spring.

NSCN: National Socialist Council of Nagaland. Naga nationalist insurgent group operating in Northeast India and parts of Burma.

Nullah: Small stream.

Nyibu: Apatani shaman.

Nyingma: The oldest of the four major schools of Tibetan Buddhism.

Nyingmapa: Someone who follows the Nyingma school of Buddhism.

Nyishi: Tibeto-Burman tribe who live in central Arunachal Pradesh. Part of the same group of Tani people that includes the Apatani, Galo, Tagin, Hill Miri, Mising and Adi. Formerly known as the Dafla.

Paan: A mildly stimulating preparation combining betel leaf with areca nut and sometimes tobacco. Chewed all over India and other parts of Asia. Stains the teeth and lips red.

Panda: Brahmin Hindu priest.

Phalap: Singpho tea.

Prasad: Food which has been blessed in a religious ceremony. Often prasad is made as a devotional offering to a god.

Puja: Religious blessing or act of worship.

Punkah wallah: A manual fan operator. The most desired were deaf because they were always within earshot of confidential conversations. A punkah is a type of ceiling fan used in the Indian subcontinent before the electric fan.

Rupee: Indian currency. At the time of my journey £1 was equivalent to 100 rupees, hence £100 is 10,000 rupees, £1,000 is 100,000 rupees (or 1 lakh).

Seven Sisters: The septet of states that make up India's tribal Northeast: Assam, Arunachal Pradesh, Nagaland, Mizoram, Meghalaya, Tripura and Manipur.

Shinka: Traditional maroon and white striped dress worn by Monpa women. Made from heavy silk yarn or wool.

Shiva: Hindu god.

Singpho: Kachin tribe found in Arunachal Pradesh, Yunnan and Burma.

Stupa: A Buddhist shrine.

Sumo: 4WD vehicle used as a shared taxi all over Northeast India.

Sutra: A Buddhist scripture. Often written on parchment and wrapped in silk.

Tai: Ethnic group of people spread over southern China, Indochina and Northeast India. The Ahoms, who ruled the Brahmaputra Valley for six hundred years, were a Tai people.

Tashi deleg: 'Hello' in Tibetan.

Terton: A term within Tibetan Buddhism. It means a person who is a discoverer of ancient hidden texts or terma. Many tertons are considered to be incarnations of the twenty-five main disciples of Padmasambhava, otherwise known as Guru Rinpoche.

Trakzen: Flat, round discs of Tibetan bread made from either millet or barley flour and water.

Tsampa: Tibetan staple food made from roasted barley flour or occasionally wheat flour.

Tshatsha: Devotional Tibetan icons moulded from mud.

Tulku: A reincarnated lama.

Tumo: A Tibetan form of meditation that raises your body temperature. Very useful for lamas and hermits who live in freezing conditions. Extremely difficult to learn.

ULFA: United Liberation Front of Assam. Established in 1979 for the purpose of creating a 'sovereign socialist Assam'.

Vaishnavite: A follower of Lord Vishnu, one of the principal Hindu gods.

Vajra: A thunderbolt or mythical weapon – both a Hindu and Buddhist term.

Yoni: Sanskrit for vagina/vulva.

LIST OF TRIBES IN
ARUNACHAL PRADESH

How many tribes there are in Arunachal Pradesh depends on who you talk to, as different people categorize tribes in different ways. For example, some will just class the Adi as a single tribe, as I have here, while others will divide them into three or four sub-groups. Please note that this list does not include refugee groups, such as the Chakma and Hajongs.

Adi	Memba
Aka	Meyor
Apatani	Mishing (also known as
Bangni	Miri)
Galo	Monpa
Idu Mishmi	Nocte
Digaru Mishmi	Nyishi
Miju Mishmi	Sherdukpen
Khampa	Singpho
Khampti	Tagin
Khowa	Tangsa
Lisu	Wancho

Endnotes

Chapter 1: The Forgotten Land

'As I write this in May 2016 the Indian government is drafting a new law':

https://www.washingtonpost.com/news/worldviews/wp/2016/05/06/cartographers-beware-india-warns-of-15-million-fine-for-maps-it-doesn't-like/

http://www.dailymail.co.uk/wires/afp/article-3576724/India-seeks-impose-15-mn-fine-false-maps.html

http://www.thehindu.com/news/national/all-you-need-to-know-about-the-draft-geospatial-information-regulation-bill/article8576523.ece

'The US backed Naga rebels':

https://www.theguardian.com/world/2003/jan/14/india.lukeharding

https://www.theguardian.com/travel/2010/dec/11/india-nagaland-jonathan-glancey

Chapter 2: All I Need Is a Hero

'a plastic bag containing a man's severed head':

http://www.hindustantimes.com/india/

human-head-found-at-famous-kamakhya-temple/story-
GS1WmXkQ9XgjkoHVjqZODJ.html

'So far an estimated 30,000 people have died':
http://www.upi.com/India-offers-truce-to-separatist-
rebels/27811096913206

http://www.csmonitor.com/World/Asia-South-Central/
2009/1209/p06s04-wosc.html

Chapter 3: Tea and Unicorns

'nearly ninety people have been beheaded':
http://www.hindustantimes.com/india/assam-7-arrested-
for-branding-63-yr-old-woman-witch-beheading-her/
story-It61ec8KBkxg9adVDlXN0M.html

https://www.theguardian.com/world/2015/aug/08/five-
women-killed-india-jharkhand-villagers-suspecting-witchcraft

http://www.bbc.co.uk/news/world-asia-india-33605244

'a five-lakh rupee (around £5,000) fine for calling or
identifying a witch':
http://www.thehindu.com/news/national/other-states/
assam-assembly-passes-bill-to-end-witchhunting/
article7538350.ece

Chapter 4: Where's John?

'Two days later the Indian Army and Assam Police launched a
joint combat operation':
http://www.satp.org/satporgtp/countries/india/states/
assam/data_sheets/majorincidents.htm (See reference to
16 February)

http://www.india.com/news/india/four-ulfa-nscn-k-
militants-shot-dead-954289/

CHAPTER 6: OPIUM COUNTRY

'More illegal opium is grown in Arunachal Pradesh than any other part of India':

    http://indianexpress.com/article/india/india-others/
    arunachal-pradesh-emerges-as-largest-opium-producer-
    in-country-raises-security-concerns/

CHAPTER 8: TRIBAL GATHERING

'At the same time, he ... cancelled the licences of Greenpeace and 9,000 other foreign-funded NGOs':

    http://www.bbc.co.uk/news/world-asia-india-32747649

    http://www.firstpost.com/india/from-greenpeace-to-
    ford-foundation-modi-govts-controversial-crackdown-
    on-ngos-2812196.html

    http://www.telegraph.co.uk/news/worldnews/
    asia/india/11845586/India-bans-foreign-funds-for-
    Greenpeace-in-latest-crackdown-on-charities-with-
    Western-ties.html

    http://www.huffingtonpost.in/2015/04/29/ngo-license-
    modi-governme_n_7172150.html

    http://www.ibtimes.co.uk/india-narendra-modi-government-
    cancels-greenpeace-licence-receive-foreign-funds-1518469

'The Dibang Dam, due to be India's largest, was approved on the back of an environmental impact assessment that was labelled farcical by many observers':

    http://www.business-standard.com/article/economy-policy/
    rejected-by-experts-dibang-hydro-project-gets-green-nod-
    115062400037_1.html

    https://www.theguardian.com/environment/india-
    untamed/2015/may/30/indian-government-to-review-
    hydroelectric-dams-two-river-basins

http://www.indiawaterportal.org/articles/no-impact-assessment-study-done-dibang-hydropower-project

http://www.theguardian.com/environment/india-untamed/2014/oct/22/indias-largest-dam-given-clearance-but-still-faces-flood-of-opposition

CHAPTER 13: THE HEART OF THE LOTUS

'In response to renewed Chinese claims on Arunachal Pradesh, in October 2014 Modi announced a plan':
  http://www.bbc.co.uk/news/world-asia-india-29639950

CHAPTER 15: GOODBYE TO PEMAKO

'"Cheating!" exclaimed Dorje. "Everyone in India cheats.':
  https://www.telegraphindia.com/990823/the_east.htm#head7

CHAPTER 17: A RISKY BUSINESS

'the Indian government blocked any further recovery efforts by the US military. When this unofficial moratorium was lifted in September 2015, the same happened again':
  This was told to the author via email by a relative of a US pilot killed in the crash and in no way represents the author's personal interpretation of facts. See also:
  https://thewire.in/30303/no-closure-yet-as-us-india-continue-to-resist-returning-the-remains-of-wwii-dead-in-arunachal/
  https://usindiamonitor.com/2017/02/15/families-of-world-war-ii-arunachal-mia-soldiers-still-waiting-for-justice/
  http://economictimes.indiatimes.com/news/defence/

missing-aircraft-from-ww-ii-shrugging-off-chinese-
concerns-government-allows-us-search-missions-in-
arunachal/articleshow/49067505.cms

Chapter 18: The Sela Pass

'I've been told that voters were paid between 300 and 1,000
rupees ... each to rally for a particular party': This was told
to the author and in no way represents the author's personal
interpretation of facts.

'Sixteen people were killed by a single landslide':
 http://indianexpress.com/article/india/india-news-india/
 arunachal-pradesh-tawang-landslide-heavy-rains-
 2765246/

'Just two weeks after we met, Lobsang was arrested again, this
time charged with some dubious allegations about insulting
the abbot of Tawang Monastery. When several hundred local
people gathered outside the police station to protest peacefully
against his arrest, the police opened fire on the crowd.':
 http://timesofindia.indiatimes.com/india/Tawang-in-
 Arunachal-Pradesh-erupts-in-protest-over-Lamas-arrest/
 articleshow/52074726.cms

 https://www.internationalrivers.org/blogs/433/
 police-kill-two-anti-dam-protesters-in-north-india

Select Bibliography

Allen, Charles, *The Search for Shangri-La: A Journey into Tibetan History*, Little, Brown and Company, 1999

Bailey, F. M., *No Passport to Tibet*, The Travel Book Club, 1957

Baker, Ian, *The Heart of the World: A Journey to the Last Secret Place*, Penguin, 2004

Baruah, Tapan Kumar, *The Idu Mishmis*, Directorate of Research, Government of Arunachal Pradesh, 1988

Butler, John, *Travels and Adventures in the Province of Assam, During a Residence of Fourteen Years*, Smith, Elder & Co, 1854

Cox, Kenneth (ed), *Frank Kingdon-Ward's Riddle of the Tsangpo Gorges: Retracing the Epic Journey of 1924–5 in South-East Tibet*, Garden Art Press, 2001

David–Néel, Alexandra, *Magic and Mystery in Tibet*, University Books, 1965

Elwin, Verrier, *The Aboriginals*, Oxford University Press, 1943

Elwin, Verrier, *A Philosophy for NEFA*, Directorate of Research, Government of Arunachal Pradesh, 1957

Elwin, Verrier, *India's North East Frontier in the 19th Century*, Oxford University Press, 1959

Ghosh, Amitav, *The Glass Palace*, Random House, 2000

Glancey, Jonathan, *Nagaland: A Journey to India's Forgotten Frontier*, Faber and Faber, 2011

Graham Bower, Ursula, *The Hidden Land*, John Murray, 1953

Hamilton, Angus, *In Abor Jungles: Being an account of the Abor Expedition, the Mishmi Mission and the Miri Mission*, E. Nash, 1912

Hamilton, James, *Lost Horizon*, Macmillan, 1933

Johnson, Amy L., *Letters Lost then Found*, Splattered Ink Press, 2015

Karunakar Gupta, *The Hidden History of the Sino-Indian Frontier*, Minerva Associates (Publications), 1974

Kingdon-Ward, Frank, *Assam Adventure*, Jonathan Cape, 1941

Kingdon-Ward, Frank, *Himalayan Enchantment*, Serindia, 1990

Koerner, Brendan, *Now the Hell Will Start: One soldier's flight from the greatest manhunt of World War II*, Penguin, 2008

Lovell, Julia, *The Opium War*, Picador, 2011

Roerich, Nicholas, *Shambhala*, Nicholas Roerich Museum, 1978

Sarkar, Niranjan, *Tawang Monastery*, Department of Cultural Affairs, Government of Arunachal Pradesh, 1981

Shand, Mark, *Queen of the Elephants*, Jonathan Cape, 1995

Shand, Mark, *River Dog: A Journey Down the Brahmaputra*, Little, Brown, 2002

Singh Rawat, Indra, *Indian Explorers of the 19th Century*, Ministry of Information and Broadcasting, Government of India, New Delhi, 1973

Williams, J. H., *Elephant Bill*, Penguin, 1950

Woodcock, Martin, *Collins Handguide to the Birds of the Indian Sub-Continent*, William Collins Sons & Co Ltd, 1980

ACADEMIC PAPERS

Chaudhuri, Sarit, 'Plight of the Igus: Notes on Shamanism Among the Idu Mishmis of Arunachal Pradesh', *European Bulletin of Himalayan Research* 32, 2008

Datta, Aparajita, 'Fading Fauna, Forgotten People', *Down to Earth* magazine, 2005

Kour, Kawal Deep, 'Opium, Empire and Assam', *International Institute for Asian Studies*, 2012

Rahman, Mirza Zulfiqur, 'Territory, Tribes, Turbines: Local Community Perceptions and Responses to Infrastructure Development along the Sino-Indian Border in Arunachal Pradesh', Institute of Chinese Studies, 2014

Sharma, Jayeeta, '"Lazy" Natives, Coolie Labour and the Assam Tea Industry', *Modern Asian Studies* 43, 2008

INDEX

abela, 136
In Abor Jungles, 187
Ahom ruins, 41
Aksai Chin, 9
Alinye, 162, 166
Allied Labour Corps, 79
Amazon, 123, 125
amrahla, 164
'ancient ones', 198
Angriem Valley, 165
ani, 321, 322
animal sacrifice, 5, 90, 92, 113,
   117, 124, 125, 130, 132, 161,
   204, 262, 265, 267, 268, 272,
   273, 341
Anini, 115–16, 117, 118, 133,
   137–8, 143, 146, 157, 159–60,
   161, 168, 182
Anjaw District, 103
antelope, 156
Apatani Valley, 256, 274, 301
Apatani Youth Association, 264
apong, 188
Arizona, 280
arms-dealing, 37
Arunachal Pradesh, xi, 5–65
   passim, 96–7, 110–19, 339
   (*see also individual places within*)
   Chinese claims on, 216
   dam dum flies, 128
   electricity arrives in, 135
   final images, 336

isolated nature of, 6
landscape, 100, 264
population growth, 155
roads, 296–7
tourism, 307
urban population, 155
during WWII, 280–1
Asian elephants, 34, 80–2
   lassoing, 73–4
Assam, xi, 61
   early history of, 5–16 *passim*,
      31, 52
   education provision, 237
   electricity arrives in, 135
   gin, 45
   medical provision, 202
   'must-sees', 41
   national anthem, 40
   New Year, 340
   populous nature of, 30, 37, 56,
      61, 133, 134
   restaurants, 27
   tea trade, 7, 32, 42, 53, 284
   towns and villages, *see by
      individual name*
   traditional dress, 54, 338
   traffic, 110, 297–8
   Upper, *see* Upper Assam
Assam Railways & Trading
   Company, 52
Assam State Transport
   Corporation, 47

Assam Valley, 134
Assam Witch Hunting
    (Prohibition, Prevention and
    Protection) Act (2015), 46
Atlanta, 59
Atunli, 121–2, 135, 136
Australia, 240
ayahuasca, 165
Azadpur Mandi (market), 11

Balipara, 298
Bangkok, 316
Bangladesh, 10, 18, 20, 51, 75,
    76, 92
baptism, 265, 272
Baptists, 264, 270
BBC, 11, 17, 339, 340
bears, 123, 131, 156, 171, 230,
    244, 285, 300
Bengal, xi, 11, 20, 95, 141, 295
    New Year, 340
    tigers, see tigers
Berlin, 68
betel nuts, 18
beyuls, 175, 176–7, 181, 210, 230
Bhalukpong, 298, 299
bhang, 252
Bhutan, 5, 8, 153, 214, 296, 319,
    322, 327
Bihar, xi, 52, 253
Bihu (Assam New Year), 340
bijou gompa, 204
birds, see individual types of bird
Blue Peter, 270, 271
Bodoland, 31
Bombay, 132
Bomdila, 300–5, 317, 333, 335
Bon, 175, 219, 226, 228
Border Roads Organisation, 101,
    252, 313
Borneo, 78
Bos grunniens, 304
Brahmaputra River, 5, 7, 8, 12,
    15, 17, 20, 24, 36, 39, 41, 49,
53, 100, 111, 134, 139, 142,
    178, 186, 187, 259, 337 (see
    also Tsangpo River)
Bramdung Chung Ani Gompa, 322
Bristol, 126
Britain, 6–7, 8, 153, 240, 259–60,
    291, 334
brokpa, 319, 322, 327, 332
Buddhism, 175–8, 194, 197, 198,
    215–18 passim, 220–2, 232,
    299, 302, 304, 308
    'burials', 319–20
    Nyingpa school of, 219
buffalo, 26
bulbuls, 97
Burma, 5, 6, 8, 11, 14, 30, 37, 51,
    54, 56, 57, 59, 61, 64, 71, 76,
    83, 84, 88, 92, 97, 143, 261,
    277, 278, 281, 291
Burma Road, 280

Calcutta, 7, 44, 340
The Calcutta Statesman, 187
Cambodia, 87, 313
Canada, 240
cannabis, 252
Catholicism, 73
CBI (theatre), 57, 61–2
Central Asia, 179, 303, 335
Chabua, 53, 281
chang, 205, 206, 212, 219, 224,
    225, 232, 234–6, 244–5, 248
Changlang, 54, 56, 60
Channel 4, 11
Chhuluk, 140
Chiang Mai, 67
chickens, 26, 31, 90, 118, 149, 152,
    161, 233, 256, 267, 269, 272,
    273, 285, 294
Chime Yangsang Ne, 176
China, 7–10 passim, 14, 37, 140,
    153, 157, 162, 201–2, 212,
    216, 226, 259, 277, 280,
    309–10, 316, 318, 335

exports to, 95
   tea trade, 42
   in WWII, 53, 56
China–Burma–India (CBI)
      (theatre), *see* CBI (theatre)
Chinese medicine, 37–8, 44
Chittagong Hill Tracts, 75, 92
christening ceremonies, 28
Christianity, 72, 113, 161, 179,
      219, 265, 270–3, 339
CIA, 10
Circuit House (hotel), 99, 104–5,
      143–4
'city of tea', 50
Claridge's, 170
'Class 1 jungies', 52
clouded leopard, *see* leopards
cobras, 58
Cold War, 10
*Collins Handguide to the Birds of the
      Indian Subcontinent*, 97
common leopards, 83
communion, 219
'coolies', 52, 58
'curtain mountain', 210

dakinis, 194, 220, 221, 249
dam dum flies, 128, 159, 204,
      227–8, 246, 289
Dambuk, 184
Damroh, 190
dao, 61, 78, 81, 92, 113, 118, 121,
      125, 128, 131, 146, 163, 186,
      262, 266, 283, 289
Daporijo, 250, 252, 256
Darjeeling, 141, 143
Dark Ages, 179
Dehra Dun, 139
Delhi, 11, 12, 13, 24, 53, 56, 71,
      113, 128, 193, 203, 237, 339
*The Delightful True Stories of the
      Supreme Land of Pemako*
      (Lelung Shepe Dorje), 177
Dembuen, 162

Denmark, 85
Deopani River, 112, 118
Devakotta, Mount, 194, 204, 210,
      214, 215, 220, 223, 226, 228,
      229
Dharamsala, 206, 237, 245
Dibang Dam, 134
Dibang River, 15, 118
Dibang Valley, 88, 111, 116, 133,
      138, 147, 155, 161, 164, 183,
      232
Dibrugarh, 49–51, 53, 74, 76
   'city of tea', 50
   Great Earthquake (1950), 49–50
Digboi, 53
Dirang Dzong, 301, 303, 335
Discovery Channel, 11
Diwali, 11
Donyi-Polo, 190, 203, 273
dorje, 192
Dorje Phagmo, 176, 197
Dri River, 137
Dri Valley, 161
drilbu, 192, 326
drug addiction, 74
drugs, 37, 86–102 *passim*, 222, 252
   non-hallucinogenic, 125, 165–6
ducks, 26, 231
dysentery, 58, 166, 248

East India Company, 6
East Pakistan, 10
East Siang, 184
Edinburgh, 46
Ela, 129
elephant boys, 73–4
elephant safaris, 35–7, 39
England, *see* Britain
engoko, 113, 122, 151, 153, 170,
      185
Etalin, 119, 133, 135
Everest, Mount, 116, 170, 172, 178

Falls of Brahmaputra, 178

Festival of Colours, *see* Holi
(festival)
First World War, *see* Great War
Fodor's Guide, 176
folktales, 78, 111
Fortnum & Mason, 178
France, 89

Gallipoli, 143
Gallipoli, 47
gambura, 156, 283–5, 292
Gandhi Suspension Bridge, 195
Ganges, 20
Garuda (eagle), 23
Garuda Rock, 247
geese, 31, 39, 165
Germany, 278, 291
Glastonbury, 128
Glencoe, 161
globalization, 124, 136, 339
goats, 2, 23, 26, 31, 40, 47, 93, 110,
207, 272, 292, 298, 337, 340
gods/goddesses, *see* individuals by
name
Golo, 161
Google Earth, 13, 144
Great Earthquake (1950), 49–50,
98, 133
Great Escapes, 11
Great Trigonometrical Survey of
India (1863), 139–40
Great War, 8, 143, 180, 259
Greenpeace, 134
grumbling ox, 304
Guidebook to Pemako (Guru
Rinpoche), 194
Gulf of Thailand, 67
Guru Rinpoche, 175–91 *passim*,
203–4, 212, 217–23, 230,
236, 237, 243
Guru Rinpoche Day, 232
Guwahati, 16, 17–22, 24, 27, 64,
71, 113, 160, 163, 269, 333,
338

Guwahati University, 144
gyaling, 234
Gymkhana Club, Jorhat, 42–4

Hamburg, 107
Hanoi, 19, 28
Harvard University, 245
Headspace, 249
Hell Pass, 57
Herat, 15
The Hidden Land (Graham Bower),
29, 261, 274, 293
Highway 37, 31
Himachal Pradesh, 17, 339
Himalayan barbets, 97
Himalayan black bears, *see* bears
Himalayas, 5, 8, 11, 14–16, 30, 76,
84, 100, 111, 175, 178, 179,
226, 249, 302, 317
'the Hump', 57
Hindi pop music, 105, 196, 207,
248
Hindu:
customs, 99
festivals, 251–2, 340 (*see also
festivals by name*)
mantras, 25
mythology, 195 (*see also gods/
goddesses by name*)
shrines, 72
Hindu mythology, 23
Hinduism, 23
*History of the Relations of the
Government with the Hill Tribes
of the North-East Frontier of
Bengal* (Mackenzie), 186
Ho Chi Minh Trail, 19, 87
Holi (festival), 251–3
Holland, 73
'holy mountain of glass', 148
hoolock gibbons, 76
hornbills, 97
Huawei, 99
Human Planet, 11

human sacrifice, 12, 23–5
hummingbirds, 97

igu, 124–5, 129, 131, 132, 133,
    159–72
ili moo, 130
Illustrated War News, 79
Independence, 53
Indian Ocean, 56, 95
Indian tea trade, 42
India's Got Talent, 128
Indo-China Frontier Highway,
    216
Indochina, 19
ini la free, 163–4
Inner Line Permit, 7, 9, 185
Inni Maselo Jinu, 124, 129, 163,
    339
Inspection Bungalow (hotel), 117,
    120, 143–6, 160, 168, 170,
    293
Iran, 335
IST (Indian Stretchable Time),
    145
Itanagar, 165, 279

Jagar, 226
Jairampur, 61
Jamuna, 20
Jang, 306, 323, 325, 332
Japan, 53, 56, 57, 62, 79, 259, 260,
    261, 262, 277, 280, 291
jathaap, 205
Jawaharlal Nehru State Museum,
    276
Jefferson Barracks National
    Cemetery, 291
Jharkhand, 46
Jorhat, 41–5
Jorum Top Pass, 274

Kachin, 71, 95
Kailash, Mount, 20, 23, 247
Kalimpong, 198

Kamakhya (temple), 1, 22, 23, 24,
    194, 223, 340
Kamalabari Vaishnavite
    (monastery), 41
Kameng River, 15, 299, 336
Kamlang River, 96
Kangto, Mount, 302
Kansas, 33
Karoi, 281–4, 288
Kashmir, 9
Kathmandu, 199
Kaziranga, 35, 36–7, 38, 46, 251,
    254
Kepang La Pass, 201
khatas, 218, 243, 247, 317, 331
khepa, 166–7, 171
khinyu, 161
khundu, 124, 125
Khupa, 99, 102, 103–6, 107, 194
Krishna, 19
Kunming, 57

Ladakh, 9, 302
Lakshmi, 195
landslides, 15, 50, 99, 108–15
    passim, 133, 177, 182, 299,
    311
Laos, 90, 313
Led Zeppelin, 17
Ledo, 56, 59, 60
leopards, 6, 17, 18, 76, 79, 288,
    339
lepidoptery, 13
Lhasa, 146, 307, 308
'life consecration', 219
'little Tibet', 303
Lohit District, 113
Lohit River, 15, 99
Lohit Valley, 88
Lorraine, 62
Lost Horizon (Hilton), 179, 180,
    219
LSD, 222
lucky charms, 29

lung-ta, 200

Ma-Kum, 54
McMahon Line, 8, 9, 201, 259
magic, 12, 13, 46, 113, 150,
    163–70 *passim*, 176–7, 180,
    186, 194, 198, 205, 207, 227,
    249, 291–2, 320, 332 (*see also*
    mysticism; sorcery)
Mahacotta, 216–17
Majuli Island, 41
malaria, 16, 30, 42, 52, 59, 154,
    279
Malaysia, 56
Malini, 135
Manali, 11
Margherita, 53, 54, 56, 59, 61
market towns, 184
Maryland, 180
Mathun River, 137, 147, 151, 160
Mathun Valley, 144–5
Mayodia Pass, 119
meditation, 23, 69, 194, 198–9,
    207, 222–3, 235, 249, 308,
    322, 326
mekhela chadar, 338
mela shikar, 73
merum, 185
Miami Vice, 75
Miao, 64–5, 74, 75, 76, 84, 86
Michigan, 279, 291
Milan, 131
Mipi, 147–9, 156, 157–8
Mishmi Hills, 88, 89, 97, 109,
    132, 141
Missouri, 291
mithun, 92, 124–32 *passim*, 136,
    156, 157, 164, 165, 204, 208,
    212, 230, 235, 236, 262, 265,
    272, 273, 289, 304, 338
Mizoram, 265
Mondulkiri Death Highway, 87
Mongolia, 77, 78, 111, 177, 303
monkeys, 96, 319, 337

monsoon, 15, 30, 32, 37, 41, 58,
    82, 103–19 *passim*, 338
Mu-La, 151
mudslides, 58
Mumbai, 11, 170
Myoko (festival), 265, 267
Mysore, 198
mysticism, 24, 161, 175–8, 198,
    249 (*see also* magic; sorcery)

Naga Hills, 30, 260
Nagaland, 10, 11, 14, 37, 44, 51,
    59, 60, 61, 77, 78–9, 265
Namdapha, 71, 75, 76, 77, 81, 84,
    100, 164
Nameri eco-camp, 337
Nameri National Park, 298
Nani Intaya, 129
National Geographic, 11
National Socialist Council of
    Nagaland, 60
Native Route, 13
Navratri (festival), 340
nen jurma, 326
Nepal, 37, 72, 117, 118, 120, 153,
    168
Nestorianism, 219
New Orleans, 271
New York, 131
Niagara Falls, 142
Nigeria, 271
Nimati Ghat, 40
No Passport to Tibet (Bailey),
    138–9, 263
Noa-Dihing River, 72, 80–1, 84
Norfolk, 186
North East Frontier Agency, 9, 98
Nyering, 204
nyibu, 267–8, 269, 272

obesity, 240
Omaha Beach, 62
Opium Wars, 42
Orissa, 46, 52, 160

ox, 304
Oxygène, 47

Pacific Ocean, 56
Padma, 20
Padma Shri, 230, 246
Pakistan, 10, 175, 335
paleo-Mongoloid peoples, 77–8
panda, 22, 340–1, 342
pandas, red, 76, 312
Pangsau Pass, 57, 61
Paradise Hotel, 42
'The Paradox of our Age' (Dalai
    Lama), 240
Parshuram Kund, 99–100
Pasighat, 172, 183, 184, 186, 188,
    282
Patkai Hills, 14, 30, 54, 55, 59, 77
Pattaya, 67
Paynigem, 244
Pearl Harbor, 277
Pemako, 148, 176, 177, 178,
    180–1, 192, 194–9, 202–10,
    211–14 *passim*, 216, 220, 221,
    225, 227, 231, 236, 242–56,
    323
Pemako Falls, 8
People's Liberation Army, 9
Philippines, 78
pigs, 118, 130–1, 136, 151, 157,
    165–6, 203, 207, 272, 273,
    294
pilgrimage, 100, 139, 148, 177,
    181, 193, 194, 198, 199, 206,
    220, 223, 229, 246, 311
pilgrimage rock, 215, 234
Planet Earth II, 17, 339
poaching, 37–8, 84
ponies, 244, 317, 319
population growth, 14, 30, 71,
    84, 180
Potala, 307
Pragjyotishpura, 18
prasad, 236

Protected Area Permits, 194, 299
protector deities, 177, 214, 228,
    236
puja, 18, 22, 54–5, 194, 195, 213,
    228, 231–3, 236, 237, 248, 340
Punjab, 253
pythons, 6, 288

'rainbow body', 212
Real Madrid, 328
reh (festival), 117, 160
reincarnation, 198, 199, 204, 206,
    212–13, 235, 249, 260, 308
Research Publication Department,
    276
Revivalism, 264, 271
rhinoceros, 34, 36–8
rickshaws, 17–18, 19, 30, 31
The Riddle of the Tsangpo Gorges
    (Kingdon-Ward), 178
river burials, 319–20, 339
River Dog (Shand), 12, 29
Riwo Tula, 230
roadside shrines, 101, 304
rock pythons, *see* pythons
rockfalls, 108
Roedean School, 260
Roing, 111–13, 116, 119, 122, 133,
    136, 144, 169, 183, 276
rollers, 97
Rolling Stones, 17
Royal Bengal tigers, *see* tigers
Royal Geographical Society, 70,
    141
Royal Palace (hotel), 51
Royal Society for Asian Affairs, 13
Russia, 7, 8, 285

sabre-toothed tigers, 70
sacred vaginas, 1–2, 24, 197
Sadiya, 93, 157
Sagalee, 282, 293
Salankam, 102
Santa Barbara University, 213

Saraswati Puja, 54–5
Sarawak, 78
Sati, 23
    yoni of, 1–2, 24
Saturday Night Fever, 334
Scotland, 30, 147, 149
The Scream, 70
scrub typhus, 58
The Search for Shangri-La, (Allen), 219
Second World War, *see* World War II
Sela Pass, 294–314 *passim*, 333, 338
selfies, 33, 55, 87, 115, 253, 334
Serengeti, 34
Seven Sisters, 5, 11
Sex Pistols, 19
shamanism, 5, 12, 68, 78–9, 117, 124–33 *passim*, 157, 162–3, 194, 267–9, 339 (*see also* Donyi-Polo; *igu*; *nyibu*)
Shambhala, 178
Shangri-La, 175–91 *passim*, 203, 219, 241
Shillong, 113
Shiva, 22, 23, 100–1
A Short Ride in the Jungle (Bolingbroke-Kent), 11
Siang, 20
Siang River, 15, 184, 191, 197, 202
Siang Valley, 135, 172, 176, 181, 182, 187, 198
Siberia, 123
Sikkim, 140, 141
Silipo, 232
Simla Conference, 8
Singapore, 56
Singik Hotel, 250, 253–5
Sino-Indian War (1962), 9, 300
Six O'Clock News, 54
Skype, 213
snakes (*see also individual types of snake*), hibernating, 76
snow leopards, *see* leopards

sorcery, 24, 45–6, 175, 249
South Africa, 38, 69, 82, 240
South Park, 107
Southeast Asia, 31
State Bank of India, 160
Stilwell Road, 57, 59–61, 280
Strike Force, 83–4
Subansiri Area, 261
Subansiri River, 15

Talo River, 124, 133
Tantric ritual, 24–5, 176
Tashigong, 215, 228–30, 238, 248, 250, 338
    disappearing way of life of, 239–41
Tawang, 14, 216, 295, 296, 299, 300, 302, 304–10, 311–13, 315–30 *passim*, 331–2, 335, 339
    macaques, 312
Tawang Chu Valley, 315
Tawang Galdan Namgey Lhatse Monastery, 308
Tawang Monastery, 314
tea gardens, 53
terma, 177
terton, 177
Tewkesbury, 66
Texas, 278
Tezpur, 9, 337
Tezu, 106, 108–9
Thailand, 67
Tibet, 7–9 *passim*, 20, 30, 64, 78, 88, 173–256 *passim*
    account of, 138–9, 263
    customs, 301
    landscape, 97, 111, 300
    'little', 303
    tourism, 71
    weather, 326
Tibetan ponies, *see* ponies
Tibetan swords, 262
Tibetan turquoise, 264

Tibetology, 326
tigers, 6, 34, 38–9, 58, 79, 80, 84,
     163–5, 243
   jawbones, as weapon, 262
Tirap, 56, 60
Titanic, RMS, 114
Top Gun, 300
tourism, 38, 73, 76, 104, 166, 180,
     185, 194, 254, 298, 307, 310
trakzen, 208, 246
Transport of Native Labourers Act
     (1863), 52
Treaty of Yandabo (1826), 6
trikonasana, 249
Tropic of Cancer, 11
tsakundu sangpo, 207
tsampa, 199, 219
Tsangpo, 176
Tsangpo River, 6, 8, 137–58
     passim, 187 (*see also*
     Brahmaputra River)
tshatsha, 217, 243
tshe-bang, 219
tulku, 212–13, 217–19
Tuting, 181, 194, 195, 197, 199,
     201, 202, 204, 210, 213, 214,
     216, 232, 246, 247–8
twitching, 34, 85, 337

United Liberation Front of Assam
     (ULFA), 31, 53, 60
United Press (UP), 60
United States (US), 8, 10, 240,
     277–8, 279–80, 284, 291
Upper Assam, 44, 47, 52–3, 115,
     277, 281
Upper Subansiri District, 250
utkatasana, 249
Uttar Pradesh, 24, 253, 340

vajra, 326
Victoria Falls, 142
Vietnam, 37, 38
Vietnam War, 10, 238
Vietnamese medicine, 37–8
Vijaynagar, 216
Vishnu, 23

Wakro, 88, 91–9, 100
Walong, 99, 141
Western Front, 79
Wild Grass, 40
Wild Grass (resort), 34–5
Wiltshire, 274
Women's Institute (WI), 211
World War I, 8, 143, 180, 259
World War II, 53, 59, 61–2, 188,
     260, 274, 277–80

yak, 129, 302, 304, 310, 313, 316,
     319, 322, 323, 326, 327,
     331–42 *passim*
Yandabo, Treaty of, 6
Yangsang Chu River, 194, 197,
     202, 220, 230, 232
Yangsang Chu Valley, 194, 202,
     245
Yarlung Tsangpo, 20
Yingkiong, 181, 188, 190, 191,
     195, 250
yoga, 29, 69, 214
Yoldong, 209, 210, 211, 213, 226,
     227, 243
Yunnan, 78, 92, 95, 111, 281

Zen Buddhism, 298
Ziro, 264, 270, 274